I0820847

A Voice of Their Own

STUDIES IN RHETORIC AND COMMUNICATION
General Editors:
E. Culpepper Clark
Raymie E. McKerrow
David Zarefsky

"Hear O Israel":
The History of American Jewish Preaching, 1654–1970
Robert V. Friedenberg

A Theory of Argumentation
Charles Arthur Willard

Elite Oral History Discourse:
A Study of Cooperation and Coherence
Eva M. McMahan

Computer-Mediated Communication:
Human Relationships in a Computerized World
James W. Chesebro and Donald G. Bonsall

Popular Trials:
Rhetoric, Mass Media, and the Law
Edited by Robert Hariman

Presidents and Protesters:
Political Rhetoric in the 1960s
Theodore Otto Windt, Jr.

Argumentation Theory and the Rhetoric of Assent
Edited by David Cratis Williams and Michael David Hazen

Rhetorical Dimensions of Popular Culture
Barry Brummett

A Voice of Their Own:
The Woman Suffrage Press, 1840–1910
Edited by Martha M. Solomon

Edited by Martha M. Solomon

A Voice of Their Own
The Woman Suffrage Press, 1840–1910

071.309
So47

The University of Alabama Press   Tuscaloosa and London

WITHDRAWN

LIBRARY ST. MARY'S COLLEGE
193875

Copyright © 1991 by
The University of Alabama Press
Tuscaloosa, Alabama 35487–0380
All rights reserved
Manufactured in the United States of America

∞

The paper on which this book is printed meets the minimum requirements of
American National Standard for Information Science-Permanence of Paper for
Printed Library Materials, ANSI Z39.48-1984.

Library of Congress Cataloging-in-Publication Data

A Voice of their own :   the woman suffrage press, 1840–1910 /   edited by
Martha M. Solomon.
    p.   cm.—(Studies in rhetoric and communication)
    Includes bibliographical references (p.   ) and index.
    ISBN 0-8173-0526-2
    1. Women—Suffrage—United States—Periodicals—History.
2. Women's rights—United States—Periodicals—History.   3. Women's
periodicals, American—History.   I. Solomon, Martha.   II. Series.
PN4888.W65V65   1991
071'.3'082—dc20   90-23922

British Library Cataloguing-in-Publication Data available

LIBRARY ST. MARY'S COLLEGE

To Wil Linkugel, who began the quest
to rescue women's rhetoric from oblivion,
and to Karlyn Kohrs Campbell,
whose dedication and contributions
to the quest have inspired us all,
we dedicate this volume
with respect and affection.

Contents

A Voice of Their Own

1

The Role of the Suffrage Press in the Woman's Rights Movement

Martha M. Solomon

> To be bound by outworn customs and traditions, and to be hampered by every known obstacle which could be put in one's path, and then to have the world calmly look on and tell you it was no use it was the divine will, was growing too absurd to be longer tolerated with dignity or accepted with self-respect. The soul within me refused to beat out its life against barred doors, and I rebelled.
> —Anna Howard Shaw, "Select Your Principle of Life," 1917

When Anna Howard Shaw spoke these words to students at Temple University, she had devoted almost thirty years of her life to working exclusively for woman suffrage, eleven of those (1904–15) as president of the National American Woman Suffrage Association (NAWSA). Her rebellion had dated from her thirteenth year, 1860, but the general agitation for woman's rights stretched back much further. What became the organized movement for woman suffrage after the Civil War had its roots in the earlier, broader efforts for woman's rights.

In part, identifying the start of the efforts for woman's rights in general and suffrage in particular is a question of definition. Philosophically, modern concern about women's roles and status reached back at least to Mary Wollstonecraft's controversial book *Vindication of the Rights of Woman*, first published in 1792. Jane Rendall, admitting that the relationship is complex and confused, sees Enlightenment thought as one impetus toward a reconsideration of women's roles.[1] Personally, both Elizabeth Cady Stanton and Lucretia Coffin Mott, two key figures in the early stages of the American woman's movement, traced their dedication to the World Anti-Slavery Convention in 1840, at which, after a heated debate, the delegates denied seats to women representatives, Coffin Mott among them.[2] The discussion begun there continued over several years, while both Cady Stanton and Coffin Mott were engaged with family matters.

The Stanton family's move to Seneca Falls, New York, provided a direct stimulus for more dramatic actions and in 1848 produced a crucial event, which marks a convenient starting date. Faced with the drudgery and isolation common to many women, Cady Stanton later recalled:

The general discontent I felt with woman's portion as wife, mother, housekeeper, physician, and spiritual guide . . . and the wearied, anxious look of the majority of women, impressed me with the strong feeling that some active measure should be taken to remedy the wrongs of society in general and of women in particular. My experience at the World's Anti-slavery Convention, all I had read of the legal status of women, and the oppression I saw everywhere, together swept across my soul, intensified now by many personal experiences. It seemed as if all the elements had conspired to impel me to some onward step. I could not see what to do or where to begin—my only thought was a public meeting for protest and discussion.[3]

Despite the facts that the local newspaper issued only one notice of the meeting and that Seneca Falls was a small, rather remote town, the convention attracted some three hundred people.[4]

From this modest beginning, the movement to gain equal rights, greater protection, and improved opportunities for women grew and expanded, extending directly even to contemporary efforts for the passage of the Equal Rights Amendment. As Eleanor Flexner observes, "Beginning in 1848 it was possible for women who rebelled against the circumstances of their lives, to know that they were not alone—although often the news reached them only through a vitriolic sermon or an abusive newspaper editorial. But a movement had been launched which they could either join, or ignore, that would leave its imprint on the lives of their daughters and of women throughout the world."[5]

Although both participants in the struggle and later scholars have chronicled the details of the agitation for woman's rights and suffrage, much remains unexplored.[6] One question that is still largely unanswered is how the small gathering in Seneca Falls blossomed and evolved into a group that could mount a large-scale, sustained, and finally effective campaign for woman's rights. The answer to that question is clearly complex; no one answer can suffice. But one crucial aspect of that answer must focus on the process by which the gathering at Seneca Falls molded itself into a social movement with

sufficient viability to achieve its goals. Because all human cooperation entails communication, that process of transformation into a
social movement will have rhetorical interaction at its core. Probing
one dimension of that rhetoric is the goal of this volume.

The rhetoric involved in the struggle took many forms. Ample evidence exists, for example, that oratory was one important element.
Certainly, the public speeches and later addresses to legislative
groups were crucial in garnering support for suffrage. The recent
two-volume study of many of those texts by Karlyn Kohrs Campbell
provides much information and insight about those efforts. Press
reports of those speeches, although often not favorable, reached
many who could not attend. Editorials, even negative ones, also
spread the message. But workers themselves recognized the vital
importance of another rhetorical medium: the periodical edited and
published by sympathizers. Through this channel, the movement
could reach, educate, and inspire scores of women who could not be
tapped by other means. Controlling the content themselves, supporters could give their cause the fullest, fairest, and most sympathetic
coverage. Such periodicals will be the focus here.

Understanding the roles of periodicals in the agitation for suffrage
involves an appreciation for the nature of social movements, an understanding of the sources and particular rhetorical problems of the
woman's rights movement, and some knowledge of the diversity and
extent of those publications.

The Nature and Tasks of Social Movements

With the increased interest in the rhetoric of groups involved in
social and political activism has come the task of defining exactly
what is meant by the term *social movement*. Scholars, unwilling to
settle for the kind of loose test Justice Potter Stewart offered about
pornography—"I know it when I see it"—have approached the task
of defining movements from a host of perspectives. Despite dis-
parities in their definitions, most scholars would probably agree that
certain features characterize all social movements. Among those
features are: some degree of organization; a position outside the established order, which will mount some opposition to the movement's efforts; a focus on social change (whether pro or con); and a
necessary reliance on persuasion rather than coercion to achieve its
ends.[7] Herbert Simons, focusing on the "uninstitutionalized" aspects of movements, argues that this unique status generates a peculiar set of persuasive demands.[8] For example, as a movement

develops, it needs to adapt its persuasive strategies to reach new audiences.[9] Moreover, coping with the internal demands of membership and with the demands of a public audience requires different kinds of leadership within the movement.[10] The job of gaining new members while maintaining a consistent sense of group identity also requires unusual rhetorical acumen. But the first and most difficult task for many embryonic movements is gaining adherents, which entails generating a sense of community. As Ernest Bormann observes, "A pressing rhetorical problem for aggregates of individuals moving toward a sense of community is the creation of a common identity. People create a common consciousness by becoming aware that they are involved in an identifiable group and that their group differs in some important respects from other groups. . . . To come to such awareness, the members need to identify their collective self."[11]

Some movements can draw on established groups or can rely on geographical propinquity for their members; in a sense, they begin with an established community.[12] Others face a formidable task in simply reaching potential supporters. The difficulties of this task are exacerbated if potential members are dispersed geographically, heterogeneous in their backgrounds, unconscious of the issues salient to the movement, and limited in their sense of political, social, and personal power. Under such circumstances, a movement's initial task is to create some basis for that sense of community that will serve as a foundation for the group's activities.

Joseph R. Gusfield, in developing a concept of community as generated through symbolic interaction, observes: "The appeal to act as a member of a community, to give special consideration to fellow members, and to place their aims above those of others and of the self must presuppose a recognition of the reality of the community and of the member's affiliation to it. The 'consciousness of kind' thus depends on perceiving that there is such a kind and that one is part of it."[13] Among the requisites for developing this sense of kind, Gusfield continues, are some sense of a common history and some shared attitudes toward past and present events.[14] For social movements, then, generating a sense of community often requires transforming the previous perceptions of history and of present society among potential members, and later, the public as a whole.[15] Nowhere was that challenge more evident or more acute than in the calls for altering women's roles that evolved into the woman's rights movement in the nineteenth century.

The Development of the Woman's Movement

As Leland Griffin argues in his application of Kenneth Burke's theories to an understanding of social movements, all such efforts begin with a rejection of an established order.[16] The woman's movement is no exception, in that it began with a rejection of the social stereotypes defining women and the women's roles that emerged in the early nineteenth century. In response to the growing pressures of industrialization, immigration, and urbanization, American society developed strong notions about the "proper" sphere and roles of each sex. Nancy Cott sees the period between 1780 and 1830 as "a time of wide- and deep-ranging transformation," which produced among many other things "the appearance of domesticity."[17] Men came to inhabit the public sphere; their business was the business of the world. Women, in contrast, were increasingly relegated to the home; the family and the household were their proper concerns. While men were the providers and heads of the families, women had responsibility for the life within the home, always, of course under the guidance of their husbands. As Jane Rendall argues, "Increasingly, the worlds of men and women were separated in the nineteenth century, a separation based on the growing division between the home and the place of work. . . . The starting point for women lay in the assumption that their lives and their future had to be seen in the context of their family roles. For them, in reality, there was no future outside the confines either of the family into which they were born or the one which they might themselves create, or, in default of either, the household which they might serve, as servant or governess."[18]

From this separation of roles came a division of identities. "Womanhood" became a controlling precept for women's acculturation. According to Barbara Welter, "Woman, in the cult of True Womanhood presented by the women's magazines, gift annuals and religious literature of the nineteenth century was the hostage of the home. . . . The attributes of True Womanhood, by which a woman judged herself and was judged by her husband, her neighbors and society could be divided into four cardinal virtues—piety, purity, submissiveness, and domesticity. Put them all together and they spelled mother, daughter, sister, wife—woman. Without them, no matter whether there was fame, achievement, or wealth, all was ashes. With them she was promised happiness and power."[19] Women who ventured outside the ordained roles were vigorously condemned; women who accepted these restrictions identified their rights not in political terms but in emotional ones. As one woman responded to the question "What are the rights of women?":

The right to love whom others scorn
The right to comfort and to mourn,
The right to shed new joy on earth,
The right to feel the soul's high worth . . .
Such women's rights, and God will bless
And crown their champions with success.

Thus, the early woman's movement emerged from a social context where woman's place was firmly in the home and man's in the public sphere. Women defined themselves in terms of their domestic roles and were consistently urged to see themselves as emotionally, mentally, and physically unfit for public life. This common identity allegedly provided a foundation for the social order. As one minister warned women: "Yours it is to determine whether the beautiful order of society . . . shall continue as it has been" or whether "society shall break up and become a chaos of disjointed and unsightly elements." Faced with these dire alternatives and wary of risking "that almost magic power, which in her proper sphere, she now wields over the destinies of the world," many women were content to accept their place in the home and on the pedestal they were assured they occupied.[20]

Somewhat ironically, this shared identity, which was so carefully inculcated in women of the age, in some ways provided the basis for its own rejection. Cott argues that the vocation of domesticity, which was the lot of all women, generated substantial unity among women: "Because it included 'all' women, and was endowed with social and political meaning, the domestic vocation gained enormous persuasive strength. It gave many women a sense of satisfaction as well as solidarity with their sex. . . . this canon of domesticity intensified women's gender-group identification, by assimilating diverse personalities to one work-role that was also a sex-role signifying a shared and special destiny."[21]

In particular, woman's common piety made her the moral superior of man, and with the rise of evangelical spirit during the late eighteenth and early nineteenth centuries, she was called to provide moral leadership in society. Cott reports that ministers urged the women in their congregations to "raise the standard of character" in men, to protect society against the "encroachments of impudence and licentiousness," and to "support what remains of religion in our private habits and publick institutions."[22] Many women sought to fulfill this charge solely within the confines of their own homes or in maternal and reform societies endorsed by clergy; others sought broader vistas, especially in the growing efforts toward abolition and temperance. As Cott reports, during the 1830s, two contradictory visions of women's relation to society arose out of this moral responsibility. Domesticity "gave women a limited and sex-specific role to play, primarily in the home."[23] On the other hand, some women perceived their responsibilities as extending beyond the home and into the larger social arena, particularly in ensuring a suitably community and environment for their families.

Eager to contribute their moral force to important social reform efforts, women supported temperance and antislavery societies. However, when they sought to raise their voices in meetings, they confronted strong resistance. Denied the rights to membership in such groups as the American Anti-Slavery Society, in 1833, women founded their own groups, at first sometimes relying on men to chair their meetings but gradually gaining confidence in their own abilities.[24] Only a few brave women dared to enter the public sphere and claim the right to speak to "promiscuous," or mixed, audiences. Almost always they met ridicule and criticism; often they risked violence. The Grimké sisters endured almost unrelenting opprobrium as they attempted to urge the cause of slaves. As Kohrs Campbell notes, the first steps toward a woman's movement involved simply claiming the right to speak in public.[25]

As mentioned earlier, when the World Anti-Slavery Convention refused to seat Coffin Mott and the other women delegates from female antislavery societies, she and Cady Stanton recognized the need for change. Although eight years elapsed before they called the Seneca Falls Convention, their concern and enthusiasm did not diminish. By a unanimous vote, the women there adopted the "Declaration of Sentiments," which was modeled on the Declaration of Independence and which asserted that history clearly demonstrated that men had attempted to establish an "absolute tyranny" over women. The statement went on to document the evidence for that claim. By a slim majority, they also endorsed a series of resolutions that asserted the natural rights of women and claimed for them the right to speak in public and to advocate reforms with the same fervor and in the same realm as men. In addition, the ninth resolution urged women to secure suffrage, a proposal that was so radical that Coffin Mott feared they would appear ridiculous.[26] Despite these bold claims and this dramatic action, the women present had determined that a female's chairing the meeting was too indecorous and had called on Coffin Mott's husband James to preside.[27]

The success of this meeting emboldened the women, and they called another convention in Rochester two weeks later. In 1850, they convened the first national convention, and these meetings continued on a yearly basis through 1860, with the exception of 1857, when several principal figures had small children or other family obligations. Kohrs Campbell labels these meetings and other local and state's woman's rights meetings "ideological crucibles," because in their speeches, statements, and debates, the women explored and refined their ideology. They discussed a wide range of topics, from women's roles in society to the nature of marriage and the propriety of divorce. As Kohrs Campbell notes, these national conventions were substitutes for formal organizations and helped to raise morale and to increase commitment. Indeed, the women resisted efforts to form a national organization, in part because they feared it would be cumbersome and in part because of their experiences with the oppressive nature of some formal groups.[28]

The final national meeting before the onset of the Civil War proved especially significant because of what became known as the divorce debate.[29] In 1860, the New York legislature was considering proposals to liberalize divorce laws, and the topic had been hotly debated in the public press. Cady Stanton, who had long seen marriage laws as major impediments to woman's equality, used the occasion of the convention in New York to offer ten resolutions that criticized the marriage laws and called for liberalization of divorce. Antoinette Brown Blackwell spoke against these resolutions, offering thirteen of her own. Ernestine Potowski Rose supported Stanton. Although the three women disagreed about the right course of action toward divorce, all saw the topic as appropriate for the convention. But Wendell Phillips and William Lloyd Garrison, both longtime supporters of woman suffrage, urged that the resolutions be expunged from the records of the convention, since they felt the topic of divorce affected men and women equally and was, thus, not an appropriate focus for a woman's rights convention. Others feared that such a controversial topic might hinder other efforts. The resolutions remained on the record but were not endorsed. Kohrs Campbell sees this debate as evidence of the movement's transition and as one sign of internal division within it.[30] Charles Conrad argues that this debate was less about divorce per se and more about the scope of concern appropriate to the movement. Thus, the debate was crucial to the future of the woman's movement because it marked a shift in focus to the narrower, more pragmatic goal of suffrage.[31]

The Civil War forced a disruption in the agitation for woman's rights. Many of the supporters of the movement worked earnestly for abolition and the war effort, most notably in organizing the Sanitary Commission, which became "the right arm of the Union hospital and medical services." In addition, in 1863, Susan B. Anthony and Cady Stanton organized the Woman's National Loyal League, which pledged itself to support all efforts of the government in a war for freedom.[32]

After the war, in 1866, many supporters of woman's rights helped found the American Equal Rights Association, with the idea of working for the interests of both African-Americans and women. However, developments on two related fronts began to produce divisions within that group. First, when the group campaigned earnestly in Kansas in 1867 for a referendum to enfranchise African-Americans and women, some supporters began to privilege suffrage for the freed male slaves, giving that effort priority over women's claims. Moreover, much to the dismay of Anthony and Cady Stanton, even longtime friends of woman's rights, such as Wendell Phillips and Horace Greeley, began to urge passage of the Fourteenth Amendment and to insist that woman's rights must wait, since this was the "Negro's hour."[33]

Increasingly exasperated with the American Equal Rights Association's efforts and with the press coverage of woman suffrage, during this period Cady Stanton and Anthony took advantage of an offer of George Francis Train to fund a periodical devoted to a broad range of issues affecting women, including suffrage. Despite warnings and objections from friends about Train's reputation and politics, Cady Stanton and Anthony undertook to publish the *Revolution*, which declared itself for "men, their rights and nothing more; women, their rights and nothing less." From the outset, the rather radical tone of the paper was clear.[34] One essay opined: "The ballot is not even half the loaf; it is only a crust—a crumb. . . . woman's chief discontent is not with her political, but with her social, and particularly her marital bondage. The solemn and profound question of marriage . . . is of more vital consequence to woman's welfare, reaches down to a deeper depth in woman's heart, and more thoroughly constitutes the core of the woman's movement, than any such superficial and fragmentary question as woman's suffrage."[35] Such an agenda did little to relieve the tensions among supporters of woman's rights, and never attracting a sufficient audience, the paper failed after only three years.

In May 1869, the divisions within the movement produced a formal split. At a convention called to consider only woman's rights, Cady Stanton proposed a woman suffrage amendment to the Constitution. The American Equal Rights Association was rent asunder by the debate. In frustration and anger, soon thereafter Cady Stanton and Anthony formed the National Woman Suffrage Association, with membership open only to women. The group professed concern for a wide range of issues, from child care for working mothers to divorce reform to suffrage, which it sought to pursue through a national amendment. In reaction, Lucy Stone, Henry Blackwell, and others formed their own organization, the American Woman Suffrage Association and published their own organ, the *Woman's Journal*, which proved far more successful and long-lived than the *Revolution*. The American Woman Suffrage Association focused its efforts solely on suffrage, avoiding more controversial social concerns, and pushed for state referenda to secure that right. With some tensions and competition, the two groups worked toward the common goal of suffrage, until they were finally united in 1890 in the National American Woman Suffrage Association (NAWSA), with Cady Stanton as its first president.

Between 1890 and 1910, the NAWSA, under the leadership of first Anthony, then Carrie Chapman Catt and Anna Howard Shaw, pursued suffrage through a series of state referenda, since efforts on the national level had proved unsuccessful. In fact, in 1893, over the opposition of Anthony, the group decided to meet in Washington only in alternate years, a decision that made it impossible to maintain steady pressure on Congress and the visibility in the capital that the annual convention provided. These state efforts proved exhausting and usually unsuccessful. Between 1870 and 1910, there were four hundred eighty campaigns in thirty-three states simply to get referenda before the voters. Only seventeen succeeded in bringing the issue to a vote. The period between 1896 and 1910 saw so little success that even supporters labeled it "The Doldrums," since not a single new state was won.[36]

Beginning in the early part of the twentieth century, the suffrage movement underwent a series of changes that proved vital to its success. These changes were largely the result of efforts by a group of younger women, who saw the need to adapt strategies to meet new needs.

In 1907, Harriot Stanton Blatch, a daughter of Cady Stanton, organized the League of Self-Supporting Women, later to become known as the Women's Political Union, because she saw little hope for working within the stolid, stodgy NAWSA. As she reported, "The suffrage movement was completely in a rut in New York State at the opening of the twentieth century. It bored its adherents and rebelled its opponents. . . . There did not seem to be a grain of political knowledge in the movement. . . . A vital idea had been smothered by uninspired methods of work."[37] Working from the activist British model she admired, Stanton Blatch sought to attract laboring women to meetings, organized the first open-air meetings on behalf of woman suffrage in thirty years, set up card files of members, and even started suffrage parades, which were to become an important tool.[38]

Another young worker proved even more confrontational. Alice Paul, who also saw the value of approaches she had learned in England, began to push actively for a national amendment. First, working through the Congressional Committee of the NAWSA, she started public agitation and demonstrations to force action on a national amendment. In 1913, when her tactics became too controversial for the NAWSA leadership, she formed the Congressional Union, which later became the National Woman's Party. By forcing attention to the movement and demonstrating the intensity of supporters' feelings, her tactics did much to stimulate interest in the cause.[39] When women were harassed and even imprisoned for their activities, their plights generated public sympathy.

While Paul pursued such confrontational tactics and Stanton Blatch sought new members and approaches, even the NAWSA underwent change. Carrie Chapman Catt, who replaced Anna Howard Shaw as president in 1915, realized the need for better strategic organization and political strategy. Her "winning plan," begun in 1916, was, according to Kohrs Campbell, "an administrative and tactical masterpiece designed to put maximum political pressure on Congress to pass a suffrage amendment, based on a hard-nosed analysis of what realistically could be achieved."[40]

These efforts, in tandem with the work by Stanton Blatch and Paul, ultimately proved successful. On January 10, 1918, the House approved the so-called Anthony amendment by a vote of 274 to 136, exactly the two-thirds needed.[41] Although the route through the Senate consumed a year and a half and state approval another fourteen months of arduous work, in August 1920, the amendment became law, and the call for the ballot from Seneca Falls in 1848 was finally answered.

Meeting Rhetorical Challenges

As the preceding discussion suggests, women who sought to enter the public sphere as advocates for any cause faced substantial problems. Kohrs Campbell points out, "Early woman's rights activists were constrained to be particularly creative because they faced barriers unknown to men. They were a group virtually unique in rhetorical history because a central element in woman's oppression was the denial of her right to speak."[42] Kohrs Campbell's historical analysis demonstrates quite clearly that, as the movement developed over time, its advocates faced changing rhetorical situations with different persuasive problems. Some understanding of those changing rhetorical problems is necessary for a consideration of the role of the press in the movement's development.

The first of these problems was simply the necessity of claiming a right to speak out on public issues in open forums. Although by the 1830s, women had established sewing circles and self-improvement groups, very few ventured into the public arena. Frances Wright and Maria W. Miller Stewart defied convention to speak publicly, but both met with widespread and caustic criticism. Indeed "Fanny Wrightist" became a derogatory term for any woman who mounted the public platform.[43] When the American Anti-Slavery Society was formed in 1833, women were permitted to attend but were not allowed to become full members. As a result, some women, Coffin Mott among them, formed their own Philadelphia Female Anti-Slavery Society. Despite this boldness, they felt uncomfortable in assuming the control of their own initial meeting and asked a former male slave to preside.[44]

Most scholars name Sarah and Angelina Grimké as among the first women to maintain stoutly their right to the public platform. But when the Grimké sisters became speakers for abolition, they first limited their efforts to small "parlor gatherings" of women only, because addressing a "promiscuous," or mixed, audience of males and females was virtually unthinkable. Even such circumspect efforts evoked stern criticism. A group of church leaders wrote a "Pastoral Letter from the Council of Congregationalist Ministers of Massachusetts," which, without naming the Grimkés, took them to task for their public efforts, claiming that such activities would render their characters "unnatural," would make them "cease to bear fruit," and would cause them to "fall in shame and dishonor in the dust."[45] Sarah answered these objections in *Letters on the Equality of the Sexes*, which asserted the biblical basis for women's public role. She argued forcefully: ". . . God has made no distinction between men and women as moral beings. . . . To me it is perfectly clear *that whatever it is morally right for a man to do, it is morally right for a woman to do.*"[46] In a speech at the second Anti-Slavery Convention in 1838, Angelina Grimké Weld extended this argument. Noting that women did not have access to the ballot to achieve change, she urged them to ignore criticism and use the right to petition to prompt action. The right to such activity is, she averred, God given, and women must exercise it if they were to fulfill their moral responsibilities.[47]

Such early pioneers helped establish women's right to work as public reformers and to speak in open meetings, but that violation of decorum was only warranted by their concern for significant moral issues. And even after they claimed their right to the public platform, women faced personal criticism, ridicule, and harassment for their efforts. Science and religion combined to combat their claims and to warn of dire consequences if they persisted in their "mannish" behavior.

The transition from public activity in behalf of others to work in their own interests was difficult. In fact, most women only reluctantly acknowledged their own oppression. These early leaders faced the difficult task of raising the consciousness of other women.[48] This task entailed several processes. Among them, were: first, offering a persuasive analysis of the barriers women faced in common; second, convincing women of their own ability to effect social change; and, finally, molding them into an organized, committed group. In essence, each woman had to become convinced that she shared many of the same problems and faced many of the same barriers as other women. She had to come to perceive herself as part of an extensive, oppressed group and to be persuaded of her right and ability to seek remedies. These tasks had to be accomplished while offering her an alternative role model to the prevailing, restrictive social stereotypes. The "true woman" ideal had to be transformed into that of a "new woman." To be acceptable to many women acculturated into fixed social roles, this "new woman" had to evince allegiance to traditional values as she embraced new roles and responsibilities.

In public meetings and lectures, movement leaders and participants could provide the arguments and discussion to raise their listeners' consciousness and could even enact this "new woman" for some audiences. Still, limitations of both time and geography restricted their impact. Such gatherings were of relatively short duration, and without other means of communication, women could quickly lose the inspiration of the moment. By their nature, oratory and public meetings were transitory; often little trace remained of even the most dynamic exchanges.[49] Many women were unable or hesitant to attend such lectures; the very publicness of some gatherings suggested commitment. Moreover, the general press coverage of these meetings was usually quite sparse and often very hostile. For example, editorials after the Seneca Falls Convention called the meeting "the most shocking and unnatural event ever recorded in the history of womanity" and warned equal rights would "demoralize and degrade women." The New York *Herald* labeled the participants in the 1853 national woman's rights convention "unsexed in mind" and the meeting itself the "Woman's Wrong Convention."[50] While even such biased coverage was useful in gaining visibility for the movement, such press discussion was of limited value in attracting members and educating those who were curious.

Newspapers published by supporters could offer a counterpoint to such negative assessments and could, of course, provide women with the chance to consider arguments and ideas for themselves. Additionally, by presenting public issues to their readers, these newspapers subtly but effectively encouraged women to think of themselves as competent, sensible, potentially important persons and to perceive themselves as members of a group with common problems and concerns. But if those contained only "radical" propaganda or didactic materials to "instruct" readers, they were doomed to failure. Thus, newspaper editors had to find compelling ways to attract readers and to raise their consciousness. In the early stages of the movement, responding quite creatively to this challenge, clever editors used diverse strategies to attract and influence their readers. As subsequent chapters will indicate, such early journals as the *Una* and the *Lily* did not initially identify their goal of advocating women's rights. They included "morally uplifting" poems and stories and materials only tangential to the issue of woman's rights. Some even included items traditionally associated with "women's magazines," such as the gardening and grooming tips routinely used as column filler in the *Una*. By providing reports of activities related to women, new opportunities for them, and stories of individual females with unusual or outstanding accomplishments, these newspapers were able to make their readers aware of the larger community of women. If the individual reader felt isolated or insulated from the problems because of her private situation, newspapers printed stories that made her realize how widespread and pressing the difficulties were. The success stories also indicated how competent and energetic women could become. Other journals, for instance, the *Lily*, gradually linked such reform causes as temperance, to which women were already committed, to the need for changes in women's status. To a great extent, each periodical sought its niche by creating a distinctive blend of materials for various segments of the audience. But the common theme of woman's rights was subtly interwoven with other appeals.

As the movement progressed, it faced new challenges, foremost among them, attracting, unifying, and maintaining a committed following. As Kohrs Campbell notes, conventions and meetings were one avenue to accomplish this.[51] Again, each journal achieved its characteristic blend of suffrage news and other items, but each helped build community and educate readers. The content, style, and formats began to shift perceptibly. Reports of meetings, reprints of speeches, rebuttal of the opposition's points, and undisguised arguments for woman's rights became more dominant. These periodicals, such as the *Woman's Journal* and the *Revolution*, were unabashed in their advocacy for suffrage and far more straightforward in their approach. Their task was not only to raise the consciousness of their readers but also to provide supporters with information and news that would sustain their commitment to the cause.

In the wake of the passage of the Fourteenth and Fifteenth Amendments and the closing down of the judicial route to suffrage, supporters faced a long, sustained effort toward legal remedies. As attention shifted to state campaigns for referenda, the movement required committed and informed members in many areas. While it needed to provide workers with information and answers to the growing antisuffrage movement's arguments, the movement also had to sustain hopes in a period with little progress. Suffrage journals provided ways to keep members informed, to offer them arguments to use in their own work, and to reinforce their sense of purpose and progress. Some editors, such as Clara Bewick Colby of the *Woman's Tribune*, used their journals to construct a history of the movement and even to establish their own standing in it. Others, for instance the editors of the *Woman's Column*, used their press to emphasize successes, provide up-to-date reports, and offer continuing inspiration along with the news. The very publication of such works gave the movement an image of importance and endurance, which was vital to sustaining a long public campaign.

On another front, journals with more regional distribution could clearly link the woman's rights cause to more immediate concerns of their readers. The *Farmer's Wife*, thus, directed its appeal to women who were involved in the rising tide of Kansas Populism. In contrast, the *Woman's Exponent* helped solidify and inform Mormon women about not only the national suffrage movement but also the threats to their existing enfranchisement.

In summary, as the campaign for woman's rights grew and developed, its rhetorical challenges and problems changed. The task of consciousness-raising, which Kohrs Campbell sees as central to the movement, took many forms, from creating awareness of oppression and one's right to advocate changes for oneself, to sustaining a sense of community and purpose, to identifying and answering salient issues. Public speeches and meetings were important tools for the suffrage cause, but equally vital were reaching and serving women outside the mainstream of the movement.

Newspapers and journals were able to bridge the gaps of time and distance, educating and uniting women across the country. Success in California, thus, became an inspiration for women in the East, for it was evidence of the inevitable triumph of their cause. In one sense, newspapers and journals became the ties that bound women together and made them into a social movement.

The process of consciousness-raising also mandated offering replacements for old social stereotypes about the nature and roles of women. The cult of "true womanhood" had to be subtly subverted and transformed; adherents had to come to see themselves and fellow workers as "new women" who merited suffrage and were warranted in struggling to gain the ballot. The nature of newspapers permitted editors great latitude in accomplishing this task. The stories about competent, successful women encouraged readers to envision new roles and activities. The depictions that these presses could and did offer were one important element in the long struggle to gain equality for women. The multitude of strategies various editors used and the functions various journals served are the focus of the following chapters.

The Role of Newspapers in the Nineteenth-Century Woman's Movement

E. Claire Jerry

If the proverb that "the pen is mightier than the sword" be true, woman's skill and force in using this mightier weapon must soon change the destinies of the world.[1]
—*History of Woman Suffrage*, Volume I, 1886

When the editors of the first volume of the *History of Woman Suffrage* made this prediction, they were hopeful of a rapid change in woman's status. The change did not come as quickly as these women had desired, but the "pens" of woman's rights publishers certainly played a part in the development of the woman's rights movement and influenced its eventual achievements.

Overall, the role of "in-house" newspapers in social movements is unclear, because their contributions to movement leadership, membership, and organization rarely have been explored. The existence of such "special interest" newspapers is particularly significant for groups and movements that are denied access to and coverage in general circulation media. The peculiar circumstances of women and the movement for woman's rights in the nineteenth-century United States make newspapers and journals from this movement especially interesting. Most American women were often geographically isolated, of limited income, and legally dead. Therefore, traditional means of movement involvement, such as attending conventions and lectures, were unavailable to vast numbers of this movement's potential membership. However, this movement eventually achieved a large following and national prominence, aided in no small part by woman's rights publishing. This essay will trace the circumstances that surrounded the growth of woman's rights newspapers in the nineteenth century, suggesting several functions that they served in the woman's rights movement.

General Circulation Press and Women

Newspapers were a significant part of nineteenth-century American life, and women had long been participants in the growth of general circulation and special interest papers. George P. Rowell, editor of the first newspaper directory in the United States, said in 1873 that "no people are equal to Americans in their appreciation of newspapers." He continued:

It is probable that newspapers will always be popular with Americans. They are suited to the character of the people. They are the guardians of their liberties, their instructors and their companions, they but echo and repeat their opinions, and often ably defend them. They are useful, too, in business or in pleasure, and the tremendous growth of journalism in the United States can hardly be wondered at when we consider how perfect a repository of all that can by possibility be recorded, the American newspaper has become. . . .[2]

The decades immediately preceding the Civil War witnessed an unprecedented increase in newspaper circulation. Frank Luther Mott posited six reasons for the increase that occurred between 1833 and 1860: an increase in population, a decline in illiteracy, improvements in home lighting, a rekindled interest in political affairs, a decrease in price due to technological changes and lower postal rates, and an increase in the number of women readers.[3] This growth was also fueled by the advent of the "penny press," newspapers that increasingly declared their independence from partisan political control. Interest in and circulation of newspapers continued to grow dramatically in the decades following the Civil War. Rowell documented the expansion in 1885: "When we consider that in 1860 there were but 5,253 newspapers published in the United States, or one for every 6,000 of the population, while to-day the aggregate is 13,494, or one for every 3,716 persons, we can readily see that the growth in the newspaper world has more than kept pace with the extraordinary growth of the nation."[4]

As Mott indicated, the increase in the number of women readers contributed to the growth of newspaper circulation. Henry J. Raymond, who had established the *New York Times* as a one-cent daily in 1851, noted the following year: "American women read newspapers much as their liege lords. The paper must accommodate itself to this fact."[5] General circulation papers, however, met this challenge in ways antagonistic to woman's rights. From the beginning of the woman's rights movement, the press responded negatively or by ignoring the effort. For example, the press had a venomous reaction to the first woman's rights convention, held in Seneca Falls, New York, in 1848. Among other things, the convention was called a "petticoat rebellion" and the "most shocking and unnatural incident ever recorded in the history of womanity."[6] The first national woman's rights convention held at Worcester, Massachusetts, in 1850 also garnered a very unfavorable newspaper reaction, with references to it as a "hen convention." Mott reported that the general circulation magazines such as *Nation, Harper's,* and *Atlantic Monthly* covered woman suffrage, but the reports were often incomplete or unflattering.[7] In her history of women orators, Lillian O'Connor discussed this neglect in reference to speeches: "The files of the leading metropolitan newspapers contain no complete texts of addresses given by women. Moreover, there was apparently deliberate omission of any *news* concerning the public-speaking activities of women. This is borne out . . . when Miss [Frances] Wright went to Philadelphia to speak, the editor of the Philadelphia *Gazette* refused to run a paid advertisement for the lectures on the ground that 'it was not agreeable to some of his friends.'"[8] O'Connor added that Horace Greeley's *New-York Tribune* was, for a time, an exception to the "conspiracy of silence." But by 1858, even his somewhat sympathetic coverage of women's concerns disappeared because of his fear that the radical positions that he would report from woman's rights conventions might be construed to be his positions as well.[9] Even publishers who recognized the truth in Raymond's advice of 1852 and wished to court women readers, did not report on reform activities. For example, Joseph Pulitzer, in his effort to acknowledge the increasing status of women in the 1880s, opted for increased coverage of home, fashion, and etiquette rather than woman's rights.[10] Thus, the accepted channels of communication were not open to women who wished to discuss and disseminate their political concerns.

Women's Publishing

This failure of general circulation newspapers to grant women desired coverage contributed to the growth of their special interest publications. Bertha-Monica Stearns, a journalism historian, summarizes the place of such reform periodicals: "Most of them lived only a brief period and are totally forgotten to-day; many of them were wildly absurd; nevertheless, taken together, as a group, they make their little contribution to the ever changing American scene, and supply a chapter of their own in any account of American magazines."[11] Women's "little contribution" began with Frances Wright, an early spokesperson for woman's rights. In 1828, she edited the *Free Enquirer*, a paper established by New Harmony Socialist Robert Dale Owen "for the purpose of fearless and unbiased inquiry on all subjects."[12] Women's reform publications also explored moral issues. The *Amulet and Ladies' Literary and Religious Chronicle*, begun in 1830, was against "intemperance and infidelity"; the *Female Advocate* (1832) was specifically antivice and antiprostitution; and Mrs. Probosco's *American Woman* (1845) was a "denunciation of masculine failings."[13] Women publishers were also active in the abolition cause. Most notable among these were Lydia Maria Child (*National Anti-Slavery Standard*, 1841), Julia Ward Howe (*The Commonwealth*, 1851), and Mrs. C. C. Bentley (*Concord Free Press*, 1851).

Gradually, woman's papers expanded from their single-issue concerns to an all-encompassing range of topics. An early example of this was Elizabeth Aldrich's *Genius of Liberty*, published in Cincinnati from 1851 to 1853. The masthead of this paper read, "Devoted to the Interests of American Women," and it was not limited to any single reform. Rather, Aldrich called for the inclusion of women in all aspects of society: "We must encourage action; aid the crawling of the sex, out of an old bed of idleness, ignorance, and irresponsibility, foster their movements in any direction that looks like the Right, the Beautiful and True. While we are laboring for an enlargement of the sphere of woman, let us not forget the duties and responsibilities that are on every hand, and calling loudly for their faithful performance."[14] Woman's rights, as a specific subject, became the sole focus of a newspaper in 1852, when Anna W. Spencer published the *Pioneer and Woman's Advocate* in Providence, Rhode Island. According to the *History of Woman Suffrage*, "Its motto was 'Liberty, Truth, Temperance, Equality.' It was published semi-monthly and advocated a better education for woman, a higher price for her labor, the opening of new industries."[15]

In spite of these examples, during the antebellum years, most woman's rights activity revolved, not around publishing, but around the holding of conventions. As the breadth of coverage in the woman's publications demonstrated, women were seeking many reforms at these conventions. For example, the call to the 1850 Worcester, Massachusetts, national convention gave as its purpose: "to consider the question of Woman's Rights, Duties, and Relations." These questions included her education, avocations, interests, rights as an individual, and functions as a citizen.[16] Lucretia Coffin Mott explained most clearly the broad-based purpose of these conventions in her opening address at the 1853 New York Convention:

It may be well, at the outset, to declare distinctly the objects of the present Convention. Its purpose is to declare principles, not to descend into the consideration of details: the principles, namely, of the co-equality of woman with man, and her right to practice those arts of life for which she is fitted by nature. These are our great principles, and the assertion of them is our only present purpose. When they shall have been recognized, then it will be quite time enough to speak of the proper mode of carrying them into universal practice. . . . This is called a "Woman's Rights Convention," but, I apprehend, the phrase "Human Rights" would more appropriately express its principles and its aims. . . .[17]

Ten national conventions were held yearly from 1850 to 1860; there was no convention in 1857. Susan B. Anthony and Ida Husted Harper summed up this period of activity: "National conventions were held in various States for the purpose of agitating the question and creating a favorable public sentiment. These were addressed by the ablest men and women of the time, and the discussions included the whole scope of women's wrongs, which in those days were many and grievous."[18]

The Civil War brought virtually all of this woman's rights activity to a halt, including the conventions and most woman's rights publishing. Northern women, who had dominated antebellum woman's rights work, concentrated their wartime efforts on assisting the Union cause, in the anticipation that their efforts would be rewarded with suffrage legislation when hostilities ceased. However, women were ignored when the war was over, as the Republican party, declaring that this was "the Negro's hour," pushed for a Fourteenth Amendment that enfranchised only African-American males and excluded women. As states began to debate the issue of African-American male enfranchisement, women began simultaneous campaigns for woman suffrage.[19]

The first major campaign for woman and Negro suffrage took place in Kansas in 1867. This campaign, which the women lost by a vote of twenty-one thousand to nine thousand, had long-range impact on both the suffrage movement and the feminist press.[20] During the Kansas campaign, Susan B. Anthony and Elizabeth Cady Stanton, recognized national leaders of the suffrage movement, realized that the American Equal Rights Association, formed at the end of the war to further both woman and African-American suffrage, was willing to sacrifice woman suffrage to achieve African-American success. In addition, the failure in Kansas led Anthony and Cady Stanton to two decisions. First, they decided a woman suffrage newspaper was needed to lobby independently for woman's enfranchisement. They later said of this decision: "Our three most radical papers—the *Tribune*, the *Independent*, and the *Standard*—were closed against us. We could not get an article in either, pointing out the danger of reconstruction on the old basis of castle and demanding the recognition of woman in the new government. . . . Thus ostracized, we tried to establish a paper of our own."[21] Second, they began to think in terms of suffrage campaigns on the federal level, aimed at a constitutional amendment; they felt that state-by-state legislation was going to be a needlessly slow and inefficient means to their end. Both of these decisions eventually led to a split in the suffrage movement that took twenty years to mend.

In an effort to achieve their first goal, that of a suffrage newspaper, Anthony and Cady Stanton made an alliance with George Francis Train, a southern, proslavery Democrat. This unusual business alliance gave rise to the first important woman's paper to emerge after the Civil War, the *Revolution*. Published from 1868 to 1871, the *Revolution* marked a turning point in the status of woman's newspapers. Lynne Masel-Walters concludes: "The newspaper set down for the first time in a major national forum arguments for women's equality that are still being used. And it began a century-long tradition of women's political journalism. The *Revolution* inspired the establishment of several contemporaneous suffrage publications, including the *Woman's Tribune* and the *Agitator*."[22]

In addition to its importance as a suffrage newspaper, the *Revolution* played other roles in suffrage history. Marion Marzolf describes some of its results: "Although it lasted for only a little over two years, it was instrumental in broadening the reputation of Stanton as a writer and in arousing more conservative feminists to action."[23] As Marzolf implies, the *Revolution*, in combination with Anthony and Cady Stanton's move toward federal agitation, contributed to the split among national leadership. Anthony and Cady Stanton's alliance with Train was anathema to suffragists who had come to the movement from abolition, most notably Lucy Stone. Stone, her husband, Henry B. Blackwell, and other abolition/suffrage leaders, such as William Lloyd Garrison and Mary A. Livermore, supported the Republican position on "the Negro's hour." They also maintained, even after the Kansas defeat, that state and local referenda were preferable to national suffrage activity. Moreover, the Stone-Blackwell faction, offended by the range and radical tone of the topics covered in the *Revolution*, refused to support it. These disagreements led Anthony and Cady Stanton to withdraw from the

American Equal Rights Association and, in July 1869, to form the National Woman Suffrage Association (NWSA).

Feeling unwelcome and unwilling to compromise, Lucy Stone and Henry B. Blackwell countered this action with the formation of the American Woman Suffrage Association (AWSA) in January 1870. More critical for the history of the suffrage press, however, was their establishment of a competing paper, the *Woman's Journal*. In addition to Stone and Blackwell, the original editorial board of the *Woman's Journal* included experienced publishers like Julia Ward Howe, Mary A. Livermore, and William Lloyd Garrison. Begun as a conservative response to the more radical *Revolution*, this paper had, in the words of Marzolf, "little social awareness of issues beyond suffrage," in hopes of "reduc[ing] the amount of controversy and hysteria surrounding the issue."[24] The *Journal* began with much more stable financial backing than did the *Revolution* (within a year Train had left the country and his support had withered). Backed by the New England Woman Suffrage Association of Boston, the *Journal* was the unofficial organ of the newly created AWSA. This informal relationship was good for circulation in that, according to journalism historian Anne Mather, "it attracted socially active women not yet prepared to bear the feminist banner."[25] Because it was supported by the less extreme wing of the movement, the *Journal*'s audience included moderate, conservative, professional women of the upper and middle class who were interested primarily in suffrage alone.[26] Since the *Revolution* could not survive against this type of competition, in 1870, the *Woman's Journal*, and by implication the AWSA, had sole possession of the national suffrage newspaper market.[27]

The *Woman's Journal* was not the only suffrage paper to emerge during this period; state and local papers sprang up, and died, with great regularity. In 1873, Rowell reported the existence of four suffrage papers: the San Francisco *Pioneer*; Boston's *Woman's Journal*; *Woodhull & Claflin's Weekly*, published in New York City; and Abigail Scott Duniway's *New Northwest* out of Portland, Oregon.[28] By the following year, the list had expanded to six and new suffrage papers continued to emerge, although there was occasional fluctuation in their number and location.[29] For example, in 1879, the Rowell listing was down to five suffrage papers, only two of which had existed in 1873.[30] By 1884, however, the number of suffrage publications had risen to nine:

San Francisco, *Woman's Herald of Industry*
Denver, *Queen Bee*

Indianapolis, *Woman's Own*
Lafayette, Indiana, *Our Herald*
Boston, *Woman's Journal*
Beatrice, Nebraska, *Woman's Tribune*
New York City, *Fortschritt*
Portland, *New Northwest*
Salt Lake City, *Woman's Exponent*[31]

This expansion of the suffrage press continued, with no fewer than thirty-three papers appearing between 1870 and 1890.[32]

The Role of the Press in Reunion and Victory

The two suffrage organizations, the NWSA and the AWSA, remained apart for almost twenty years. The NWSA continued to push for a constitutional amendment, while the AWSA lobbied on a state-by-state basis. The NWSA was without an official newspaper after the death of the *Revolution* in 1870, although the *Woman's Tribune* presumed to fill this function. In contrast, the AWSA spoke through the pages of the *Woman's Journal*. Except for a few women who held memberships in both organizations and except for the few times when both groups campaigned in the same place at the same time, these two associations had little official contact. At the same time, between 1870 and 1890, there was little success in the extension of woman suffrage. Maud Wood Park, one of the movement's own historians, described the period between 1869 and 1890 as "twenty years of constant effort and constant defeat."[33] Both suffrage organizations acknowledged that their in-fighting had contributed to this failure. Although talk of reunion circulated as early as 1870 and again in 1880 and 1884, problems of ideology and leadership could not be resolved.[34] Gradually, however, the good of the cause overcame the personal animosities that had existed between the two groups since the split in 1869, and serious reunion proceedings began in 1887.

The suffrage press is significant in this merger because the issue of an official suffrage organ was a major topic during negotiations. Of concern was the relationship between the *Woman's Journal* and the *Woman's Tribune* and the role of each in the movement. The *Journal*, as described above, was the organ of the more moderate suffragists and focused primarily on suffrage. It was publicly, if unofficially, recognized to be affiliated with the Massachusetts Woman Suffrage Association, the New England Woman Suffrage Association, and the AWSA.[35] The *Woman's Tribune*, aligned with the more liberal views of Elizabeth Cady Stanton and Susan B. Anthony, was never again formally affiliated with a suffrage group after the Nebraska State Woman Suffrage Association dropped it after only one year's backing. However, Anthony represented it in state campaigns as the "organ of the National Association."[36] The AWSA perceived this claim as an attack on them. The issue of an official newspaper was raised at a negotiation meeting between Anthony and Stone on December 21, 1887. Anthony apparently compromised, because the *Woman's Journal* retained its semiofficial status. (It was not named the official organ of the National American Woman Suffrage Association until 1910, after the *Tribune* had folded.[37]) Whatever the reason, the issue of an organization newspaper was resolved, as were other issues, and the reunion was completed in February 1890 at the first convention of the National American Woman Suffrage Association (NAWSA).

Reunion did not lead immediately to a widespread extension of woman suffrage, although the first few years were promising. In the first year of the reunion, Wyoming was admitted to statehood with woman suffrage in its constitution. In 1893, Colorado passed woman suffrage, and in 1896, Idaho and Utah joined the suffrage ranks. These early gains were promising, but fourteen years would pass before another state would be added to the suffrage cause.

Various reasons have been posited for the slowness of the suffrage pace, including the strength of the liquor lobby, which equated woman suffrage with Prohibition; the southern states' rights argument, left over from similar battles about African-American suffrage; women's own apathy, based on their acceptance of the ideology that "a woman's place is in the home"; and men's fear of women's political power. The arguments of the antisuffragists are not the focus here, since they have been examined in depth elsewhere.[38] What is important is that women's level of activity was not at fault. Carrie Chapman Catt and Nettie Rogers Schuler, in their history of the suffrage movement, cataloged the amount of effort that took place between 1868 and 1920:

During that time they [American women] were forced to conduct fifty-six campaigns of referenda to male voters; 480 campaigns to urge Legislatures to submit suffrage amendments to voters; 47 campaigns to induce State constitutional conventions to write woman suffrage into State constitutions; 277 campaigns to persuade State party conventions to include woman suffrage planks; 30 campaigns to urge presidential party conventions to adopt woman suffrage planks in party platforms; and 19 campaigns with 19 successive Congresses.[39]

The turning point in this activity came in 1917 with victory in New York. The example set by New York led to suffrage amendments in Indiana, Maine, Missouri, Iowa, Minnesota, Ohio, Wisconsin, and Tennessee in 1919. Maud Wood Park argued that it was these "state gains that carried us over the top."[40] Just over a year elapsed before the necessary thirty-six states ratified the amendment, which became part of the Constitution on August 26, 1920, seventy-two years after Seneca Falls.

This history of the final years of the suffrage movement provides a context for the final years of the suffrage press. In the years following the turn of the century, the movement and the press, which had grown together in the nineteenth century, diverged. As more states passed suffrage legislation and victory became increasingly sure, the suffrage press declined in size. Of the fourteen major suffrage newspapers that were published after 1900, only two survived past 1917. The following chart reflects the process:[41]

Year of Final Issue	Number of Papers That Folded
pre–1910	2
1910–1915	4
1916	1
1917	5
post–1917	2

In the most telling year, 1917, when victory seemed assured, almost three-fourths of the suffrage newspapers folded. This is not as incongruous as it might at first appear. Historians Anne Firor Scott and Andrew M. Scott provide the first potential reason in their discussion of general press coverage of the movement. In an analysis of the *New York Times*, they find increasing attention paid to suffrage as the final New York referendum drew near: "From December 1915 to March 1916, only six suffrage stories appeared on the first five pages of the *Times*, and many that did appear were printed along with engagement, marriage, birth and death notices. By July coverage began to pick up, and two and three column articles replaced the earlier brief paragraphs. By late summer editorials and letters to the editor appeared in considerable numbers. . . ."[42] This trend toward suffrage as news continued, and coverage expanded from 1916 through the passage of the Nineteenth Amendment. Anne Messerly Cooper, from a content analysis of ten daily newspapers, concludes that "by 1920, suffrage had taken its place as a page-1 topic at or near the top of the news agenda. . . ."[43] Suffrage newspapers, which had functioned to provide news of the movement to supporters and rationale for passage to foes, were no longer necessary. The general circulation press was now serving these purposes.

What accounted for this change in press coverage? Lauren Jeanne Kessler, who studied the relationship between the general circulation press and the suffrage press in Oregon, offers conclusions that could be applied to the entire country. She argues that a group that has been denied access to the press can only gain entry after the "group attains legitimate status within the society" and after social acceptance is attained.[44] She concludes that male editors purposefully and systematically denied women access to the press as a means of "symbolic annihilation," i.e., a denial of social existence.[45] An extension of her argument, then, is that as woman suffrage gained more and more popularity and as the movement attracted increased national attention, the editors were forced to cover the speeches, conventions, and lobbying activities as news.[46] This analysis, consistent with the chronology of events throughout the country, echoes the claim of the television documentary "The Female Rebellion," which argued that the press did not support woman suffrage until after the Senate had passed the amendment and ratification appeared inevitable.[47] Both the suffrage press and the suffrage movement were subsumed into activities of the newly formed League of Women Voters following ratification of the amendment.[48] Nonetheless, seventy-two years of suffrage activity and ninety-two years of feminist publishing had left their mark on American women forever.

Conclusion

The events of the nineteenth century involving woman's rights and woman's publishing led to a body of journalism that served several functions for the woman's rights movement. Comparing the purpose statements of nineteenth-century woman editors, examining the content of their papers, and considering the critiques of several scholars reveal numerous functions. First, these papers reached a less homogeneous audience than did lecturers and convention speakers. For example, this varied audience could include women from divergent social classes and, very importantly, men. With readership estimates ranging from a few hundred to several thousand, the papers were obviously being read by more than a few active middle-class women. Second, newspapers could reach larger numbers of people than could any single speaker. By definition, conventions and lecture meetings were limited to the seating capacity of the auditoriums, whereas newspapers could be printed in large

numbers, and individual copies could be shared among several readers. In addition, editors often argued, the written word had a longer-
lasting impact than individual movement activities, in that it could
be read and reread, continually reinforcing and reintroducing movement claims. Clara Bewick Colby, editor of the *Woman's Tribune*,
stated it as follows:

The spoken word has its power for the day, but for building up a new line of
thought in the popular heart there must be the written word, which shall be
quietly digested and made part of the reader's own thought. Then the
change in belief comes irresistibly. . . .
   But while the lecture amuses and interests for an hour or two, often the
many cares and interests of our complex life sweep away the impression
immediately, while the paper read in quiet moments gradually makes conviction, and the reader instead of being transitorily influenced by the opinion of another, builds up opinions of his [sic] own from the logic of events, a
faith that cannot be shaken.[49]

   The fourth function of movement newspapers was to bring together women who were separated by geography. In her study of several suffrage journals, Linda Claire Steiner posits that "suffrage
periodicals drew together geographically isolated women into an
emotionally bonded community sharing a set of values, concerns,
and way of looking at the world."[50] She concludes:

Thus mass media enable geographically dispersed members to participate
symbolically in the central dramas and myths of that group, to engage in
symbolic action. . . . For those nineteenth century women frustrated by
their cultural, social and physical isolation at home, the suffrage papers
offered identity within a new and larger community claiming a socially significant purpose. Furthermore, suffrage periodicals involved new women in
an [sic] national arena, reorienting them to national (and presumably more
important) problems, and connecting them to national myths and objects of
reverence or celebration.[51]

Steiner's analysis also articulates a fifth role, that of bringing the
national groups into contact with the members. As Lauren Kessler
observes: "In addition to acting as forums for ideas, the feminist
press enhanced intramovement communication and aided in internal organization. Especially in the nineteenth century, when national communications and transportation networks were not yet
developed, feminists from New England to the Northwest were
linked through the pages of their newspapers and periodicals. Feminist publications helped boost the morale of their readers. . . ."[52]
However, women could not appreciate this contact if they were unaware of their needs. Therefore, the papers also served to reach

women who might not think of themselves as feminists or woman's rights activists, who might not be aware of their frustration. Lucy L. Correll, wife of an early woman's rights publisher, explained that once apathetic women were reached, "they were soon awakened to a new consciousness of their true status wherein they discovered their 'rights' were only 'privileges.'"[53]

Finally, woman's rights newspapers helped identify and create movement leaders. As in studies of the antebellum black press, a list of woman's rights movement leaders closely parallels a list of newspaper publishers. Susan B. Anthony, Elizabeth Cady Stanton, Lucy Stone, Amelia Bloomer, Paulina Wright Davis, and Abigail Scott Duniway were but a few of the women who filled both categories. Others sought leadership through their journalistic endeavors. Clara Bewick Colby attempted to use her paper, the *Woman's Tribune*, to catapult herself into a position of national prominence that she was never able to achieve by election.[54]

In sum, woman's rights newspapers fulfilled a variety of functions in the nineteenth century, functions made necessary by the special needs of women and the special concerns of the movement for woman's rights. Although most nineteenth-century woman's rights editors did not live to see the success of the causes for which they fought, Clara Bewick Colby spoke for the goals that motivated their activity in the face of discouragement when she articulated the goals of her own paper: "to present an epitome of the best that comes under its observation whether in person or place, deed or speech; to fight all forms of wrong by encouraging the good. . . . What a beautiful paper it would be that should be devoted only to a recital of the good and brave deeds that each day are performed by our glorious humanity."[55]

The *Lily*, 1849–1856
From Temperance to Woman's Rights
Edward A. Hinck

> "Emancipation of Woman from Intemperance, Injustice,
> Prejudice, and Bigotry"

> It is woman that speaks through the *Lily.* It is upon an important
> subject, too, that she comes before the public to be heard.
> Intemperance is the great foe to her peace and happiness. It is that,
> above all, which has made her home desolate, and beggared her
> offspring. It is that above all which has filled to the brim her cup of
> sorrows, and sent her mourning to her grave. Surely she has the
> right to wield her pen for its suppression. Surely she may, without
> throwing aside the modest retirement, which so much becomes her
> sex, use her influence to lead her fellow mortals away from the
> destroyer's path. It is this which she proposes to do in the columns
> of the *Lily.* (January 1849, 3)

The Origin of the *Lily*

In the early 1840s, six men took a vow in a Baltimore tavern and
resolved themselves to spread the gospel of temperance.[1] Known as
the Washingtonians, they delivered temperance speeches all over the
country, including Seneca Falls, New York, where Amelia Jenks
Bloomer and other female temperance activists thereafter formed
the first Ladies Temperance Society.[2]

Temperance organizations of the time, which were composed
mainly of males, excluded women from the public sphere of their
activities. Although temperance was recognized as a significant
woman's issue, and women were allowed to form their own temperance societies, their activities were constrained by customs pre-

venting women from speaking out as public advocates for their causes. These factors led the Ladies Temperance Society of Seneca Falls to consider the creation of a temperance journal that would allow them to express their views while remaining within the sphere of "true womanhood" reserved for them by a male-dominated society. In Dexter Bloomer's words: "But though public sentiment did not then sanction the appearance of women speakers even to advocate so good a cause as Temperance, yet they could use their pens in its support. Mrs. Bloomer did this quite frequently as we have seen, but the little society in Seneca Falls concluded that it must have a paper of its own, and on the 1st of January, 1849, such a paper was commenced in that place."[3]

A paper was planned, but last-minute obstacles arose tempting the committee to cancel the project altogether. Thinking they would be the subject of male ridicule if they did not follow through with the paper, especially after they had taken money for subscriptions, Amelia Jenks Bloomer, a member of the organization and an officer, insisted on completing the project.[4] Ultimately, Jenks Bloomer was responsible for seeing the first issue through to publication, did most of the work on subsequent issues, and after a year became the first woman in the United States to edit and publish her own journal.[5] The *Dictionary of American Biography* noted that "in 1850 the heading of her paper 'published by a committee of ladies' was dropped and Mrs. Bloomer's name appeared alone as publisher and editor and a new heading 'devoted to the interests of women' was added."[6]

The journal, named the *Lily*, appeared for the first time on 1 January 1849. Although Jenks Bloomer was never satisfied with the name, she did not change it. With yearly subscriptions at fifty cents, circulation increased from two or three hundred for the first issue to six hundred or eight hundred by the end of its first year and to over four thousand by 1853. At its peak, probably around late 1853 or early 1854, the *Lily* enjoyed a circulation of six thousand, due in part, perhaps, to the notoriety of the costume named for its editor, the bloomer.[7]

Originally devoted solely to "temperance and literature," the character of the *Lily* began to change toward the end of the first volume. By January of 1853, the *Lily* had become devoted to the "Emancipation of Woman from Intemperance, Injustice, Prejudice, and Bigotry," and finally, in January of 1854, to equality for woman.

From 1849 to 1853, Amelia Bloomer published the *Lily* in Seneca Falls, distributing it by mail. In 1853, Amelia's husband, Dexter, sold his interest in the *Seneca County Courier* to invest in the *Western Home Visitor*, published in Mt. Vernon, Ohio, where the couple relocated and where she continued publishing the *Lily* from 1853 to 1854. After a year in Ohio, the Bloomers moved to Council Bluffs, Iowa, which as a frontier town lacked modern printing presses and was located hundreds of miles away from the nearest railroads. Because publication and mailing of the *Lily* from her new home was impractical, Jenks Bloomer sold the *Lily* to Mary Birdsall of Richmond, Indiana. Birdsall continued publication for two years and "then suffered it to go down."[8]

Although Jenks Bloomer authored many of the articles, Elizabeth Cady Stanton, Susan B. Anthony, Jane Grey Swisshelm, and other interested readers contributed letters, articles, and columns. While an editorial policy was evident in the responses Jenks Bloomer wrote to her readers, for the most part, the editor gave priority to well-written pieces on the subjects of temperance, woman suffrage, and the welfare of women.

The *Lily* is significant because it was a forum that circumvented the prohibition on the public appearance of female advocates in the nineteenth century. As a historical artifact, its pages function as a remarkable record of the ways in which early feminists used language to shape effective appeals and persuasive arguments, to raise feminist consciousness, and to provide model roles for feminist activists.

The rhetorical impact of the *Lily* was significant because it reaffirmed readers as "true" women in the sense of being moral, pious, and concerned with the domestic tranquillity of home and family. While this strategy was essential, given the nature of the audience, the *Lily* widened the sphere of what could be considered feminine through its use of indirect argument in narrative mode via poetry and literature, and then, later, direct argument. The distinctly feminine tone, the focus on domestic and maternal issues, and the analytical discussions of causes for their plight helped women to transcend their limited sphere of activity within an actual home. By arguing that intemperance was a threat to all women, the *Lily* helped shape the temperance issue as a universal concern for women. This approach widened the basis of activities open to women, by revealing that the fundamental values of society needed to be reordered if women were to obtain the necessary power to effect legislative change. To facilitate a change in the concept of woman, the *Lily* helped its readers visualize themselves as reformers in a historical tradition of all great humanitarians. By presenting women with a moral precedent, transformed as a moral imperative to act as reformers, the *Lily* helped legitimize actions outside the domestic sphere.

Characteristic Features

The format usually consisted of a cover story and a poem on the front page, which often developed moral themes. Inside were columns, news stories, and articles. Four broad categories of content are evident: moral literature, particularly short stories and poetry; columns and articles devoted to the domestic interests of women; temperance literature taking the form of moral injunctions, appeals, and news items; and woman's rights literature, including articles, appeals, and news items.

These categories are not mutually exclusive because in the journal's evolution many articles spanned these divisions. For example, after its first year of publication, appeals for temperance began to reflect a concern for woman's rights. Also, stories about successful women operating as professionals outside the domestic sphere not only fall within the category of "moral literature" or as examples of "columns devoted to the interests of women" but, arguably, can be classified as examples of woman's rights literature, in the sense that they provided historical and contemporary instances of female abilities, as well as constituting important role models for those women who had no other concept of womanhood save that imposed by a male-dominated culture. In short, the distinctions among these four types of content were clearest in the first volume of the *Lily*. Importantly, the changes in the *Lily* after volume one were due to the influence of Elizabeth Cady Stanton; as a result of her increased contributions to the columns of the *Lily*, these distinctions in content become more problematic as the interconnections between woman's rights and temperance became more complex. After volume one, temperance gradually receded as a primary concern of the journal and equal rights took precedence. Still, each category merits some discussion.

Moral Literature

The first issue of the journal provides a good example of the moral tone and instruction in many stories. A short story, "The Old Cloak," instructed young ladies to develop their intellects, to minimize their vanity, and to act prudently if they hoped to be successful in attracting a desirable husband (January 1849, 1–2). This story and later ones captured the audience's attention through dramatic narrative, while the characters provided contrasts between good and evil motives. Reading such stories, the audience realized that feminine vanity, then an acceptable concern for a woman, deprived other women of independence. If this reason was insufficient to alter attitudes, the vain woman also learned that men favored women with intelligence and common sense over women who pursued the latest fashions. Finally, this particular story revealed the ways in which the vanity of youth contributed to woman's dependence or, at least, foiled her attempts to gain independence.

A second major feature of the *Lily* was the inclusion of poetry. In all issues surveyed, two or more poems appeared. Often the poems attempted to evoke some feeling of pity, sadness, sentimentality, or religious fervor, usually but not always in connection with the issue of temperance. For example, in the first issue, "Lines" expressed the purpose and hope of the temperance advocates (January 1849, 1). The voice of woman was symbolized by the lily, which is pure, lifegiving, and virtuous; it carried a message to "outcast wanderers" who had forsaken their homes, family, and friends for alcohol; and it expressed the fervent hope of gradual conversion through steady work in the face of disappointments. Hence, it seemed appropriate to initiate the new journal with an example of moral rebirth that expressed both the purpose of the journal and the hope of the new temperance society.

Columns and Articles: Education and Models

In addition to stories and poetry, monthly columns contributed to the development of women's intellect by furthering their education. Early in the first volume, for example, a discussion of the "Nebular Theory of the Universe" begins, with subsequent issues focused on diverse aspects of how the universe was formed. In one issue, the author examined "gravitation, magnetism, and the plurality of the worlds" (March 1849, 19), in another, "the moon" (June 1849, 44). Generally, such columns provided women with scientific information and discussion that usually came from a formal education, which many of the audience had no opportunity to receive.[9]

A second kind of column provided information to young ladies, especially young mothers or girls soon to marry, about health, fashion, or household care. In Jane Swisshelm's "Letters to Country Girls," for example, the author advised her readers and answered their correspondence on a variety of issues, including health care for women (July 1849, 52), the kinds of dresses that "country girls" should sew and wash (October 1849, 74), the right of women to vote and hold office (August 1850, 60), and her opinion of drunkards (October 1850, 78).

A third kind of column was exemplified by Elizabeth Cady Stanton's series "Henry Neil and His Mother." In addition to this column, Cady Stanton wrote another series entitled "Letters to Mothers," which dealt with the problems of bringing up children (September 1851, 66). Although "Letters to Mothers" was restricted to more traditional concerns for women, Cady Stanton's conversations between the fictitious Henry Neil and his mother on issues of government, law, and economics reflected a subtle rhetorical strategy. Although discussion of these matters was normally reserved for men, Cady Stanton's columns appealed to mothers who had strong convictions about government and laws, especially as they related to the issue of temperance. Since mothers were responsible for raising their sons within the domestic sphere, issues concerning government, law, and economics were important for other women to learn about so that they might instruct their sons in ways to fight intemperance. This column, then, reveals one way in which the sphere of "true womanhood" was widened to include activities normally reserved for males. Cady Stanton remained within the traditional concept of "true womanhood" by focusing on ways in which mothers could contribute to the education of their sons; however, at the same time, she enlarged the domestic sphere by including discussions of matters normally reserved for men, educating her audience in the ways of government, law, and economics, and by providing the resources for her readers to instruct their children in those same areas, so that they, too, might become effective temperance advocates.

Another important aspect of the *Lily*'s content was the inclusion of stories about female role models. In the first issue of the *Lily*, the "Widow of Rona," a woman who had saved lives by lighting a warning beacon for incoming ships during storms, was portrayed as having "saved more lives than Davy's safety lamp and thousands of pounds to the underwriters, yet seldom has she been prevailed upon to receive any award" (January 1849, 11). Late in volume one, the image of the ideal woman changes. Benevolence is replaced with competence outside the domestic sphere. In "Female Printers and Editors," the *Lily* reprinted sixteen examples of female publishers and printers who had written and published during the Revolutionary War. The article was prefaced with this statement: "We would particularly commend it to the attention of those sensitive ones who think a woman incapable of doing anything beyond the narrow sphere of her own home, and who are shocked at the impropriety, and cry out against the indelicacy and want of modesty in those who dare venture upon a similar step at the present day. Verily our grandmothers knew their rights and could maintain them" (November

1849, 87). Stories of this nature are included in many issues of the *Lily*. They were drawn from history, e.g., "What History Says of Woman?" (April 1851, 31), and contemporary models, e.g., "Mrs. Elizabeth Fry—From Sketches of Reforms and Reformers by H. B. Stanton" (December 1849, 90) and "The Female Doctor" (July 1851, 49), a biographical sketch of Laura Maria Catherine Bassi, who had struggled in Italy to acquire a doctorate in philosophy. While these stories did not argue explicitly that women could legitimately act outside the domestic sphere, they did present female models who proved women could function successfully in the public arena.

Temperance Literature

The *Lily* was also a place to reinforce temperance attitudes; throughout are appeals to "Shun the Wine Cup."[10] In such articles, contributors, describing the evils of intemperance, encouraged readers to avoid any contact with alcohol. Other appeals blamed the continued liquor traffic on those who did not actively participate in the battle against intemperance. In "Who Is Responsible for the Traffic in Intoxicating Drinks?", the *Lily* answered: ". . . the People. Yes it is upon the people, and especially upon those of wealth and standing in our society, that the weight of condemnation must fall. They have it in their power to put a stop to the deadly traffic, but use their power, and lend their influence, instead to sustain and defend it. . . . Those who remain silent on this subject, and do nothing for the good of our cause, even though temperate themselves, are equally guilty with the oppressor" (January 1849, 12). Other pieces throughout the *Lily* served to dramatize the destruction caused by alcohol. In one anecdote, "Crazy Jane," the authors report on their visit to an asylum where they noticed a girl who, they claim, had once been very beautiful. After inquiring into her history, they discovered that her husband came under the influence of alcohol, was inebriated much of the time, and once beat her. That act of cruelty was too much for the young girl, whose hopes of a happy marriage were blasted by her husband's vice, alcohol. Becoming insane, she was placed in the asylum to finish her wretched life (January 1849, 16).

When such emotional stories were combined with an appeal for total abstinence, they created an appeal based on an implicit form of an argument from the irreparable.[11] For example, consider this description of a gradual fall into the clutches of alcohol: "By slow, but certain approaches, it cases the chains around the husband of a fond and virtuous wife—it gradually palsied his intellect and brutalized his affections—it led him into bad company, and destroyed his at-

tention to business—it made him sour, morose and cruel. . . ."[12]
The argument was most effective when it included a moment of
remorse. In this appeal, the implications of taking a single drink
became clear only in the final moments of the narrative. The effect
was to telescope the reader's experience into the future in the hope
that it would frighten him/her from taking the first drink. In the
following excerpt, a fictitious father experiences such a moment of
remorse, warning the reader of alcohol's destruction:

Again the child was quiet and soon it fell asleep. Jenny crept closer in the
dark corner and tho't it was warmer, though the snow still blew in, and the
cold piercing wind still howled and moaned. The thin and delicate frame
ceased to shiver and shake as it had all day, and she contentedly fell asleep
with Willy clasped closely in her arms. That was a sweet long sleep—for
they never awoke. . . . The father's heart was full of remorse at the misery
and death he had caused—but it was too late, for them and for him. He
could not conquer his appetite. He had trifled with the wine cup. He like a
thousand others had said, I can take care of myself! I can let it alone if it
injures! I am not such a fool as to drink in excess.[13]

Finally, the *Lily* provided concrete evidence of alcohol's devasta-
tion in reports of individuals who had recently been found dead as a
result of their intemperate habits. These news items were always
short, but vivid: "'Cut His Throat:' Henry Rhienerker was found
dead in his bed on the 13th inst., in Twentieth Street, with his throat
cut, and a razor clenched fast in his hand. He was very intemperate and
did not live with family" (February 1849, 24). Or, "A Man by the
name of George Whitcomb shot his wife and child at Rindge, N.H.,
lately while in a fit of intoxication" (November 1849, 84). Because
the *Lily* contained many examples of such dismal results from intemperate lives, advocates always had on hand several examples to
employ in support of their cause.[14]

The *Lily* also served as a source for news about the temperance
movement. Announcements of other states and counties passing
antiliquor laws,[15] advertisements for public lectures by temperance
advocates,[16] and reports from various temperance conventions were
included in the *Lily*. These articles provided encouragement to temperance activists by reporting progress in the fight against intemperance and reminded readers of their responsibilities to the
movement by showing them how much was gained for them in the
victories of temperance advocates across the nation.

But more importantly, the coverage of temperance issues empowered women to serve as agents of change. Toward the end of the
first volume, when Jenks Bloomer was uncertain of continuing the
Lily's publication, this letter encouraged her to continue her fight

against intemperance, by arguing that social action was appropriate given woman's occupation of the domestic sphere and given woman's ability to feel, to think, and to act for the good of humanity:

We are all interested in the success of this paper—but more especially is woman. The *Lily* pleads her cause in two ways. First, by a continued warfare on one of the greatest enemies of her domestic peace—intemperance; and next, by a practical manifestation of woman's capacity to feel, to think, to act; and by the eloquence of her pen to do much for suffering humanity. Those who claim to be interested in what they call "woman's rights," should do what they can to sustain this paper, for although its pages may not be filled with that subject, yet the fact that its editor is a woman, is a great argument on that side of the question; then too, the interests of the whole human family are so linked together that whatever is done for the elevation of one class effects [*sic*] all (December 1849, 95).

Woman's Rights Literature

By volume three, the content of the *Lily* had become more explicitly activist.[17] Although the columns imparting interesting information to women did not disappear, articles that engaged in social criticism began to appear. For example, throughout volume three run columns entitled "Equality of Rights to Woman" and "The Democratic Review of Women's Rights," both authored by a radical who penned her work "Senex." Each installment offered detailed, careful argument in support of the burgeoning equal rights movement. In part seven of "Equality of Rights to Woman," Senex provided a sample of her ability to reveal weakness in the arguments of the opposition:

The argument is, some women at some times could not conveniently perform the duties of Judge, Legislator, military commander, because of the duties of the nursery. Therefore all women should at all times be excluded from all political franchises: or in shorter form, because some women are and will be mothers, all women shall be nothing else. This is making maternity not merely an inconvenience, but a crime—inflicting the penalty not on the delinquents alone, but on all the sex alike—not only on one age but on all ages (part 7, March 1852, 20).

Volumes three and four also witnessed an increasing number of articles on such topics as "Equality of the Sexes" (May 1851, 36), "Defense of Women's Rights" (May 1851, 36), "Woman's Rights" (April 1851, 28), and "Female Education" (April 1851, 4). While previously these pages had been filled with moral injunctions to abstain from drinking, the *Lily's* content now focused on the question of equal rights.

In addition to the many arguments and discussions, there were reports of conventions on temperance and woman's rights (September 1851, 67). Letters were printed from various women who could not attend these conventions but who wanted to contribute their thoughts to the movement. Speeches delivered at the conventions were reprinted together with the proceedings and minutes of these meetings.

In essence, volumes three and four viewed temperance only in relation to equal rights. In this regard, the *Lily* underwent a transformation from a journal devoted simply to temperance and literature to one that marked the progress of the broader woman's rights movement. This transformation can be seen most clearly in the purpose statements of the journal. The first issue of volume one began as a "woman's journal devoted to Temperance and Literature" (January 1849, 1). The publication of volume four witnessed a change to "a monthly journal devoted to Emancipation of Woman from Intemperance, Injustice, Prejudice, and Bigotry . . ." (March 1852, 24). And finally, volume five stated: "It will continue to labor zealously and earnestly for the emancipation of woman from the crushing evils of Intemperance—from the cruel enactments of unjust laws made without her consent—from the destructive influences of Custom and Fashion—from the mistaken views of duty and personal effort, and for her true position in society of perfect and entire equality in all that relates to her social, civil and religious rights and duties" (July 1853, last page).

This transformation was due, in part, to the influence of Cady Stanton's contributions to the journal. As Jenks Bloomer noticed the increasing interest in woman's rights issues and activities, she adapted both content and purpose statements to reflect the changing identity of the journal. Attention is now turned to the ways in which the first two volumes redefined the concept of true womanhood and enabled early woman's rights activists to articulate their grievances, recognize common concerns, develop arguments for change, and lay the groundwork for organizing a social movement.

Rhetorical Functions of the *Lily*

In one sense, the audience for the *Lily* is quite easy to describe. It was composed mainly of women: wives, mothers, sisters, daughters, aunts, grandmothers, and widows, all of whom allegedly had potential influence over men. At the time of publication, the intended audience had to have fifty cents for the yearly subscription, were probably Christians, and quite likely were members of a local temperance society. This "immeasurable" influence, according to the *Lily*, was to be the road to temperance reform (April 1849, 29). Because women had no power to alter laws, the strategy of the *Lily* was to appeal to women's sense of piety, their maternal instincts, their status concerns, and their religious values. Much of the rhetoric of the *Lily* assumed a shared value system evident by the heavy reliance on scripture for support of the notion of drinking as sin.

Also, the journal did little to change attitudes of those who believed in moderate drinking. Drinking was an absolute issue: those who drank were sinners; those who abstained were righteous. In this regard, temperance appeals within the *Lily*, whether poetic, literary, or directly expressed, constituted a divisive rhetoric. These assumptions narrowed the basis of appeal, limiting the degree to which the movement could generate further support. Moreover, by alienating so many different groups—rum sellers, intemperates, non-Christians, social drinkers, husbands—temperance advocates generated opposition to their cause. For these reasons, reform based on a narrow ideology of total abstinence was likely to be unsuccessful.

Initially, temperance advocates were concerned with moral behavior, and Jenks Bloomer represented that part of the *Lily's* audience that saw temperance issues strictly in moral terms. But moral literature would lead women to the more fundamental concern for woman's rights. Because the *Lily* encouraged women to express their feelings through moral literature, the journal allowed women to share a common understanding of their plight through poems, stories, articles, and columns. As they confronted the cultural and legal barriers to a temperate society, they discovered that their inability to protect themselves from intemperance was due to a sexist social order. In this respect, the *Lily* contributed to the early women's rights movement by revealing how temperance issues stemmed from the problem of unequal rights. But because their actions were narrowly circumscribed by social custom, the only ways in which they could alter those customs would be through actions prescribed for them by the prevailing social order. Only through moral literature, then, could women begin to reshape what it meant to be a woman, try on new roles as humanitarian reformers, and ultimately widen the sphere of "true womanhood."

Redefining "True Womanhood" through Moral Literature

Poems and stories provided a unique means of altering roles and transforming the audience into temperance advocates. Through literature the paper could reorient values and perspectives on behavior where arguments were not yet considered appropriate for women.[18] Moreover, the dominant concept of "true womanhood" made moral literature the appropriate form of discourse for contemporary feminist roles. Because arguments were inappropriate for women, temperance rhetoric was required to find its form in a nondiscursive mode, in this case, narrative.[19] Feelings were within the realm of piety reserved for women in the nineteenth century. Before arguments could be made, women needed to become aware of the issues of oppression. As Suzanne Langer notes, ". . . feelings have definite forms, which become progressively articulated."[20] Thus, what were to be the rationales for enlarging women's sphere had to begin as ideas in works of art—literature and poetry. Langer concludes, "To understand the 'idea' in a work of art is therefore like having a new experience than like entertaining a new proposition. . . ."[21] For example, in "The Old Cloak," the selfishness of one character became apparent only when contrasted against other more desirable characters. By reading the story and comparing their mode of conduct to that of the other characters, young girls were able to acquire a perspective on their own behavior and, thus, bring their conduct closer to the model portrayed in this story and others. Thus, the stories and poems offered "new experiences" for women to reflect on, and from these reflections came a greater awareness of the issues that women needed to address.

The columns of the *Lily* marked changes in the image of the ideal woman. For example, in the article "Ultraism," the author provided an elaborate definition of "ultraism," which more simply meant "active in effective radical reform" (November 1849, 87). In responding to claims that woman's rights radicals were guilty of excess in the way of ultraism, the author pointed to examples of past "ultraists": Columbus, the Pilgrims, Benjamin Franklin, Patrick Henry, Robert J. Fulton, John Howard (a contemporary prison reformer), Martin Luther, Lafayette, Charles Wilberforce, and Elizabeth Fry (for prison reform efforts). For each name, the author gave reasons why the example fit within the category of ultraist. The result was a series of men who served as examples legitimizing the acts of reform by women. Elizabeth Fry stood alone but not overlooked as an example of a woman's capacity to achieve on an equal level with men. Attacking the only female example would call into question the other examples. Challenging the work of such men as Franklin, Henry, and Fulton would run counter to widely shared premises for model careers. Attempting to dissociate Elizabeth Fry from the list would risk the charge of nit-picking and reveal unfounded prejudice against women on the basis of their sex. Thus, ultraism was moved from having a negative connotation to having a positive one; consequently, the cause of women's reform was placed in the tradition of other great humanitarian efforts.

In another article entitled "What History Says of Woman?" a number of examples of female rulers were provided for the readers: Queen Zenobia; Margaret of Denmark, Norway, and Sweden; Isabella of Spain; Elizabeth of England; Catherine of Russia; Zinga of Angola; Blanche of Castille; and Caroline of England in her husband's absence (April 1851, 31). These eight examples proved that women had ruled nations in the past with the "divine approval" usually reserved for royalty and that they had shaped an image of self-respect for early radicals by providing them with examples from a tradition of feminine royalty.

These articles chronicled a process by which examples of capable and self-reliant women were accumulated and detailed for the audience. Also, they provided a wide range of instances where women functioned competently outside their socially relegated sphere and grounded those examples in socially legitimate situations. Hence, it became appropriate for women to think of themselves in terms of new roles—as printers, citizens, reformers, activists, leaders, doctors, and university professors. These examples gave shape to an image of women as capable, intelligent, and self-reliant agents.

The shift in self-image was gradual, however. Many women found it difficult to speak out in public and to feel comfortable moving beyond the domestic sphere. Part of the difficulty lay in the transformation of how women perceived themselves in relation to what was then considered the "male's" sphere. That transformation was hindered by the remnants of the "cult of domesticity." For wives, the *Lily* had this advice: "If a man is thus weak, and easily tempted, let it be woman's part to lend strength to his weakness, and instead of leading him on in the dark road to ruin, let her rather guide his footsteps into the path of virtue and sobriety, and show him by her own life of purity an example worthy of imitation" (February 1849, 23). This quotation reflects at least two of the four defining characteristics of woman: piety and purity. The role of woman in this excerpt was not one of advocate. Women were still constrained within the domestic sphere and were to use their "superior" character to reveal a more moral course of action.

The *Lily* did not limit advice to the role of wife only. In a later excerpt, the *Lily* admonished mothers to consider how great their influence might be in the matter of leading their sons from ruin: "Woman does not realize her immense influence in social and domestic life. No custom, however time honored, will continue long, if 'the ladies disapprove;' whatever is wrong in good society continues to exist because such evils, are at least *tolerated* by them. Still greater is the Mother's influence. . . . Whatever the mother loves is sacred to the child; whatever she abhors he shuns" (April 1849, 29). Again, woman's influence was limited to social and domestic life. In this article, the mother's influence is regarded as having more impact than that of a public speaker. Despite the presence of some role models of women as advocates and the appearance of some pieces that began to outline new roles for women, the concept of "true womanhood" as it related to the domestic sphere was still very much alive and was often reinforced by the *Lily*.

Accustomed to the limited versions of woman as wife and mother, the development of a more flexible role would not transpire until women realized the close connection between their status as citizens and their status as women. Rather than understanding the need to enact the role of woman as citizen, women needed first to see the relationship of temperance as dependent upon the broader issue of woman's rights. Until then, women remarked, "if we may not go ourselves to the polls, let us give the men over whom we have an influence no peace, until they consent to make our votes their own, and deposit them for us."[22]

Forging the Connections between Temperance and Rights

Gradually, the assumption that woman could only influence through her power in the domestic sphere lost currency. The shift was subtle. In the same issues demonstrating that woman's influence on temperance was tied to her domestic sphere, statements appeared that claimed for woman the right to speak in public. The right to speak, however, soon became integral to the temperance cause. At this point, the relationship between temperance and the broader issue of woman's rights was bridged. Once it became clear that woman could not effect her rightful moral influence until she had the right to advocate just policies granting her equal rights under the law, the early temperance activists came to see equal rights as their fundamental concern. This change in perspective was due principally to the influence of Elizabeth Cady Stanton.[23]

Temperance became linked to equal rights when women realized that intemperance threatened woman's sphere—the home. Since women had no property and lost all legal existence in marriage, alcohol consumption threatened their existence. Initially, temperance efforts were not so much a defense of self but a defense of woman's sphere. Gradually, awareness grew that if woman was to preserve her domestic sphere, she would have to fight to prevent alcohol from invading her world. This was in line with the narrow sphere of domesticity prescribed by society for her. But to halt the menace of alcohol, she needed first to speak out. In responding to the question of what woman could do to stop intemperance, the *Lily* stated:

She is called upon as she loves her own peace of mind—as she loves the happiness of those with whom she is connected in life, to come forth and do what she may to banish the evils of intemperance from the land. —We have long felt this to be her duty. We have long felt that woman was called upon to act, and act efficiently in the work of advancing the great temperance cause . . . we recommend the formation of Female Temperance societies. We believe they may be the means of doing much good. With us, as with men, more may be done by combined effort than singly; and we can thus make our influence more surely felt. We believe such associations may be conducted in a manner becoming the retiring modesty of our sex—without noise or parade, and in accordance with the strictest rules of propriety. The influence we exert in the community is not like the noisy bubbling brooklet, whose source is merely the pool formed by the summer shower, but like the quiet course of a deeper stream, "which ever hath a peaceful, silent flow." (February 1849, 21)

Two aspects were noteworthy here. First, women had a duty to act in defense of the home. Second, women were advised to form temperance societies, distinctly female in membership. Both elements contributed to a sense of community among women who perceived a need to violate some constraints of the domestic sphere if they were to protect it. This sense of community was an important first step in the formative stages of the early woman's rights movement. By articulating a duty to act in defense of the home and by suggesting that women had much to gain from organizing, the *Lily* revealed a fundamental basis for shared values among women. As women organized themselves in these early temperance societies, they gained experience in advocacy, in leadership, in creating networks, and in mobilizing political support for their cause. These skills and resources would be refined as the early woman's rights movement matured.

By the fourth issue of volume one, the temperance advocates perceived an inherent need to change the laws of the present system:

How little those know of the blighting curse entailed upon mankind by the legalized poison *alcohol*, who have never had its miseries visited upon them. They sit at ease in their quiet, comfortable homes, surrounded by unencumbered blessings, little thinking of the sorrows which are breaking the hearts of many tender and delicate beings like themselves, who were reared in affluence, caressed, and beloved by fond parents, and kind friends, but who are doomed to toil on, and drag out a weary life of misery and want. . . . And why is all this?[24]

The answer given by the *Lily* in this piece was that the sale of liquor was legal. The next step was to define rum selling as a crime.[25] From here, the *Lily* attacked the present system: "Those calling them-selves gentlemen and claiming the highest respectability—those to whom wealth and talents have been given—those who should be patterns of morality and goodness—those who should be foremost to relieve our land from this curse—who should be ever ready to succor the oppressed—these are they who uphold and sustain the cruel and deadly work. It is the gentlemen wine drinkers who stand in the way of temperance reform."[26] Those who had the power to act would not. As a result, the *Lily* defined the opposition and the solu-tion—new laws. But new laws would require that the readers either appeal to relevant agents of change or acquire the necessary political capital to act themselves. Since the woman's temperance movement had defined its audience so narrowly, its appeals alienated relevant agents of change. The only hope for relief from intemperance lay in the acquisition of an alternative power base.

In reporting temperance news, the *Lily* seized on a dramatic and symbolic action by Caroline M. Sweet, reporting in the August 1849 issue of the *Lily*: "Finding that 'moral suasion' was worse than useless, and knowing the law had no protection for her, she took the law into her own hands, and did what lay in her power to punish the thief who was stealing away not only her living, but the life of her husband."[27] Sweet smashed some kegs of alcohol. Although she was fined ten dollars for the action and made to pay fifty dollars in damages, the act of violating the law illustrated the dissatisfaction with the status quo. Thus, temperance became closely tied to the nature of women's survival. The *Lily* provided this endorsement: "There is a point beyond which endurance ceases to be a virtue. If the rulers of our land will do nothing to stay the ruin caused by intoxicating drinks—if they will do nothing to protect the innocent wife and children from being crushed and trodden to the earth by the tyrant rum-seller, then it is time that woman bids defiance to our unjust laws, and shows a spirit and determination to protect herself" (August 1849, 62).

Temperance, then, became an outgrowth of unjust laws, which were part of a much larger and insidious social structure of sexism. The tenth issue of volume one articulated the now clearly recog-nized connection between intemperance and woman's rights:

It is not our right to hold office or to rule our country, that we would now advocate. . . . But woman has her rights which she knows not of or know-ing, disregards. She has rights of which she deprives herself. She is willing to sit down within the narrow sphere assigned her by man, and make no effort to obtain her just rights, or free herself from the oppressions which are crushing her to the earth. She tamely submits to be governed by laws as man sees fit to make and in making which she has no voice. We know that many of us think that we have rights enough, and we are content with what we have; but we forget how many thousand wives and mothers worthy as ourselves, are compelled by the unjust laws of our land, to drag out a weary life and submit to indignities which no man would bear. It is stated that thirty thousand die annually from the effects of intoxicating drinks; an equal number of drunkards must stand ready to fall. Think of the wives and mothers of this great number—of their untold griefs—of their hidden sorrows—of their broken hearts—of their hunger and nakedness—their unwearied toil to procure a bare pittance to save their little ones from starvation—of the wretched life they lead, and the unmourned death they die. Think of all this, and then tell us not that woman has her rights." (October 1849, 77)

This statement explains how woman's vulnerability to intemperance was seen to be a direct result of her legal status. Intemperance threatened woman because she was "compelled by the unjust laws of our land, to drag out a weary life and submit to indignities which no man would bear." By comparing woman's status under law to that of men, the article focused attention on the source of injustices against women. Woman's station would be greatly improved if inequality under the law were to be eradicated. Once woman obtained equal rights, they would have the power to protect themselves.

When women realized that inequality was the source of their problems, interest shifted from moral issues to equal rights issues. Where strict temperance appeals based on moral abstinence seemed common in the first two volumes of the *Lily*, subsequent issues focused increasingly on woman's rights issues. These later issues served as a place for early activists to present rationales for change, refute arguments defending the status quo, articulate and reinforce shared values, and communicate news of the growing woman's rights movement. Thus the *Lily* not only contributed to reshaping the image of woman but later functioned as an important channel of communication for early activists.

Conclusion

As the early woman's rights movement began to form, the *Lily* reflected its development and provided an arsenal of facts and arguments that women could use to advance their cause. Most important, however, is that the *Lily* fulfilled two critical requirements for social change: it confronted women with their own powerlessness within the prevailing social order, while reshaping the image of woman in ways that empowered them to act as reformers without violating their traditional roles. Thus, the *Lily* was an important conduit for much of the discourse that laid the foundation for the early woman's rights movement.

The *Una*, 1853–1855

The Premiere of the Woman's Rights Press

Mari Boor Tonn

"A Paper Devoted to the Elevation of Woman"
"Out of the Great Heart of Nature Seek we Truth"

With these words emblazoned on its masthead, the *Una* premiered in Providence, Rhode Island, in February of 1853, the brainchild of Paulina Kellogg Wright Davis, a wealthy, young Rhode Island socialite and fervent crusader for woman's rights.[1] Although another woman's newspaper, Amelia Jenks Bloomer's *Lily*, had begun publication in 1849 as the organ of the local ladies' temperance society,[2] the *Una* is acknowledged as the first "feminist" newspaper to spring from the fledgling woman's rights movement of the nineteenth century.[3]

Wright Davis served as the paper's sole editor until Caroline Healy Dall joined her in January of 1855, the same month that the struggling monthly also changed publishers and moved to Boston. In October of that year, the *Una* ceased publication entirely, three months short of a three-year run. Although the *Una*'s existence was brief and racked with financial hardships, the small periodical broke ground for the myriad of woman's rights newspapers that would follow.

The *Una*'s debut came four and a half years after the benchmark Seneca Falls Convention engineered by Elizabeth Cady Stanton and Lucretia Coffin Mott. A similar convention three years later was largely the result of the organizational efforts and financial backing of Wright Davis, who had emerged as a strong and vibrant voice for female emancipation.[4] Although early feminists were buoyed by the relative success of such conventions, Wright Davis recognized that other means were needed to circulate the woman's rights message accurately and to recruit the members crucial for the advancement of the cause. In what Wright Davis feared would be the final issue of the *Una*, she explained her rationale for launching a paper devoted entirely to the interests of the woman's movement:

The idea is false that political papers do not and will not misrepresent this movement, no other class of reformers have been so unwise. The Temperance people with a work far less delicate and subtle in its character, far less likely to be misunderstood, have their papers in every part of the country. The anti-slavery people with a work aiming only at the enfranchisement of three millions of human beings, have their organs, and feel that without them they can do but little, while this work, which aims not alone at the elevation of woman in this country, but throughout the whole world, and at the regeneration and harmonizing of the whole human family, is left with no other medium of communication than the chance notices of political or other papers. (December 1854, 376)

Wright Davis possessed several characteristics essential for a venture as daring as initiating a woman's rights press: familiarity with other kinds of crusades, sufficient capital, organizational skills, and the courage to stand against custom. Orphaned at the age of seven, Paulina Kellogg was reared in upstate New York by an aunt whose religious devotion prompted her niece to consider missionary work as her life's vocation. Instead, at the age of twenty, Paulina married Francis Wright, a wealthy Utica merchant, whose premature death left her economically secure but painfully aware of the privileges that money alone could not grant her. Although she was free from the financial concerns that plagued the lower class, Paulina's life was affected by laws and social customs that constrained all women. For example, after she married Thomas Davis of Providence, the congressman reportedly was often embarrassed by his wife's unconventional behavior, which included her controversial decision to be the first woman to lecture on female anatomy and physiology, thereby providing American women with the only accurate information about their bodies available to them. Paulina also defied decorum by publicly championing abolitionism and spiritualism.[5]

Because Wright Davis conceived the primary mission of her paper to be humanitarian, she selected the mystical name of Una, which signified truth. In the prospectus of the first issue, Wright Davis explained the publication's name and articulated its purpose as grounded in natural rights philosophy:

Our purpose is to speak clear, earnest words of truth and soberness, in a spirit of kindness. To discuss the rights, sphere, duty, and destiny of women, fully and fearlessly; and our aim will be to secure the highest good of all. So far as our voice shall be heard it will ever be on the side of freedom. We shall not confine ourselves to any locality, set, sect, class or caste, for we hold to the solidarity of the race, and believe that if one member suffers, all suffers, and that the highest is made to atone for the lowest. (February 1853, 4)

Clearly, Wright Davis initially envisioned the paper's target audience as all women, who, although diverse in terms of individual circumstances, shared much by virtue of being female. Initially, Wright Davis pursued two directions to gain a diverse readership for the *Una*. First, she sought to attract and air the concerns of women who worked, were immigrants, or were in the lower socioeconomic strata. Unlike some of her contemporary woman's rights advocates who embraced a natural rights argument largely to address the concerns of middle-class white women, Wright Davis's commitment to a natural rights philosophy was more thoroughgoing. For example, besides treating subjects such as suffrage, marriage and divorce, temperance, and woman's health, early issues of the *Una* also included numerous articles on topics more relevant to the concerns of lower-class and immigrant women, such as poverty and child labor. Wright Davis thus perceived that sex should be a more salient basis for identification than class or economic status. Her desired audience was, in truth, women as an oppressed group.

Besides targeting women outside the middle class, Wright Davis also sought to attract readers whose interests might extend beyond the narrow realm of material offered by other periodicals. Because such papers devoted solely to light fare had limited potential in advancing woman's development, Wright Davis chose not to emulate other popular woman's reading of the day. As she explained in the first issue, "Women have been too well and too long satisfied with Ladies' Books, Ladies' Magazines, and Miscellaneous; it is time they should have stronger nourishment . . ." (February 1853, 4). Thus, Wright Davis conceived of the *Una* as "alternative" reading for women, which she hoped would shatter the myths surrounding women's situation, interests, abilities, and "role" rather than perpetuate them in the manner of popular woman's reading. As Wright Davis argued, replacing the portrait of the "idealized" woman with the "real" woman was necessary for progress to occur: "We ask to be regarded, respected, and treated as human beings, of full age and natural abilities, as equal sinners, and not as infants or beautiful angels, to whom the rules of civil and social justice do not apply" (June 1853, 73). However, while Wright Davis recognized the need to provide women with factual information about their real condition, she also recognized that a paper comprised entirely of argumentative essays might not pique the interest and garner the support of those women not already sympathetic to the movement. Women accustomed to and satisfied with journals replete with fiction, poetry, and housekeeping tips were unlikely subscribers for a paper that represented a radical shift from such a format. In early issues, Wright Davis struck a compromise between ideological advocacy and more pragmatic marketing concerns; often she included short stories and poems that imitated the style of popular journals but were "feminist" in substance. Passages from a poem entitled "The Market Woman" by F. [Frances] D. Gage are representative:

She stands behind her market stall
    That woman strong and bold,
While many an idler passes
    With heartless sneer, and cold.

They roll their eyes disdainfully
    And prate of "human sphere,"
And say no woman, kind and true
    Would be a lingerer here. . . .

Not womanly, I ask her,
    One cold and rainy morn,
Why she came forth to brave the storm,
    She said, "to sell my corn."

"Lady, for four long toiling years,
    I've mourned a husband dead—
I have six little ones at home—
    And I must earn their bread.
. . . .
Go to, ye prating ones, and learn
    That woman's holiest sphere,
Is only filled by duty done,
    Without remorse or fear.
. . . .
The mother working for her child,
    The wife for those she loves,
Can never leave her woman's sphere
    If in the right she moves.
    (October 1854, 339)

Although Gage's poem mirrored the style of "sentimental" fiction and poetry, the poem clearly argued that "woman's sphere" was an artificial cultural construct that damaged women. Not only did the concept of "woman's sphere" as home-centered deny the existence of many poor women and single mothers, society's vehement disapproval of women's public activities further oppressed women who were forced into the public arena through unfortunate circumstances. Gage's poem articulated the double-bind for such women: society defined woman's duty as caring for her family, but if that responsibility required a woman to work outside of the home, society castigated her.

Additionally, in the first issue, an essay entitled "The Truth of Fiction, and Its Charm" suggested that fiction and poetry could also express woman's peculiar situation, likewise serving consciousness-raising and identification-building functions for the movement:

Making no pretentions to and limited by none of the laws of narrative, truth and historic fact, [fiction] brings the truth of nature—the probable, the possible, the ideal—in their broadest range and utmost capabilities into the service of a favorite principle, and demonstrates its force and beauty, and practicality, in circumstantial details, which like a panorama, presents an image so like an experience that we realize it for all the purposes of knowledge, hope and resolution. (February 1853, 5)[6]

In short, when Wright Davis launched the *Una*, she believed that for the paper to aid in advancing the cause of women from all classes and circumstances, it had to be bought and read by women from all classes and circumstances. Thus, she shaped the substance and style of her paper to attract a broad spectrum of female readers.

Although Wright Davis hoped for a broad readership for the *Una*, the paper's subscription records indicate that it served largely those individuals already committed to and active in the cause. During the *Una*'s first and most prosperous year, total annual subscriptions numbered fewer than five hundred, although initial response to the new publication was encouraging. Immediately following the first issue in February, over one hundred sixty persons sent in their annual one-dollar fee, and Wright Davis received enough requests for the first issues that periodic notices soliciting extra copies from subscribers were posted in subsequent issues. However, the list of recruits steadily diminished each month, and by November, new subscribers numbered only twenty-five. Of these names on the rolls, many were veteran woman's rights advocates or were closely connected to individuals who were. Quite predictably, leaders such as Lucy Stone, Elizabeth Cady Stanton, Lucretia Coffin Mott, Susan B. Anthony, William Lloyd Garrison, and Elizabeth Blackwell were regular subscribers, as were frequent contributors to the journal such as Frances D. Gage, many of whom accounted for more than a single subscription each. Other Motts, Stones, and Blackwells frequently swelled the subscription lists.

Like most woman's rights journals that followed it, the *Una*'s demise resulted primarily from financial difficulty. Although Wright Davis argued justifiably that the one-dollar annual fee was a modest sum necessary to meet the paper's expenses, the women that the *Una* targeted were frequently incapable of or reluctant to pay that amount. As Lynn Masel-Walter notes, few females in the nineteenth century had money of their own, and those who were employed were often poor women who worked out of necessity to feed families and could neither afford nor justify such a "luxury." Married women frequently met resistance of spouses who regarded woman's rights issues as immoral, threatening, or both.[7] In the *Una*'s first July issue, Wright Davis addressed some of the more unusual problems in collecting subscription fees: "The pecuniary interests of our paper will not be promoted by sending us uncurrent money:—and we would suggest to gentlemen who have a counterfeit bill in hand, that there are more honorable ways of disposing of it than to hand it over to the wife to pay for her paper . . ." (July 1853, 151).

Wright Davis's naïveté in dealing with potential and delinquent subscribers also weakened the *Una*'s economic base. By her own admission, she sent first issues to many individuals who had not subscribed, in the hopes that the paper itself would garner their philosophical and financial support. She then ran notices, replete with appeals to "honesty" and "decency," asking for those individuals to either mail the annual fee or return the paper to the publisher, which some actually did. By December of 1854, the editors hailed the issue as the last in an emotional, melodramatic farewell to readers:

We cannot bring ourselves to announce the death of our dear Una, for she has been to us a perpetual joy. At her birth, all gentle and good spirits were invited, but as in the Fairy tale it seems, there was one for whom no cover was laid, and in her malignity she bids her sleep till the true night [*sic*] shall arise who will dare and overcome all obstacles to waken her into life again. . . .

We have striven in vain to convince women that they need an organ which could give to the future a correct history of this revolution and which would be a true and just exponent of our views and principles of action. (December 1854, 376)

As Wright Davis had hoped, the altruism of an anonymous individual postponed the *Una*'s demise temporarily, and the publication continued for several more months without interruption. But uninterrupted also were the requests for subscription payments, which became more strident in tone and more frequent after the paper changed publishers. In May of 1855, the editors appealed for canvassers to solicit subscriptions, offering commissions to any who were successful. Three months before the *Una* folded, the new publisher posted a lengthy notice stating that no money had been received in the six months since he had assumed publishing responsibilities. A later notice reminded subscribers that fees had been overdue for ten months, adding that "printers want their pay and must have it. Paper-makers want theirs, and will have it. . . . As for the publisher, he has already learned *to live on air . . .*" (October 1855, 360). In October of 1855, the publisher apologized for the delay of the issue, citing "a variety of circumstances we have no room here to mention," and promising the next would "be issued in better season" (360). That issue never appeared.

The "variety of circumstances" that plagued the paper's latest issues may have included the fatigue of the *Una*'s small staff. As Masel-Walters notes, many suffrage papers failed, in part, because they depended so heavily upon the energy and time of a single woman. When her strength began to wane under the heavy burden of the publication or when other duties warranted her attention, the journal usually folded.[8] The *Una* was no exception. Although Caroline Healy Dall assisted Wright Davis in editorial responsibilities during the paper's final ten months, both women complained of the difficulty in juggling the demands of their public enterprise with the demands of their private lives as women:

[W]e cannot write, Mr. Publisher, till, in New England parlance, we have put everything to rights. . . . We must see all things attended to, or ghosts of neglected duties haunt us, and your wants sink into insignificance; but when all is quietly settled we are sometimes disposed to talk very gravely about housekeeping, although we must own that we do not believe that woman's emancipation will ever be achieved or political economy make much advance, while she is compelled to go through the belittling details of the isolated household. . . . (May 1855, 72)

Thus, ironically, a paper dedicated to the belief that women were able and should be allowed to function in both the public and private world may have failed, at least in some measure, because the women editing the paper *were* functioning in both worlds simultaneously.

Characteristic Features and Approaches

As noted, early issues of the *Una* provided an eclectic approach to subjects of relevance to women. The standard format of these issues included the following: an introductory fictional work (usually serialized); poetry by subscribers or established poets; a minimum of one expository piece on some aspect of woman's condition; a listing of educational or vocational opportunities for women; book reviews; letters to and from the editor; advertisements for woman's rights tracts; and column fillers such as proverbs, famous quotations, or household, parenting, and gardening tips. On a less regular basis, the following kinds of pieces were often included: proceedings and/or speeches from woman's rights conventions; petitions involving woman's rights legislation; excerpts from anonymous diaries and journals; information about health and beauty care; discussions of art; and clippings from other papers (some foreign). The following titles from the introductory issue suggest the eclectism of the *Una*'s early offerings: "The Real Controversy between Men and Women," "Working Out Taxes," "Women as Physically Considered," "Schools of Design for Women," "Health of the Skin," "The Truth of Fiction, and Its Charm," "Long Lane" (short story), "The Beautiful" (poem), "Shadowy Sounds" (poem), *Bleak House* (book review), *Woman's Record* (book review), and excerpts from *Female Dominion* (play by Goethe).

The articles, literary pieces, letters, and speeches printed in the *Una* were contributed from a variety of individuals, including such movement notables as Ernestine Rose, Lucy Stone, Elizabeth Cady Stanton, Angelina Grimké Weld, Antoinette Brown Blackwell, and William Lloyd Garrison. After the paper changed editors and publishers, the following group of regular contributors was established and listed in each issue of the paper: Healy Dall, Cady Stanton, Frances D. Gage, Mrs. E. Oakes Smith, Mrs. E. Cheney (Paris), Mrs. Peter, Elizabeth B. Peabody, and Lizzie Linn.

Some of the most poignant and powerful contributions, however, came from women whose full identities were never divulged. The circumstances of their lives that these anonymous women discussed suggested that they were the women most severely oppressed by a society that denied them equal rights: women who did not enjoy the privileges of class and beauty and wealth, and who were, therefore, those most sorely penalized by society's codification of the "ideal" woman as pure, pious, delicate, and lovely. One such woman, an invalid known only as Emma, wrote frequent and lengthy letters to "Dear Una." Wright Davis responded, speaking to all women who shared in Emma's circumstance. Through Emma, the socially, economically, and culturally deprived gave voice to their fears and frustrations and their disenchantment with a movement they believed ignored them:

How came you to think that the article in Putnam's magazine, "Woman and the Woman's Movement," would amuse me? You know or ought to know, that I have not the head for such things as Mr. James writes. . . . I am as you know neither a radical nor a blue. I have not the courage required of the one nor the talents of the other. But there is something in me that makes me weary of this eternal crowd of make believers and emptiness. My infirmity makes me sedentary; I am unattractive in person and the forecast of my future makes me serious. . . . I cannot even earn the right to sleep in such idleness as my conditions of life compel. (April 1853, 54)

Similarly, in a serialized offering entitled "Stray Leaves from a Seamstress's Journal," an anonymous working woman detailed the bleakness of her life and her prospects:

A rent of five dollars per month. I have two small rooms, a cooking stove, a dresser, two beds, and a few other useful articles to serve in the way of housekeeping. A sick mother and two young sisters depending upon me. Four backs to clothe, four mouths to feed, and one pair of hands to do it. One with a heart strong enough to say I will. But "how" is the question. . . . Many times in the past I have longed for responsibilities, now I understand all its meaning. I must not make my own theories of failure, for I have said that a woman was equal to any emergency, that she had worlds of latent strength to be developed at the right time. But will my fierce pride, my unbending spirit bear [up] . . . ? (June 1853, 68)

Obviously, letters such as those from Emma and the diary from the impoverished but eloquent seamstress added to the personal tone of the publication, as did other contributions. Augmenting the journal's tone of intimacy were the personal friendships between Wright Davis and other prominent individuals in the movement, which were clear in the informal familiarity that characterized their writing. The journal's tone was often almost conversational, with Wright Davis frequently addressing open letters to her readers and prefacing specific articles with commentary in which she revealed to the reader her own reactions. Moreover, although Wright Davis alone served as the paper's editor for most of its duration, she scrupulously avoided the personal pronoun "I," using instead the more inclusive "we," "us," and "our" to foster a spirit of sisterhood and camaraderie.

The major themes treated in the *Una*, although broad in scope, were all related to the paper's motto, "The Elevation of Woman." In the first issue, Wright Davis articulated the journal's general direction in terms of content: "In our editorial service we shall discuss with candor and earnestness, the Rights, Relations, Duties, Destiny, and Sphere of Woman, Her Education—Literary, Scientific, and Artistic, Her Avocation—Industrial, Commercial, and Profesional [sic], Her Interests—Pecuniary, Civil, and Political" (February 1853,

2). Significantly, all arguments advanced by the paper were colored by Wright Davis's commitment to a natural rights philosophy. Wright Davis, Stone, Cady Stanton, and other contributors contended that because a woman was undeniably accepted as a member of the human race, she should be afforded all rights inherently hers by virtue of being born human. That same philosophy buttressed the *Una*'s official support of abolition; Wright Davis, who viewed institutionalized slavery as a blatant violation of the African-American's natural rights, encouraged measures to end that oppression in such articles as "Teaching Negroes to Read." Indeed, the arguments against slavery and the legal and social oppression of women often took parallel form; slavery was frequently used as an analogy to refute theological, biological, and sociological rationales for woman's "proper sphere." The *Una* used the natural rights philosophy as the major premise to argue for suffrage, for equity in education, employment, and wages, and for the restructuring of laws dealing with property rights, inheritance, and divorce, which treated women as nonpersons.

Issues less directly connected to natural rights were poverty, temperance, child labor, health concerns, and laws governing acceptable grounds for divorce. Essays in the *Una* argued that, because all humans possessed certain inalienable rights, they should be afforded an existence free from the threat of constant hunger, violence, and illness. In an attempt to help women and their children break out of the vicious cycle of poverty, the *Una* offered numerous articles on educational and training opportunities for women, on types of new employment that were opening to women, such as typesetting, and on the locations of successful community homes as alternatives to squalid tenement housing. The journal advocated revising divorce laws to enable women to dissolve marriages to intemperate husbands who were frequently violent and often provided inadequately for their families. Additionally, the *Una* argued that poor health training and the lack of courses for young schoolgirls served to keep women oppressed by keeping them ignorant of their bodies and making them constant victims of sickness and disease. As partial remedy, the journal offered women instruction on personal hygiene, nutrition, cooking procedures, and the correct use of alcoholic tonics and medications.

The only issue that sparked any noticeable contention among members of the movement was the frequent discussion of woman's perceived "moral superiority," a debate that hinged on what Karlyn Kohrs Campbell describes as the tension between "personhood" and "womanhood."[9] The position advanced by Wright Davis, Cady Stanton, and others was that neither sex enjoyed the privilege or responsibility of moral superiority, and they warned of the pitfalls in exalting woman as the inherent moral superior of man. Although some woman's rights advocates embraced the argument that allowing women to enter the public sphere to vote, work, become educated, and enter politics would "purify" it, the *Una*'s position was that the expediency argument could also be used to restrict women from certain activities, serving to stymie real progress for women. To Wright Davis, the moral superiority argument was merely a variation on the concept of the "idealized" woman, which was promulgated by the very theologians and popular literature that most advocates for woman's rights fought against. In the spirit of compromise, some articles posited that woman's nature was merely different from man's, rather than superior to it. Foreshadowing arguments of our own day, a contributed essay entitled "The Intellect of Woman" argued that the sexes should view their differences not as competitive but as complementary: "We affirm no superiority, for her, as we allow none to him, in the things not relevant to their respective differences of nature. It would be grossly unphilosophical to speak of the skill and cunning of the hand, as superior to the strength of the foot, or the acuteness of vision as transcending the delicacy of the ear" (March 1853, 24).

The *Una*, by devoting relatively limited space to the views of the movement's opposition, strategically denied its legitimacy. When mentioned at all, the paper, in some of its rare moments of humor, trivialized and ridiculed the opponents, their arguments, and their actions. The proceedings of one woman's rights meeting, which was infiltrated by persons committed to the superiority of males, described a hired hisser as proving his own inferiority "by imitating very badly the sound peculiar to a goose" (July 1853, 138). The opposition's points were most visible in theological discussions, primarily because religion provided the base from which most arguments supporting woman's oppression grew. These arguments were generally debunked through the use of satire or irony. For example, to illustrate the absurdity of society's censorship of women speakers, William Lloyd Garrison noted the irony of allowing women to "sing" but not to "speak" that "our Redeemer liveth" (July 1853, 138).

Regardless of the issue under discussion, a recurring argument in the *Una* was the need for women to take control in changing their existence. The Reverend Mayo, a frequent contributor, posited that the most effective method for woman's advancement was involvement and enacting the right to belong: "It is one thing to prove the absurdity of social customs," he argued, "and another to change them. Associations are stronger than arguments; and women will be recognized in new positions, not so much by proving that she belongs there, as by making herself strong enough to take them" (February 1853, 6).

Although Wright Davis never wavered in her allegiance to the major themes to which she committed the paper in its initial issue—the rights, duties, education, interests, and avocations of women—the manner and extent in which these various themes were treated changed significantly over time, altering the tone of the paper and possibly its readership.

The *Una*'s first issue contained sixteen pages, a length that increased by only a few pages in subsequent issues. Although the size, the price, and some of the standard features of the *Una*—the letters to and from the editor, for example—remained constant throughout its short life, the *Una* evolved gradually and subtly to the extent that the final issue bore little substantive resemblance to the original effort. On the surface, the most salient change was the new publisher's decision to include advertising to increase revenue, thereby decreasing the amount of space devoted to other offerings. More significant substantively was the change in the focus of the paper. The variety of contributions, which had given the *Una* its unique sparkle, its poignancy, and its broad appeal, were replaced by longer, more esoteric pieces, apparently geared to the intellectual elite of the movement. Lengthy letters to the editor from frustrated and inspired women from all classes and regions became sparser, while the number of long essays and letters discussing cultural topics such as music, sculpture, painting, and the like increased. Sample essays from later issues included "Sculpture—Paul Akers," "Gobelin Tapestry," "Confucius and His Teachings," "The First Statue of Canova," "The [Sculpture] Works of Miss Hosmer," "New Approaches on Photography—Daguerrotypes on Wood," and a series of essays from a correspondent in Florence, Italy, discussing art treasures in that city. The number and the length of book reviews in later issues also increased, as did their focus on critical analysis. While religious discussions in the early *Una*—such as the article entitled "Paul vs. Silencing Women"—were elementary enough for broad consumption, similar discussions in subsequent issues became progressively more esoteric, targeted toward the intellectual reader who was well grounded in theology, philosophy, and culture. This narrowing of the targeted audience was clear in later essays entitled "Lessons on God's Providence as It May Be Traced in History" and "The New Catholic Goddess," the latter of which discussed the theological and feminist implications of the Vatican's recent clarification on the doctrine of immaculate conception. Fiction and poetry assumed a larger role, while clippings from other papers, quotations and proverbs, and short pieces of general interest became fewer. During the last months, the tone of even the more general "household" offerings was occasionally more sophisticated, as illustrated in a piece entitled "A Brief Chemico-Physiological Essay on Milk."

As the *Una* evolved, it also assumed a more international flavor. Although news of the sister movement in England had punctuated the *Una*'s pages from its inception, later issues expanded international coverage to include discussions of events and individuals from various regions of the globe. In its final months, the periodical offered translations of literary works authored in other countries and debated the "moral superiority" of foreign female monarchs and leaders over their male predecessors and counterparts. Essays such as "Bologna and Its Women," "Female Education in France," "The Rough House—From Brace's Social Life in Germany," "Circassians and the Sale of Beautiful Slave Girls," "A Female Prime Minister," and "A Journey through Canada" became common fare. Individuals from other countries especially appeared to intrigue the editors, who chose to publish pieces on such persons as Cassandra Fedele from Venice, Maria Gaetana Agnesi, Marie Cunitz, and Miss Murray, the sister of a Scottish duke. The European travels of the American movement's leaders were closely chronicled, as were similar trips made within the country in the course of championing certain legislation.

Ironically, the newspaper that was pledged to "fidelity to all" continued to treat issues *about* all women but seemingly ceased to speak *to* all women in its final months. Although the *Una*'s shift from a journal with mass appeal to a more cosmopolitan periodical is clear, the rationale behind the shift is not. Whether lower-class women such as Emma ceased contributing to the *Una* or whether the editors merely rejected those offerings is uncertain. Circumstances such as Healy Dall's involvement as an editor during the paper's last year possibly influenced its focus. However, the shift to more intellectual articles may have been purely pragmatic on at least two fronts.

First, the *Una*'s dire financial circumstances may have prompted the editors to target and court better educated and more economically secure women who had the means to support the paper financially. In a related vein, the new male publisher's concern for marketing the paper may have eclipsed any allegiance he might have had to treat issues relevant to all women, regardless of their ability to pay their subscriptions.

Second, an attempt to avoid treating women's concerns in the same manner may have steered the editors in new directions. For example, although the editors realized the obstacles that religious teachings presented for women, repeated articles treating Saint Paul's position toward women may have struck the editors as excessive duplication. In one of the last issues, the editors discussed the pressures of continually producing vast amounts of fresh material and alluded to the difficulty of not having the financial resources to pay contributors: "Please furnish copy, says our publisher. Yes, sir, we wish we were made of copy, like 'the man who was made of money,' and had nothing to do but put our hand into our bosom, and draw forth page after page, filled with 'thoughts that breathed and words that burned,' but we are not, nor have we a mint of money, otherwise you should feel no anxiety as to where printers' pay is to come from" (May 1855, 72).

Interestingly, the demands of the publication on the editors also altered the tone of their own writing in significant ways during the *Una*'s last months. The spirit of sisterly camaraderie and optimistic idealism that characterized early editorial contributions gave way to less kind depictions of women who criticized the movement, the paper, and the editors themselves. Romanticized claims from the early issues assume an ironic tone when juxtaposed with entries made months later. Wright Davis's naive assumptions about the *Una*'s reception, the demands of editorship on her personally, and its singular potential for changing the status of women are clear in the introduction she wrote for the paper's premier issue: "Our antagonisms will grow less, because we shall see through a brighter medium, that the interests of the sexes are identical. . . . We mean also never to be in a hurry, never to get ambitious, avaricious, or ill-tempered, and to set all kinds of traps for sunbeams, and then with a liberal hand shower them on our friends. We mean to win by love and reason" (February 1853, 3). Unfortunately, "love and reason" were inadequate to win over all women to the cause, and the editors' "antagonisms" toward their critics increased rather than diminished, as evidenced in an issue of the *Una* published over two years later:

Now we, the women's [sic] rights women, have been accused by Eliza Cook, in her widely circulated Journal and in several other smaller papers and periodicals, of having less regard for our homes and domestic duties than we should have; in other words, we are represented as slatternly housekeepers, careless wives and mothers, and neglectful of hospitality, "given to loud talking and much gadding abroad." . . .

. . . those frivolous women, who think only of dress, or rather who vegetate through life and never think at all, are forever hurried to death in their busy idleness, altering dresses that seemed faultless in style, making one bow longer, and another shorter, one flounce fuller, and another more scanty; doing up laces, and paying morning visits that they have not a shadow of interest in, glad when they find their *very dear friends* out and can leave a card. Ah, this woman dust lies deep over the earth. (May 1855, 72)

Thus, consciously or unconsciously, the *Una* evolved in significant ways from a paper that was a mouthpiece for all women, to a paper that progressively reflected the interests, circumstances, and feelings of its editors: wealthy, cultured, and well-educated white women, overwhelmed at times by the demands of their endeavor, and sensitive to the personal criticism their endeavor engendered.

Rhetorical Function and Impact

Because social movements depend upon a variety of rhetorical agents and agencies, the *Una* was not conceived as a replacement for conventions and other types of valuable meetings already established as part of the movement, but as a supplement to them. Indeed, the primary functions of the *Una* duplicated, in large measure, those of the woman's rights conventions: disseminating information about woman's condition, recruiting members into the movement, providing members with arguments to counter the opposition, and developing a common ideology for the movement. However, as a journal, the *Una* was both forced to and able to perform these functions differently. A letter to the *Una* from H. M. Tracy Cutler just three months after the paper's debut concurred with Wright Davis's rationale for augmenting the platform with the press because of the latter's unique capacity to advance the cause: "The pen is the all powerful lever. With the press to multiply its impressions, it far surpasses the power of Grecian eloquence. Success to all who dare to use it freely, boldly" (May 1853, 63).

Although Tracy Cutler's claim of the print medium's superiority is clearly arguable, such newspapers as the *Una* did have certain distinct advantages over the public platform. Although in some respects, woman's rights conventions already performed one of the paper's primary functions—providing a variety of accurate information *about* women's existence *to* women on a large scale—the *Una* sought to enlarge the scope of the message, to expand the audience for it, and to issue the information more regularly. While years sometimes separated major conventions, the *Una* was available to subscribers on a regular monthly basis. Particularly significant was the paper's unique potential to reach vast numbers of women unable to attend the conventions for various reasons such as distance, financial constraints, family responsibilities, or spousal resistance. Because the paper frequently published speeches and proceedings of these conventions, readers could participate in them vicariously, with the added advantage of having the more tedious discussions omitted.

Moreover, the *Una* was a potentially powerful agency to recruit individuals into the movement. While conventions catered largely to those persons who were already committed, a newspaper could reach those women who were personally dissatisfied with their condition but who were not yet politically involved for various reasons. For women too timid to attend meetings where members of their sex took such "radical" steps as speaking in public, a newspaper fashioned somewhat after other popular women's journals may have seemed more familiar, safer, even innocuous in comparison, yet still intriguing.

Like the conventions, the *Una* also performed the function of arming committed women with arguments and evidence to counter the traditional arguments used by the opposition to perpetuate woman's oppression. In this respect, the advantage that a newspaper had over public meetings was its permanence. Although the general themes of information obtained aurally are often retained, specifics are frequently and rapidly forgotten. By contrast, the *Una* enabled women to repeatedly return to its pages to refamiliarize themselves with its content.

As an impetus for social change, the *Una*, like the conventions, had as one of its primary functions the forging and refining of the movement's ideology. As an open forum to which readers were encouraged to contribute ideas and debate them, the journal was an avenue for the movement to define itself in terms of issues and overarching philosophy. The spirited debate over the natural rights argument versus the expediency argument provided the most salient example in the *Una* of the movement's attempting to establish a clear basis of identity for its members.

In addition to these functions that the *Una* shared with woman's rights conventions, the journal fulfilled at least three other functions that had significance for the movement, all three of which are subsumed under the larger function of altering the self-perception and aspirations of women individually and as a group. First, as the initial newspaper to treat a multitude of woman's rights issues, the *Una* served as a touchstone for later woman's journals, and its female editors served as positive role models for the women who subscribed to it. Second, the journal helped to undercut the confining stereotype of "true womanhood" by creating in its pages an image of a multidimensional woman who was interested in art, politics, literature, commerce, international affairs, and woman's rights, as well as more traditional issues such as cooking, fashion, childcare, and hygiene and health. Third, and most significantly, because the journal treated the concerns of women from all classes and encouraged dialogue among them and commentary by them, the *Una* provided a unique avenue for women of all circumstances to find commonalities as women. It is in this sense that the *Una* and its editors were most remarkable. Astutely, Wright Davis recognized that she was unable to speak empathetically for women who were socioeconomically unlike herself. She not only encouraged lower-class women to contribute, but when they did, she responded. Moreover, Wright Davis's responses indicated that she was changed by what these women wrote, a process that served as a model for the changes in awareness and attitude that might have occurred in the *Una*'s readers, many of whom resembled Wright Davis socially and economically. In cutting through barriers that served to keep women isolated from and ignorant about each other, such as class, the *Una* provided a means to encourage sisterhood and a collective identity, a necessary precursor to eventual empowerment.

Obviously, the most salient characteristic distinguishing the *Una* from other woman's rights newspapers was its position as the first paper of that kind. In the same manner that Seneca Falls became a model for woman's rights conventions that would follow, the *Una* set the stage for subsequent woman's rights periodicals. Although short-lived, the *Una* suggested the potential for such a woman's rights venture and possibly helped dispel misgivings about the feasibility of similar endeavors. Similarly, to their readers, Wright Davis and Healy Dall themselves served as exemplars of woman's potential accomplishments outside of the domestic sphere. In this sense, both women editors enacted their argument that women were intelligent, responsible individuals who were capable of functioning in public leadership positions such as business. Moreover, the fact that both women openly named themselves as the paper's editors was in itself a significant message. Although many women had demonstrated impressive business and organizational skills through their work in voluntary societies, fewer were willing to assume openly the credit for their accomplishments. Even movement luminaries such as Cady Stanton and Coffin Mott, who had spearheaded Seneca Falls just four years earlier, bowed to propriety and relinquished the role of chairing that meeting to Coffin Mott's husband, James.[10] Thus, because Wright Davis's enterprise was viewed as radical for her day, readers who subscribed to the *Una* were accepting—or at least not rejecting—a new conception of woman.

In a related vein, the admixture of content in the *Una* painted a portrait of a well-rounded woman pursuing self-actualization. The image of a woman interested in public, cultural, *and* domestic issues may have helped relieve the tension experienced by women who believed they were forced to choose between the traditional domestic role for women and the nonconventional role of woman's rights advocate. The *Una*'s "woman" potentially helped to dissolve this artificial dichotomy and the accompanying threat for women who felt pulled in two directions. Like contemporary readers of *Ms.*, readers of the *Una* were made aware that many women who wanted political, legal, and social change and intellectual stimulation still regarded themselves as "women" who enjoyed caring for their appearance, their homes, and their families. Moreover, this multidimensional image of woman possibly neutralized the opposition's contention that woman's rights concerns were alien to the existence of most women and that advocates of change firmly rejected traditional social values. Contrary to the opposition's negative portrait of woman's rights activists as "semi-women" and "mental hermaphrodites,"[11] the woman who emerged from the *Una*'s pages was an appealing blend of homemaker, nurturer, cultured intellectual, and social reformer, a marked, but still attractive change from the "true womanhood" ideal. In this respect, the *Una* potentially served to enhance the self-image of the women who read it. Unfortunately, this attractive balance was lost in the *Una*'s later issues, where esoteric articles on art, foreign dignitaries, music, etc., far outweighed more traditional fare.

The *Una*'s most significant function for the movement was the unique and varied manner in which it crossed class boundaries to raise the consciousness of all women and create identification among them. Unlike many feminist journals succeeding it, which, as Masel-Walters notes, largely ignored "the factory operative, the domestic employee, or the home-bound piece worker,"[12] the *Una*, at least in its early months, devoted considerable space to the concerns of lower-class women. Interestingly, most of the contributions treating this subject came from the working-class women themselves in the forms of letters or diaries. The prosperous Wright Davis apparently recognized her inability to empathize credibly with their plight or accurately give voice to their concerns. In the *Una*'s first issue, Wright Davis alluded to her own privileged existence, while simultaneously attempting to build identification by sympathizing with those women less fortunate than she on the basis of sex: "We shall complain little of wrongs, for individually we have suffered very few, but in our human sympathies, we have suffered from every infliction upon the dependent class to which we belong. We bear in our heart of hearts, their sorrows, and carry their griefs . . ." (February 1853, 4). In the same issue, a published letter to Wright Davis from Angelina Grimké Weld chided the middle- and upper-class women at a recent convention for miscalculating the best means to liberate the impoverished woman whose existence the wealthy misunderstood:

How can [the women in high life] truly sympathize with those in whose soul's stead they have never been[?] Charity they are willing to give to the poor, but competent wages they are not—a woman is expected to work for little or nothing. But when as a body, we feel the *burden* of making a support for *our* families, then we will open widely the hand of justice to laboring women instead of the hand of charity. The latter has debased and enfeebled women; the former will elevate, strengthen, and bless her. (February 1853, 12)

Apparently aware of her inability to empathize fully with poor women, Wright Davis compensated by relying upon authentic materials such as the diary of a poor seamstress, which she ran in the hopes that it "may help to solve the problem of our wants" (April 1853, 62). These diaries, the fictional stories set in the homes of poor families, and the interaction between the paper's readers and the editors provided the clearest examples of the *Una*'s crossing class barriers to build identification and raise the consciousness of all women. The most striking instance was the evolution in attitudes that was reflected in the regular correspondence between Wright Davis and an invalid who signed her letters to the editor "Emma." Although Emma's letters were unlike the lucid polemical essays that often graced the *Una*'s pages, her words were hauntingly thought-provoking for the reader, for the paper's editors, and for Emma herself.

Emma's words expressing the anger, anguish, and desperation that characterized the daily existence of many women of her time served several important functions. First, her discussion of the social and psychological obstacles facing ordinary women helped educate those more gifted and privileged, lessening the estrangement between these two groups in the process. In a related vein, the feelings of unattractiveness, inadequacy, and unworthiness as a woman that Emma voiced about herself and those she knew were not class specific. In this sense, Emma spoke forcefully to and about all women who shared those self-perceptions, cutting across every kind of social line to bond women together as women. Moreover, the initial distance between Emma and Wright Davis and their resolution of it through dialogue generated identification, not merely between them, but with all women who participated vicariously in the pair's debate.

Second, Emma's unusual eloquence and candor and her strong

emotionality made her especially convincing to traditional women who were less comfortable with rigorous argument and confrontational strategies as a means of exploring ideas. Her seriousness of tone, self-deprecation, and decorous letter-writing mode built her ethos as a pious traditional woman, compelling women who identified with her to accept the unconventional ideas that she expressed.

Finally, in wrestling with the reasons for her own sense of worthlessness and discovering that they were largely external to her, Emma began to fashion hope from her despair. A sense of community with other women began to replace the isolation that characterized Emma's early letters, and she came to feel empowered in the process. For, although as an invalid, Emma was distinct from most of the *Una*'s subscribers, readers and Emma herself gradually became aware that she symbolized all women handicapped by laws and social custom.

Because Emma erroneously believed herself to be ungifted, she displayed uncanny empathy for the talented women crushed by a society that disregarded those qualities in the female sex. In one letter, she quoted a man commenting on a gifted young woman, embittered by a world undesigned for and unappreciative of her: "I rather think that she is born out of time and place; the earth is, I suppose, about a foot deep of such woman dust as she will make" (April 1853, 54). Rather than arguing with the aptness of the cruel analogy, Emma expounded on its appropriateness. Poignantly, she capsulized perhaps the movement's greatest obstacle: women who, reduced to hating themselves so intensely for their oppression, begin to view it as justified and feel compelled to deride those foolish enough to try and free them:

It seems to me that the best must die in atonement, as you say, for the worst, but when they judge themselves unworthy of such grace—they must perish for differences of their own excellencies, and their disproportion to the conditions which surround them. Woman dust! Yes, it is deep all over the earth; and the sacrifice is not yet ended. The last words that I heard from Miss F—— were a seething satire upon "woman's rights" and "strong minded women." I looked earnestly into her face; she seemed conscious of the truth her lips were falsifying, and five minutes afterwards, aside, she said to me, "I am ashamed of my sex, they are fit only for slavery, and nobody but a fool would take any trouble with them or for them."

There it was, all out and I said in my heart, "dust to dust" but alas for the crumbling of heart and hope, of power and principle, and all that is divine in woman! (April 1853, 55)

Significantly, Emma's exploration of the differences in the obstacles facing women in varying classes and circumstances led to the discovery of commonalities in the oppression of all women. Although she believed her physical infirmity rendered her less capable of contributing in a society that valued only "whole" and beautiful women, Emma also recognized that her greatest liability was her sex. Thus, Emma's physical handicap became a living metaphor for the barriers that faced all women:

This morning as I passed along the street a couple of half dressed little girls suspended their rope dancing for a moment, and gazed at me with mingled curiosity and pity. One of them said to the other, "The poor cripple, it's a pity of her." "Ah, my poor girls," thought I, "I am a cripple, indeed, and in a sense deeper, far deeper than you have the sense to know; but you are also of the sex that will teach you yet the fuller meaning of the word." (April 1853, 54)

Although Emma initially believed that her physical handicap destined her to "soon add a few more grains to deepen that growing layer of woman dust" (April 1853, 55), her letters gradually grew more optimistic concerning the prospects of avoiding that fate. Clearly, her correspondence with Wright Davis in the *Una* enabled Emma to identify with the movement's goals by feeling included in its constituency. Undoubtedly, Wright Davis's lengthy responses and generally supportive prefaces to Emma's letters enabled Emma to feel attended to as a worthwhile individual, perhaps for the first time. In one particularly poignant entry, Emma's painful struggle in trying to free herself from defeating feelings of inadequacy is punctuated by glimmers of hope precipitated by the movement and her new sense of belonging in it:

I do not know what has put me in this vein of philosophizing today, unless it be the recent contact with a logical mind. I am not sure that I have done justice to the apprehensions which I have been trying to alter, but failure in this would (unintelligible) less matter, if I could escape an oppressive sense of my own insecurity. I think and dream and talk far above the pitch of my own life. I cannot resolve to deserve my own self respect. Perhaps it is this which has put me on the defence or apology for the delinquent ladies of my set.
But can we do that we are capable of, and—don't laugh at me—it would suit us to do? There are, it seems to me, two modes of serving the cause—one direct and the other indirect; both of which are equally right and necessary to the great end. But the trouble is that the indirect requires *genius*, of which we perhaps have very little among us; and the direct demands *courage*, of which we certainly have not much. . . .
The very thought of all this great progress strengthens me, even me. My own despair is nothing. I feel as I do on shipboard or in a railroad car; I am not of the least consequence to the movement, but it goes on and carries me

with it. It is a joy to know that we are not standing still and that my worthlessness is not fatal to the interest that I have at heart. (June 1853, 78)

Although Emma herself failed to see either the genius or the courage evidenced in her writing, those qualities were not lost on Wright Davis. Like Emma, apparently Wright Davis also was changed by the relationship between the two women. Wright Davis's early romanticized responses to Emma clearly illustrate a lack of empathy and an incomplete understanding of the dismal economic, social, and psychological conditions of lower-class women that Emma had tried to describe:

Your letter to the editor was sad in tone, sadder than real workers ever indulge in. Labor, which is prayer, brings confidence and trust to the soul. "Woman dust" may cover the earth three feet deep or so, but hope "recreates" from this very dust, true, noble, strong women; women who can labor and wait for the return of their harvest; women who can discern from afar the first gleam of light, and go cheerily to their toil, renewed and refreshed from the fountain of all good. (June 1853, 74)

Gradually, Wright Davis appeared to understand and accept as valid Emma's emotional responses to her existence: "We claim that the heart is never ignorant; because the mysteries of feeling are as full of wonder as the intellect. There is much in the soul above intellect; there are those distinct energies by which we seize upon and appropriate high truth . . ." (June 1853, 78). The extent to which Wright Davis's consciousness was raised by women such as Emma or by Davis's own working experience, which required her to "grind and work [her] brain for everyday use" (February 1853, 3), or by both, is not clear. Emma's influence on Wright Davis was evidenced, however, in the editor's borrowing of Emma's sentiment and language to describe the movement's female critics: "Ah, this woman dust lies deep over the earth" (May 1855, 72).

Although later issues of the *Una* contained dramatically fewer offerings so personal in nature, Wright Davis initially recognized the *Una*'s value in providing an avenue for the expression of woman's existence. In an early issue, Wright Davis acknowledged that Emma wrote "because you must have an utterance for your free thought" (June 1853, 74).

Thus, whether real or fictionalized, the personal accounts that were common to the *Una*'s early issues served an important function for the movement by providing characters and contexts with which most women, not just the movement's elite, could identify. The sharing of common concerns, common values, and common experiences helped to undercut the stereotypes that divided woman, creating a sisterhood from diversity.

Conclusion

Although the *Una* survived for less than three years, its appearance marked the advent of the woman's rights press, an unarguable contribution to the relatively young woman's rights movement. The *Una* served to augment and expand upon the functions already performed by woman's rights conventions: disseminating information about woman's condition, recruiting members into the movement, arming members with arguments and evidence to counter the opposition, and forging movement ideology. In addition, the *Una* and its editors functioned as role models for the movement and created in its pages an image of a new woman interested in public, domestic, and cultural issues. Particularly significant was the *Una*'s initial recognition of the interests and concerns of lower-class women and the need to embrace these women and include them in the crusade. Through consciousness-raising and identification-building strategies, the *Una* sought to bridge the isolation and alienation engendered by class to forge a sisterhood. Many other such journals, newspapers, and magazines would follow, some borrowing from ideas first presented in this small monthly, some learning also from the *Una*'s mistakes. Regardless of its "success" during its own time, the *Una*, in its search for truth, opened doors for women, which would never quite be closed again.

5

The *Revolution*, 1868–1870
Expanding the Woman Suffrage Agenda
Bonnie J. Dow

"Principle, Not Policy; Justice, Not Favors—Men, Their Rights and
Nothing More; Women, Their Rights and Nothing Less."
—Masthead of the *Revolution*, 8 January 1868

On 8 January 1868, the first issue of the *Revolution* was published
in New York City, listing Elizabeth Cady Stanton and Parker Pillsbury as editors and Susan B. Anthony as "proprietor," or business
manager. Although not the first woman's journal in the nineteenth
century, the *Revolution* was significant both in rhetorical and historical terms. It was a rhetorical forum designed specifically to disseminate arguments for woman suffrage, and the controversial positions
it espoused would serve to redefine the issues and membership of
the woman suffrage movement. Moreover, during its short lifetime,
the *Revolution* contributed to important developments in the internal leadership and organization of the movement. This essay will
examine these significant aspects of the *Revolution* as well as
provide a short history of the development of the journal.

History and Development of the *Revolution*

Parker Pillsbury, who originally coedited the *Revolution* with
Elizabeth Cady Stanton, was an experienced journalist and reformer,
having edited the *National Anti-Slavery Standard*. However, Cady
Stanton and Susan B. Anthony, with the financial backing of George
Francis Train, were responsible for the establishment of the journal.[1]
In 1867, during their campaign for a suffrage amendment to the Kan-

sas constitution, Cady Stanton and Anthony had formed an alliance with Train based on his support for woman suffrage, and he offered to fund a paper for them to promote the cause.[2]

With members of the northern, liberal press no longer sympathetic toward woman suffrage, coverage of the activities and speeches of the Kansas campaign had been virtually nonexistent.[3] A journal of their own would allow Cady Stanton and Anthony to air their views freely and to disseminate them to the public. Their only concession in their agreement with Train was to allow sufficient space in the paper for Train and his associate David Meliss, the financial editor of the *New York World*, to express their views on politics and finance. Train was an advocate of the Irish rebellion, greenbackism, open immigration, organized labor, and the Credit Mobilier and Credit Foucier systems. Meliss became a contributor to the "Financial Department" of the *Revolution*, where many of these views were advocated.[4]

However, very soon after the *Revolution* was established, Train went abroad. Because of his pro-Irish sentiments, the British government jailed him in Ireland for a year. Consequently, his financial support was uncertain, and although Meliss underwrote the *Revolution* in Train's stead for a time, the journal developed financial difficulties fairly early in its two-and-a-half-year career.[5] These difficulties eventually resulted in the sale of the paper in May of 1870 for the sum of one dollar, with Susan B. Anthony assuming responsibility for the journal's ten-thousand-dollar debt.[6]

Because of Train's incarceration in Ireland early in 1868, his direct influence on the journal was limited after that time, but the editors loyally printed the letters he sent from his Dublin cell. Although these letters usually dealt with Train's views on the Irish rebellion or the currency question, he also made cogent arguments in support of woman suffrage (see, for example, 29 October 1868, 263). David Meliss apparently edited the financial page of the *Revolution* until 1869, when Cady Stanton noted in her New Year's editorial that the financial department had been taken over by a woman editor (7 January 1869, 8).

Train's connection with the journal was not officially and publicly severed until May of 1869 (see 8 May 1869, 280). By the beginning of that year, the *Revolution* had begun to narrow its focus to issues that had a direct bearing upon women, and the editors abandoned the unrelated political issues that Train and Meliss had advocated. In July of 1869, Parker Pillsbury's name was dropped from the editorial page, and Cady Stanton was the sole full-time editor until January of 1870, when Paulina Wright Davis, former editor of the *Una*, joined her as corresponding editor.

The prospectus for "*The Revolution* of 1870," published in December of 1869, no longer claimed to discuss issues except as they were designed "to educate women for an intelligent expression of opinion at the polls, where, in the march of civilization, she is so soon to share in the grave responsibilities of government" (9 December 1869, 360). Cady Stanton also noted in the prospectus: "While we would not refuse men an occasional word in our columns, yet as masculine ideas have ruled the race for six thousand years, we specially desire that *The Revolution* shall be the mouthpiece of women, that they may give the world the feminine thought in politics, religion, and social life; that ultimately in the union of both we may find the truth in all things" (9 December 1869, 360). By this time, the financial department was virtually nonexistent; it appeared only on an irregular basis and usually included only correspondence.

Despite all efforts to keep it afloat, Anthony was forced to sell the *Revolution* to Laura J. Bullard in May of 1870. With Bullard, a very moderate woman's rights supporter, as its editor, the *Revolution* was much less controversial and became a "more literary and socially oriented journal." However, Bullard did not manage to make a success of the journal either, and within two years it had been absorbed by the New York *Christian Enquirer.*[7]

The establishment of the *Woman's Journal* as the unofficial organ of the American Woman Suffrage Association (AWSA) in January of 1870 also played a part in the demise of the *Revolution*. The more conservative *Woman's Journal*, which appealed to a broader audience than the *Revolution*, operated on a more stable financial basis.[8] Because the potential audience was not great enough to support two woman's journals, the last issue of the *Revolution* with Cady Stanton as editor was published on 26 May 1870.[9]

Content and Format of the *Revolution*

The *Revolution* was radically different from the woman's journals that had preceded it, such as the genteel and literary *Una* or *Lily*, and those that would follow it, such as the moderate *Woman's Journal* and *Woman's Tribune*. The *Revolution* was different because its editors did not conform to politically popular or expedient positions in pursuing their objectives; instead, the journal reflected the uncompromising and often controversial ideas of its creators.

In the first sixteen-page issue of the *Revolution*, the editors explained their journal's purpose and its name: "The enfranchisement of women is one of the leading ideas that calls this journal into existence. Seeing in its realization, the many necessary changes in our modes of life, we think *The Revolution* a fitting name for a paper that will advocate so radical a reform as this involves in our political, religious, and social worlds" (8 January 1868, 1). At first glance, the early issues of the *Revolution* more closely resemble an extremist political newspaper than a journal devoted to women's concerns. Early issues included a platform declaring that the journal was the official organ of the "National Party of New America," and that the *Revolution* would discuss issues as varied as "abolition of standing armies and party despotisms," "eight hours labor," "greenbacks for money," "science, not superstition," and "open doors to artisans and immigrants." This platform was probably the result of Train's influence. In the first year of the *Revolution*, much space was devoted to discussions of financial policy and political matters.

The political editorializing, the product of Cady Stanton and Pillsbury and undoubtedly influenced by Train, demonstrated a strong anti-Republican flavor, which the editors freely admitted and justified: "Our Republicans are growing more and more shamefaced. Last winter they could not present a woman's petition without an apology; now they cannot mention the name woman. Send your petitions to the Democrats, they will tell you who you are and what you want!" (22 January 1868, 39). In response to a critical letter from William Lloyd Garrison, Cady Stanton praised the Democrats and defended George Francis Train:

The Democratic party, on the contrary, has done all it could to keep our question alive in the State and National councils, by pressing Republicans, in their debates on negro suffrage, to logical conclusions. They have respectfully presented our petitions and called attention to them in every possible way. . . . So long as Mr. Train speaks nobly for woman, why should we repudiate his services, even if he does ring the charges "nigger, nigger, nigger?" though we traveled with him through nine states, and never heard him in public or private ignore the black man's rights. (29 January 1868, 49–50)

The journal was filled with news of woman suffrage activities across the country and abroad in the form of articles reprinted from other periodicals (with Cady Stanton's commentaries) and letters and articles from correspondents and subscribers. Regular correspondents included Matilda E. Joslyn Gage, Paulina Wright Davis, and Ernestine Rose. The news, confined usually to the first eight pages of the paper, was followed by a three- or four-page editorial section, including book reviews; the last pages of the journal were occupied by the financial department and the advertisements.

In 1869, Cady Stanton had begun a poetry column on the front page of the paper; it included the work of well-known poets as well as poetry specific to women's rights written by women such as Alice and Phebe Cary. The poetry column, edited by Elizabeth R. Tilton, the wife of prominent reformer Theodore Tilton, continued until the *Revolution* was sold. In the initial issue of the *Revolution* for 1870, Cady Stanton began the serialization of a story by Alice Cary entitled "The Born Thrall, or Woman's Life and Experience." The journal had rarely carried lengthy fiction before, and it was, at least partially, a ploy to increase circulation. The story's installments were carried on the front page of the *Revolution*, and Cady Stanton promoted the serial by claiming "What *Uncle Tom's Cabin* was to the anti-slavery movement, this work will be to the cause of women" (6 January 1870, 1). Alice Cary's death ended the serial shortly before the *Revolution* was sold.

The weekly journal charged a subscription rate of two dollars, which was later raised to three dollars in an effort to increase revenue. Anthony attempted to make the paper financially solvent by amassing a hundred thousand subscribers, but even at its peak, the *Revolution* did not claim more than three thousand subscribers.[10]

As editor of the *Revolution*, Cady Stanton expanded the focus of woman suffrage concerns by addressing a host of controversial social issues that had formerly been handled only indirectly by other publications and reformers.[11] Cady Stanton's attention to issues such as abortion, prostitution, marriage, divorce, and prison reform, and her portrayal of these issues as concerns for woman suffrage, greatly expanded the field of arguments relevant to suffrage. Cady Stanton promoted woman suffrage as the solution to such problems as prison reform by arguing:

Surely, mothers should have a voice in the making and administering of our criminal laws, in the treatment of these weak and unfortunate ones. When woman walks these prison halls with her love and mercy, when she is a responsible witness of the horrible punishments inflicted on her sons, from the fiendish cold shower, to the gallows, these things will all be changed. Woman knows the cost of life better than man does, hence her quick sympathy for suffering, her impulse to save and protect life. (23 July 1868, 40)

Clearly, Cady Stanton did not hesitate to use the special, sympathetic nature of woman as an argument for her right to the ballot.

On the issue of prostitution, the *Revolution* condemned the silence of other reformers, claiming, as a correspondent's article indicates, that it exacerbated the problem: "Prostitution is a social disease whose sustenance is silence, and all who treat it to its own food, by suppressing the voice, or withholding the effort which would tend in any degree to mitigate the evil, are guilty of adding that much influence toward its support. Many would-be reformers cry down vehemently any exposure of the social sore, and seem to think silence the best surgery; the smooth patch under which the evil is sure to work its own cure" (16 April 1868, 231). The editors of the *Revolution* promoted a solution to this evil in the form of new prostitution laws that would require the registration of prostitutes and houses of prostitution, and they argued for the establishment of a hospital for "the treatment of such maladies as are engendered by prostitution . . . while the disease is yet in its earliest stages—before it has utterly destroyed the lives of its victims and before hundreds of new victims have been made by infection" (9 April 1868, 216). This unmistakable reference to venereal disease was controversial at the time, and the implication of these suggestions was that women would carry them out if given the ballot.

The willingness of the *Revolution*'s editors to defend their views was demonstrated by the journal's coverage of the controversial trial of Hester Vaughn. Vaughn, a servant girl, was impregnated by her married employer and then cast out by him; she was later found near death from starvation in a tenement house, with her dead baby by her side. She was convicted of "infanticide" (a euphemism for abortion) and sentenced to be executed in Pennsylvania (19 November 1868, 312). Because the proof was not conclusive that Vaughn had consciously murdered her child or even that the child had been born alive, Cady Stanton took up Vaughn's cause, writing numerous editorials defending the young girl as the victim of her male seducer: "In the name of womanhood, we implore the mothers of that state to rescue that defenceless [*sic*] girl from her impending fate. Oh! make her case your own, suppose your young and beautiful daughter had been thus betrayed, would it not seem to you that the demands of justice should take the life of her seducer rather than her own? Men have made the laws cunningly, for their own protection; ignorantly, for they can never weigh the sorrows and sufferings of their victims" (19 November 1868, 312).

In another editorial, Cady Stanton argued that Vaughn's case had been improperly tried, citing specific legal grounds for her arguments and concluding: "This case carries with it a lesson for the serious thought of every woman, as it shows that importance that women of wealth, education, and leisure study the laws under which they live, that they may defend the unfortunate of their sex in our courts of justice, and, as able advocates, avail themselves of every advantage the law gives for their acquittal" (10 December 1868, 360). Cady Stanton visited Vaughn in her prison in Philadelphia and later wrote a letter to the *Revolution* describing the girl in sympathetic terms: "On seeing the poor girl, our interest in her was greatly intensified, and we felt more than ever convinced of her innocence. . . . She has a quiet, self-possessed manner and is gentle in her movements and speech. She can read and write, and is very intelligent for one of her class. . . . Everything about her indicates a taste for order, cleanliness, and beauty" (10 December 1868, 354–55). The *Revolution's* defense of the girl, which aroused sympathy for her case, resulted in a meeting at the Cooper Institute in New York City to rally her defenders; it certainly contributed to Vaughn's eventual pardon.[12]

Although discussion of marriage and divorce was decidedly less controversial than the coverage of scandalous criminal cases, Cady Stanton's positions on marriage in the *Revolution* were definitely iconoclastic, particularly in comparison to those of the moderates in the woman's rights movement. She stated unequivocally that she was opposed to "the present legalized marriage, and the marriage and divorce laws of most of the states in the Union, because they bear unequally on man and woman" (8 April 1869, 212). In one article, Cady Stanton described the role of "mistress" as superior to that of wife, because the "'legal position' of a wife is more dependent and degrading than any other condition of womanhood could possibly be" (15 October 1868, 233). Cady Stanton argued against the traditional position that marriage was sacred and indissoluble with fervor, as this response to an article in the *New-York Tribune* indicates: "The 'monstrous fallacy' of the *Tribune*, and all who agree with it, is that all marriages, whether of interest, convenience, necessity, or mere lust are sacred. . . . If there is hell on earth, it is found in the homes where brutal fathers, cold, joyless mothers, and little children pining for the love that never comes, are indissolubly bound together, to torment, torture, exasperate each other, until death brings release" (4 November 1869, 280). As she usually did, Cady Stanton concluded that woman suffrage was the solution to the inequality inherent in the present state of marriage: "Woman, as woman, has nothing to ask of our legislators but the right of suffrage. It is only in marriage that she must demand her rights to person, children, property, wages, life, liberty, and the pursuit of happiness. All the specific statutes of which we complain,—all the barbarities of the law—fall on her as wife and mother. We have not yet outlived the old feudal ideal, the right of property in woman" (15 October 1868, 238).

Although the *Revolution* addressed many issues that were new to the suffrage agenda and did so in a straightforward manner that was uncharacteristic of past women's journals, one refrain appeared in Cady Stanton's editorializing. In virtually every case, she asserted that the enfranchisement of women would lead to the solution of the ills she exposed. Although history has proved that the vote was not a panacea for women's problems, Cady Stanton was astute in recognizing not only that the spectrum of issues affecting women was far wider than many suffragists believed, but also in perceiving the important function of the ballot as a goal for women's rights advocates.

The *Revolution*'s Effect on the Woman Suffrage Movement

Despite its short life, scholars have agreed that the *Revolution* had a significant impact on the woman's rights movement in the nineteenth century.[13] In one respect, the *Revolution* was important because it gave the woman's rights movement a "forum, focus, and direction," as Flexner argues;[14] however, the nature of that focus and direction was even more important.

In addition to its discussion of controversial issues in relation to woman suffrage, the *Revolution* also departed from the general tradition of women's journals because it targeted lower-class women laborers as potential beneficiaries of and participants in woman suffrage reforms. From its beginnings, the woman's rights movement had focused on middle- and upper-class women, primarily because such women had the time, resources, and education to pursue reform.[15] Through the *Revolution*, Cady Stanton and Anthony attempted to create recognition of the equal stake of working women in equal rights and suffrage.

Moreover, the *Revolution*'s unswerving advocacy of woman suffrage and its consequent opposition to the Fifteenth Amendment, at a time when moderate reformers were proclaiming the "negro's hour," served as catalysts for the split of the woman's rights movement into two factions. The rift would not heal until 1890, with the formation of the National American Woman Suffrage Association.[16] Although this development was obviously detrimental to the movement in one sense, in another sense the *Revolution* was a blessing, because it kept the ideas of woman suffrage alive at a time when they were being pushed into the background for the benefit of African-American male suffrage. This opinion was not shared by other important reformers, such as William Lloyd Garrison, Wendell Phillips, and Lucy Stone, who believed that women should delay their demands for suffrage until African-American male suffrage was gained. Moreover, these moderate reformers did not believe in clouding the woman suffrage issue with discussion of other controversial social issues affecting women.[17] Consequently, the positions advocated by the *Revolution* were iconoclastic in another sense because they defined woman suffrage as a movement with an independent and multifaceted existence.

While Cady Stanton redefined the spectrum of issues affecting woman suffrage, Susan B. Anthony's concern for the plight of the working woman eventually resulted in redefinition and expansion of the potential membership of the suffrage movement. Prior to the establishment of the *Revolution*, female laborers were organized to a limited extent, primarily in the textile mills of New England. Unrelated to a desire for suffrage, their actions were motivated by desire for better wages and treatment.[18] Anthony recognized that the working woman's role in the movement had largely been ignored, and she set out to cultivate these women through the *Revolution*. Her goal was clear: to convince working women that the solution to their problems lay in the right to the ballot and, consequently, to expand the membership of the movement by appealing to them (see 17 September 1868, 181).

In August of 1868, the editors made the bold statement that "*The Revolution* exists for the one specific purpose, more than any other, of ameliorating the condition of the working woman." They clearly indicated their desire to cultivate working women as participants in the woman's rights movement when they noted: "We fixed our subscription at two dollars per year, much below a 'fair price' that we might place our paper within the reach of the working people—especially all *women* who earn their own living" (20 August 1868, 105). Anthony engineered the formation of the Working Women's Association in September of 1868 "for the purpose of doing everything possible to elevate women, and raise the value of their labor" (17 September 1868, 181). In an editorial in November of 1868, Cady Stanton boasted that the Working Women's Association had over two hundred members, and she described its agenda:

They [the members] are to meet once a month to devise ways and means to open to themselves new and more profitable employments, that thus by decreasing the numbers in the few avocations open to women, they can decrease the supply and raise the wages of those who remain. They propose, also, to demand an increase in wages in all those trades where they now work beside men for half-pay. This can only be done by combination, for one person alone demanding higher wages can effect nothing, but 5,000 women in any one employment, striking for higher wages, would speedily bring their employers to terms. (5 November 1868, 280)

Cady Stanton concluded, as usual, that the eventual success of these aims was dependent on woman suffrage: "while association will do much toward ameliorating some of the evils of our present social condition, no radical changes can be effected for woman's elevation until she holds the ballot, the citizen's only shield of protection, in her own right hand" (5 November 1868, 280). The *Revolution* dutifully reported the proceedings of all of the subsequent meetings of the Working Women's Association, and the editors established a column entitled "The Working Woman," "to record what women are doing in the various departments of labor, what new enterprises they are inaugurating, what they have already accomplished" (10 March 1870, 154).

Initially, working women were responsive to Cady Stanton and Anthony's attempts to organize them. The Association of Women Printers elected Anthony as their delegate to the National Labor Union Congress meeting in September of 1868,[19] the first such meeting to include women as delegates (1 October 1868, 200). In an editorial in November of 1868, Cady Stanton and Anthony pledged their continuing commitment to the cause of the working woman: "Until woman is awarded equal pay with men for equal work, and is permitted to enter any calling to which she is adapted, the Working Women's Associations will continue to be a necessity, and will secure a due share of attention in our columns; though all efforts for women are fragmentary and superficial until she holds the ballot in her own hand and has a voice in the laws" (26 November 1868, 328). The commitment of the *Revolution* to working women reflected not only Cady Stanton and Anthony's concern for the plight of these women but also indicated an effort to expand the scope and membership of the woman suffrage movement to include a potentially large and powerful group of women.

Although the controversial views espoused by the editors of the *Revolution* from its first issue disturbed the moderate leaders of the woman suffrage movement, the position of the journal on the question of African-American male versus woman suffrage, culminating in the controversy over the Fifteenth Amendment, was the final and decisive factor in the split in the movement's leadership in 1869.[20] In the early issues of the *Revolution*, the editors were clear about their advocacy of universal suffrage and their opposition to African-American male suffrage taking precedence over woman suffrage. In June of 1868, Cady Stanton wrote that "our political necessity today is universal enfranchisement, and those who talk merely of the extension of suffrage to a few men on Southern plantations are blind to the duties and necessities of the hour" (14 May 1868, 296). In an editorial in October of 1868, Cady Stanton refuted the position of those reformers who had proclaimed the "negro's hour" and pointed out the superiority of the *Revolution*'s position on African-American suffrage: "You see, friends, so soon as we women get a foothold among the 'white males,' instead of selfishly rejoicing in our own good fortune, forgetting all that are behind, we turn to help our colored brothers up to the same platform. The world never hears us say, 'this is the woman's hour,' for in the world of work, as in politics, we demand the equal recognition of the whole people" (1 October 1868, 200). Cady Stanton's language was not always this conciliatory, however; at times her comments had a clear racist tone: "Think of Patrick and Sambo and Hans and Yung Tung who do not know the difference between a Monarchy and a Republic, who never read the Declaration of Independence, or Webster's Spelling book, making laws for Lydia Maria Child, Lucretia Mott, or Fanny Kemble. Think of jurors drawn from these ranks to try young girls for the crime of infanticide" (24 December 1868, 392).

At the American Equal Rights Association (AERA) convention in May of 1869, the simmering controversy between the two factions in the movement became an open rift, resulting in Cady Stanton and Anthony's withdrawal from the AERA to form the National Woman Suffrage Association (NWSA).[21] The views of the NWSA were represented by the *Revolution* in Cady Stanton's editorials. Cady Stanton saw the AERA's adoption of a resolution favoring the Fifteenth Amendment, which granted suffrage to African-American males but did not include women, as a dangerous blow to the women's cause. She openly attacked the action of the AERA in an editorial:

The women in that convention did not interpret the platform of the American Equal Rights Association to mean the establishment of an aristocracy based on sex in this republic. How a man with a grain of sense could propose such resolutions is the marvel. He must have supposed the women who gathered there either gods or fools, and intended them as lofty compliments, or supreme contempt. But as they were merely commonsense women; incapable of rising above all human considerations, or sinking below the ordinary plane of manhood, they felt toward the Fifteenth Amendment, which places all women under the heels of all men, precisely as Mr. [Frederick] Douglass would have felt had it proposed to enfranchise the men of all races but his own. (27 May 1869, 328)

The formation of the American Woman Suffrage Association (AWSA) in November of 1869 by Lucy Stone and other members of the conservative Boston group of reformers gave Cady Stanton more material for her editorials in the *Revolution*. Although she exhibited some regret at the split in the movement, she did not relinquish her conviction that the NWSA held the proper position concerning woman suffrage:

In the present stage of the Woman Suffrage movement in this country a division in our ranks is rather to be deplored, for when friends disagree newcomers hesitate as to which side to join; and from fear of being involved in personal bickerings they withhold their names and influence altogether; still more deplorable is the result to the old friends themselves, when, instead of fighting the common enemy, prejudice, custom, unjust laws, and a false public sentiment, they turn, as the old Abolitionists in their divisions did, and rend each other. . . . I would say if there are people who cannot come up to our broad catholic ground, and demand suffrage for All—*even negro suffrage, without distinction of sex*, why let them have another association until they are educated for the higher platform the present Association occupies. (28 October 1869, 264)

However, the far-reaching and controversial ideas of the NWSA expressed in the *Revolution* proved to be less popular than the moderate positions of the AWSA's *Woman's Journal*; soon after the *Journal* began publishing in January of 1870, Cady Stanton and Anthony sold the *Revolution*.

The Rhetorical Function of the *Revolution*

The *Revolution* was a rhetorical tool of the woman suffrage movement in the most traditional sense: it was a discursive, persuasive forum that allowed Cady Stanton and Anthony to project their vision of the direction that the movement should take. As Lynn Masel-Walters has argued, journals such as the *Revolution* "could clearly explain the movement to the committed and the uncommitted, provide information about suffrage organizations and campaigns, and suggest feminist goals and tactics."[22] Cady Stanton offered clearly reasoned editorials that dissected the issues facing the movement, and she exposed readers to a wide variety of issues that expanded the agenda for suffrage concerns.

In contrast to more literary women's journals, the *Revolution* was characterized by logical argument and direct attention to issues. The style of the journal was graphic, hard-hitting, and clearly partisan. The arguments were often sarcastic, as exemplified by the column of a correspondent in 1868 who addressed women who did not support suffrage:

Why is it, my dear friends, that you are averse to possessing the ballot? Have you so little confidence in your virtue and firmness that you are afraid it will injure you? . . . If you should go to the ballot-box, even if there was a crowd of rough people there, you would have the satisfaction of knowing that you had an object in going there, and a most worthy object too; but when you go in other crowded places, you cannot boast of so good a reason for doing so. . . . Perhaps you think you are not capable, do not know enough. You must have a very poor opinion of yourselves, if you think the half-witted drunken man knows more than you do. He votes every year, sometimes for one party and sometimes for the other, always for the one that will pay him most. (12 November 1868, 294)

Like other forms of woman's rights rhetoric, the *Revolution* exhibited consciousness-raising techniques. Examples of the *Revolution*'s rhetoric reveal the personal tone, reliance on examples, and efforts to create audience identification that are characteristic of this approach.[23] Particularly in Cady Stanton's editorials, the writing was characterized by an informal, often highly charged tone, numerous examples of the problems of women, and a tendency to generalize from those examples to the general condition of women. For example, Cady Stanton's rhetoric on behalf of Hester Vaughn, urging readers to imagine the young girl as their own daughter, claimed that the case made it imperative for women to study law so that they might defend those in similar situations.

Although the iconoclastic implications of the *Revolution* have been discussed at length in this paper, the role of the journal in disseminating traditional arguments for woman suffrage should not be overlooked. One primary function of journals such as the *Revolution* was to provide arguments for women to use in support of suffrage in their own areas. From the beginning, the editors of the *Revolution* supported woman's right to the ballot using arguments based on natural rights and expediency. Arguments grounded in natural rights relied on "the 'consent of the governed,' the natural equality of all human beings, and other ways of setting forth the beliefs that women ought to have political equality because justice required it," while arguments based in expediency "claim[ed] that woman suffrage would benefit society."[24]

Although Cady Stanton and Anthony's rhetoric throughout their lives demonstrates a primary reliance on natural rights philosophy, the *Revolution* published arguments from both rationales, wishing to give their readers all of the ammunition possible. In an editorial in April of 1868, Parker Pillsbury argued for woman suffrage as a natural right: "If the right of liberty and the pursuit of happiness be the gift and endowment of the creator, then surely is the right to the ballot; the only possible or conceivable assurance and guarantee of it in republican governments. And on this ground, the claim of woman is no less than that of man" (23 April 1868, 248). In an earlier issue, Cady Stanton had argued for suffrage based on its potential benefits for the working man:

A disenfranchised class degrades and cheapens every branch of labor it enters. Just as slave labor crowded free labor out of the Southern States, so will the cheap labor of women crowd men out of every employment she enters, hence it is the interest of the laboring man to dignify the woman by his side—to give her the ballot, that when she strikes for higher wages, capitalists and politicians, knowing that the discontent of woman, too, can find expression at the ballot box, will take heed to a strike that has a vote behind it. (15 January 1868, 24)

In their columns, the editors of the *Revolution* also took care to refute every common argument against woman suffrage, including woman's supposed lesser intelligence, her role as a mother, and the unwomanly nature of the polls. In response to an antisuffrage article from the *New York Times*, Cady Stanton sarcastically noted: "Voting does not involve a change in the natural division of labor. All men vote here, yet they go on in their every-day occupations as well in this country, yea, better than in those countries where they do not. . . . Why suppose that if women voted, there would be a general stampede from the kitchen and nursery: that, if permitted to go to the ballot box one day in the year, they would dance round the polls the remaining 364?" (22 January 1868, 34–35).

The refutative nature of much of the *Revolution*'s rhetoric is consistent with Charles Conrad's conclusion that, as the suffrage movement encountered more explicit opposition following the Civil War, woman suffrage rhetoric became "a rhetoric of response."[25] Although the *Revolution* noted the establishment of an antisuffrage organization in February of 1870, Cady Stanton did not appear openly concerned with the competition. In response to rumors that the Anti–Sixteenth Amendment Society would present a memorial to Congress opposing woman suffrage, she wrote: "All right. Let both sides and all sides do and be their very best. In John Quincy Adams' time a petition was sent to Congress against Abolition, signed, or purporting to be signed, wholly by slaves. Twenty years hence, one report will be just as creditable to the parties, if not just as true, as the other" (5 May 1879, 282).

The editors of the *Revolution* were more concerned with promoting concrete action for woman suffrage among their readers, which they accomplished to an extent. In the fall of 1868, a sample petition for equal suffrage was printed on the front page of the *Revolution*. It said: "To the Senate and House of Representatives, in Congress Assembled: the Undersigned citizens of the State of ——— earnestly but respectfully request, that in any change or amendment of the Constitution you may propose, to extend or regulate Suffrage, there shall be no distinction made between men and women" (19 November 1868, 305).

Within two months, the pages of the *Revolution* were filled with letters from subscribers, which typically said: "I send you by this mail a petition for Equal Suffrage, signed by one hundred and eighty-five names, with the exception of forty, I have obtained them myself, by going from house to house. It is a slow process, so few have heard anything of the movement, and the whole thing has to be explained to each person" (28 January 1870, 50). These letters demonstrated that the *Revolution* was accomplishing its goal of educating people about woman suffrage. More than one petition was printed on the front page of the journal during its lifetime, and the circulations of these petitions by subscribers exposed those who did not read the journal to the arguments of those who did.

Although the *Revolution* was effective to a degree in educating women and bringing new adherents to the cause of suffrage, it differed little from most other women's journals in terms of the audience to whom it appealed. When Cady Stanton wrote of the problems of poor and disadvantaged women, clearly she was not speaking to the women she wrote about but to women who were in a position to help those who were less fortunate. Even Anthony's efforts to organize working women stemmed from the same motivation that fueled much of female benevolent reform. Cady Stanton and Anthony were not members of the working class that they were trying to aid, a problem that eventually led to the end of their relationship with the working women. While Cady Stanton and Anthony saw the organization of these women as another avenue for suffrage promotion, the women laborers were concerned with more concrete problems, such as wages and job security, and they explicitly rejected efforts by the two suffragists to push them toward suffrage agitation (see 1 October 1868, 181, 197).

In time, the female laborers left the Working Women's Association because no practical steps were taken to ameliorate their condition. The association was taken over by middle-class professional women, such as free-lance authors and independent business women.[26] Even at the beginning of the *Revolution*'s association with working women, Cady Stanton's rhetoric suggested that she was writing for a primarily middle-class audience: "Let women of wealth and brains step out of the circles of fashion and folly, and fit themselves for the trades, arts, and professions, and become employers instead of subordinates; thus making labor honorable for all, and elevating their sex, by opening new avenues for aspiration and ambition" (15 October 1868, 231). Although Cady Stanton and Anthony were unable to overcome their middle-class ideology and achieve concrete results for women laborers, they nevertheless performed a service for the movement by attending to the problems of working women. The *Revolution* relied on the middle-class audience that was behind most woman's rights reform in the nineteenth century, but through the pages of the journal, the awareness of that audience was significantly heightened.

In any final estimation, one must note that the *Revolution* lived up to the promise of its name. The journal was revolutionary in the controversial ideas it discussed, in its support of working women, and in its editors' uncompromising position about the equal importance of woman suffrage and African-American male suffrage. Without neglecting traditional arguments for woman suffrage, the *Revolution* attempted to redefine the limits and potential membership of the movement. In doing so, while it contributed to schism in the leadership of the movement, the *Revolution* kept the ideals of woman suffrage alive when they might otherwise have been forgotten. Finally, the *Revolution* contributed to the expansion of the pool of arguments needed to ensure the continued development of the movement.

6

The *Woman's Journal*, 1870–1890
The Torchbearer for Suffrage

Susan Schultz Huxman

> The *Woman's Journal* has always been the organ of the suffrage movement, and no suffragist, private or official, can be well informed unless she is a constant reader of it.
> —Carrie Chapman Catt, 1916

It was called "The Suffrage Bible" and "The Torchbearer of the Woman Suffrage Cause." Asked about its role in securing enfranchisement for women, Carrie Chapman Catt, then president of the National American Woman's Suffrage Association (NAWSA) for the second time, flatly remarked: "It is impossible to imagine the suffrage movement without it."[1] The glowing tribute was deserved. The *Woman's Journal*, which ran continuously from 1870 to 1920, was the most visible and widely distributed suffrage periodical in the nation.

Despite the abundant accolades, the *Woman's Journal* has received little scholarly attention.[2] No scholar has fully explored the *Journal* to determine the reasons for its longevity or to describe its role within the suffrage cause. This essay will examine the *Journal* with an eye to understanding its rhetorical importance. My purpose is twofold: to identify the factors that led to the *Journal*'s formation and threatened its duration during the paper's early struggling years, and to account for its rhetorical significance both as a reform newspaper and as a suffrage voice for the conservative wing of the woman suffrage movement.

Respectable Beginnings

With the advent of a rival, and more conservative, wing of the woman's movement in 1869, the American Woman Suffrage Association (AWSA), two longtime woman's rights reformers and representatives of the new organization, Lucy Stone and her husband, Henry Blackwell, moved away from New Jersey and out from under the shadow of the preexisting organization, the National Woman Suffrage Association (NWSA), and its "radical" publication, the *Revolution*. After arriving at 3 Tremont Place in Boston, Massachusetts, they convinced the New England Woman's Suffrage Association (NEWSA) to rent them one room for the operation of a paper reflecting the club's and the newly formed association's "conservative views."

Lucy Stone's dream of editing a suffrage paper of national scope received firm financial support with the generous gift of ten thousand dollars from a wealthy sympathizer of woman's rights, Mrs. Elizabeth Eddy. To complement the seed money for the project, the couple, with the help of two prominent businessmen, Samuel E. Sewall and Ebenezer D. Draper, established a joint-stock company with two hundred shares of fifty dollars each. Blackwell bought the largest number of shares, and Stone sold the remainder to members of the AWSA and NEWSA. Later the NEWSA conducted annual large-scale, well-publicized, and highly successful suffrage bazaars to keep the publication in the black. With such a well-planned financial base, the *Woman's Journal* proudly debuted on 8 January 1870, as its competitor, the *Revolution*, struggled to secure the monies to print its next issue.[3]

In attracting suffrage sympathizers, the *Woman's Journal* left no doubt about its purposes as a suffrage organ. Printed prominently as part of its masthead, the *Journal* declared that it was "devoted to the interests of Woman, to her educational, industrial, legal and political equality, and especially to her right of Suffrage."[4] The *Journal* aimed to resurrect the viability of woman suffrage for a great number of conservative, professional women and men by depicting the cause as the gateway to a host of middle-class reforms: higher education for women, full privileges in the professions, the establishment of women's clubs, and equal property rights. The new, more single-minded constituency of women activists who resisted universal reformism and "entangling alliances" needed a paper like the *Woman's Journal* to speak for limited suffrage measures, according to *Harper's Weekly*.[5] Far from being just a clearinghouse of suffrage news, the *Journal* also aimed to "fill its readers with zeal for the cause" and to "convert them into efficient, consecrated workers."[6] Its high ideals prompted at least one subscriber to write: "The object of the *Woman's Journal* is a mighty one; no newspaper in our land is charged with graver responsibilities and every writer, therefore, wields an influence."[7]

From its inception, the *Journal* was billed as "a conservative response" to the *Revolution*, "a moderate, less abrasive" journalistic endeavor than its counterpart.[8] Readers characterized its reformist tone as "encouraging, inspiring, genial, and good-natured." It had "a certain kindly grace of spirit," being "neither defiant nor obsequious." One new convert described it simply as a paper that could "corrupt you gradually."[9]

Compared to the standard fare in the long-running *Ladies Home Journal*, however, the *Woman's Journal* was anything but conventional. Rather than catering to the delicate feminine sensibilities with columns steeped in depoliticized content, such as "Domestic Happiness," "Hints for Housekeepers," and "Fashion Corner," the *Journal* aimed both in form and content to give the impression of hard-nosed, serious journalism. One glance at its layout conveyed its primary communicative function: information, not entertainment. Its title, displayed in bold calligraphy without adornment, unveiled its feminist interests. It was, after all, a "woman's," not a "ladies'," publication and its interests were decidedly larger than "home." The *Journal* resembled a city newspaper of the period in many respects: eight pages, four columns, small print, and no white space or illustrations; there was simply nothing delicate or dainty about its contents. The *Chicago Post* agreed, calling the paper "a very handsome publication mechanically and intellectually."[10]

The *Journal*'s readership clearly appreciated its intellectual image. In objecting to the drivel found in the "Ladies Column" of most large circulars of the day, one woman struck a responsive chord among its educated readers:

Let the gentlemen try what the sensation would be supposing the *Woman's Journal* should magnanimously set apart a column to gentlemen, wherein there would be found loving information concerning the cocking of a soft hat, or a minute description as to how a real Napoleonic curve can be given to an ordinary mustache, or maybe it would tell the most approved method of saying goodnight to a pretty girl on the doorstep. . . . I think the bright, earnest little ladies who come out from Vassar and Wellesley eager to do their part in the struggle of life, read the Saturday newspapers for other purposes than to ascertain the latest fancy of Worth?[11]

Indeed, the *Journal*'s readers, accurately targeted in this editorial as bright, young, well-educated, and ambitious, resented the triviality of traditional feminine subjects. Occasionally, readers even registered their disapproval of the *Journal*'s contents on these grounds.

For example, when Lucy Stone allowed a discussion of new developments in women's undergarments to continue beyond one issue, a disgruntled reader wrote: "In behalf of many of the readers of the *Journal*, I sincerely hope that the silly discussion with regard to a name for a lady's undergarment will soon subside. . . . In our excellent paper the columns should be filled with more sensible matter."[12] As cultivated thinkers, *Woman's Journal* readers were likely to hold their paper to high standards of journalistic excellence precisely because they viewed the paper as a reflection of their newfound selves; the paper was not an entertaining time-filler for domestic wives, but a symbol of progressive womanhood.

The paper's "more sensible" regular columns, which were rarely related to suffrage news, changed little in twenty years, giving the paper a predictability and stability readers probably appreciated. "Gossips and Gleanings," "Humorous," "Notes and News," "Foreign Correspondence," "Concerning Women," and "Miscellaneous," a page of poetry and short stories, were standard entries. Though strictly irrelevant to the subject of suffrage, these columns celebrated and endorsed woman's autonomy, progress, intellect, and wit since their contents were by or about nontraditional women. They also provided a sometimes comic interlude amidst the sober suffrage reports. Perhaps most importantly, the regular columns appealed to a wider readership of both men and women because they were human interest stories. The two additions to the *Journal*'s regular columns—"Letters From the People" column in 1878 and a "Children's Column" in 1884—suggest the editors' concern in attracting a broad readership.

The bulk of the newspaper, however, treated suffrage campaigns, pending suffrage legislation, AWSA proceedings, activities of the "remonstrants," and suffrage developments on the European continent with a scrupulous eye. The *Journal* faithfully recorded full transcripts of woman suffrage conventions, suffrage debates on local, state, and national levels, and political platforms that favored suffrage. Although reading them was perhaps tedious, their accuracy and completeness satisfied the most fastidious suffragist and gave readers a sense of being at the center of political activity wherever they lived.

Yet for all its careful efforts to attract a solid constituency with its professionalism and pragmatism, the *Journal* had difficulty attracting advertisers. Lucy Stone characterized her sales effort as "a hard, constant tug." True to its own high standards, the *Journal* contributed to the problem by refusing to accept liquor, tobacco, or medicinal products. Greater obstacles to advertising sales were the paper's small circulation, its absence from newsstands, the poor quality of its newsprint, and its inability to attract local businesses because of its national circulation.[13] The paper began with only two advertising columns devoted to a potpourri of products, including women's colleges, professional schools, books, dry goods, clothing, and beauty products. As the paper gained popularity, advertising space grew. But even into its second decade, Stone still compared the paper's need for advertisers to "a big baby which never grew up and always had to be fed."[14]

From 1870 to 1920, despite advertising difficulties, a fire that destroyed the printing office, name changes, several changes of editors, countless suffrage defeats, and lean subscription years, the *Woman's Journal* never missed an issue. Throughout its lengthy tenure, many organizations publicly endorsed the paper, but until 1910, none established an official connection with it. From 1870 to 1900, the *Journal* was the unofficial organ of the AWSA and the NEWSA. From 1900 to 1917, the paper was adopted by the merged suffrage organizations, the NAWSA. After this date, the *Journal* moved to New York and was consolidated with two other suffrage papers to form the *Woman Citizen*, which ran until the victory of the Nineteenth Amendment in 1920. For the next thirteen years, the paper became an independent magazine devoted to the civic interests of women. In its forty-seven years as the *Woman's Journal* proper, the price of the paper steadily dropped from its initial three dollars an issue, to sell for only one dollar an issue by 1917, while subscriptions steadily rose from a few hundred to twenty-seven thousand in the same period of time. By 1915, the *Journal* went to forty-eight states and thirty-nine countries and each year circulated two hundred thousand pages of its official woman suffrage tracts and leaflets.[15] From respectable beginnings emerged a solid, ever-present suffrage organ that outdistanced even Lucy Stone's ambitions for a successful suffrage paper in becoming a never wavering "torchbearer" of suffrage news to loyal readers everywhere.

The Editorial Team

In its formative years, the *Woman's Journal* was fortunate to have attracted six well-known, articulate reformers, who, because of their professional backgrounds in education, the ministry, medicine, journalism, the military, and business, gave the paper considerable ethos. As a founder, Lucy Stone recognized that she needed a competent supporting staff to maintain high journalistic standards for a growing and highly educated readership of women.

Yet Stone brought her own set of credentials, as well as expertise on suffrage issues and a popular following. Stone earned distinction as a courageous public speaker for abolition in the late 1840s after becoming the first woman to graduate from the "regular" course at Oberlin. Noted for her well-pitched and melodious voice, her calm air of assurance and pleasant demeanor, she had almost a magical ability to turn hecklers into respectful admirers. Soon Stone began speaking about woman's rights exclusively. After conducting several expansive speaking tours, she won the title of "morning star of the woman's movement."[16] Of his editor in chief, Colonel Thomas Wentworth Higginson said: "Lucy is the Queen of us all . . . and delights the whole country from Maine to Kentucky."[17] With her marriage to Henry Blackwell in 1855, a ceremony performed by Higginson, Stone continued to make headlines. In protest of the legal inequities facing women, she became the first woman to retain her birth name and to return her tax bill unpaid on the grounds that women suffered taxation without representation. With the onset of the Civil War, Stone enlisted in her own form of active duty by assuming the presidency of the Woman's National Loyal League. Though Stone had no experience in journalism, her sound education, speaking tours, and leadership posts prepared her effectively for the responsibilities of editorship.

Stone immediately pursued another woman with journalistic expertise: Mary Ashton Livermore, editor of the Chicago Suffrage organ, the *Agitator*. In giving Livermore the post of editor in chief, Stone arranged for her to merge her paper with the new publication. Like Stone, Livermore came from New England, had an abolitionist background, and was a gifted public speaker. Unlike her collaborator, she had originally opposed woman suffrage. But after witnessing men's moral depravities during the war while serving as an army nurse and later as a leader in the Sanitary Commission, she changed her position. Within months after returning from service, she became one of the most important figures in the Illinois woman's rights movement. Though admittedly on the "radical" side (imposing moral reform, not securing the vote, was her most urgent aim), Livermore warmed to the idea of bringing new converts to the cause. She was only with the paper its first two years, leaving for a more lucrative opportunity on the lyceum circuit, but she brought successful editing skills and a built-in constituency to the new paper.[18]

The four assistant editors, William Lloyd Garrison, Henry Blackwell, T. W. Higginson, and Julia Ward Howe, brought additional insight, stature, and legitimacy to the *Journal*. Garrison's name evoked instant recognition and respect from a good portion of the wider citizenry for his three-decade crusade for antislavery, including founding the abolitionist weekly, the *Liberator*, and organizing the "Garrisonian" wing of the abolitionist movement. His sympathies with woman's rights went back equally as far. A resilient reformer accustomed to bearing the brunt of mob violence and verbal abuse, Garrison was living testimony to *Journal* readers that vision and perseverance could bring victory to unpopular causes. His official affiliation with the *Journal* was fleeting, for after half a year he pursued other interests, but he continued to write for the newspaper periodically. When Garrison resigned his post, Henry Blackwell, with some gentle prodding from his wife, stepped in. Originally, Blackwell expressed a desire to put his business expertise to work behind the scenes managing the paper's finances, but he dutifully assumed the place of associate editor, where, despite lengthy absences to pursue business ventures across the country, he served for twenty years as the Massachusetts legislative correspondent.

A close friend of Stone and Blackwell, T. W. Higginson, joined the team to assume a substantial share of the writing duties for the first four years. Like Garrison, he had distinguished himself as an abolitionist reformer from his pulpit in the Unitarian church and as a colonel in the Union Army. As a noted intellect with ties to the ministry and the military, Higginson brought a special dimension to the paper in his ability to legitimize woman suffrage on sacred and patriotic grounds. Political differences between him and Stone diminished his role to one of several editorial contributors in 1874, finally leading to his resignation in 1884 to write for *Harper's Bazaar*.

Julia Ward Howe, a writer, lecturer, editor, lay preacher, and activist for antislavery and woman's rights, but best remembered for writing "The Battle Hymn of the Republic" in 1861, stayed with Stone and the *Journal* until her death. As the conservative anchor of the paper, Howe projected her mothering form of feminism, ever proclaiming that women were the natural guardians of social morals.

Joining this distinguished class of writers in 1883 was the only Stone-Blackwell offspring, Alice Stone Blackwell. By this date and for the next seven years, the *Journal* became exclusively a family affair, although with Stone's diminished influence due to ill health, the list of occasional contributors mushroomed to twenty.[19]

Lucy Stone displayed foresight in surrounding herself with competent writers. Over the next two decades, multiple editorship of the *Journal* by leading woman's rights figures was essential to overcoming the many obstacles that threatened to close its presses.

Surviving the Growing Pains of a Movement

The *Woman's Journal* emerged from a divisive yet dormant period in the history of the woman's movement. Woman's rights supporters had suffered political blows from a party that had earlier applauded their efforts. They were confronted with two rival organizations that purported to espouse the movement's goals. They were surrounded by a cacophony of journalistic voices clamoring for their recognition. Most damaging of all, they were dealt countless suffrage defeats between the years 1870 and 1890.

The political fallout of a Union victory, abolitionist success, and Republican leadership that accompanied the ending of the Civil War did not, as woman's rights advocates assumed, make the movement's demands more realizable. Despite heroic efforts by women to aid the war effort, to petition on behalf of the slaves, and to support Republican Reconstruction, politicians were not willing to grant woman suffrage along with black suffrage, arguing instead that the country could not accept two major reforms at once.[20] The two substantial political defeats of 1866 and 1868, and the adoption of the Fourteenth and Fifteenth Amendments, which introduced the word "male" into the Constitution in connection with the vote and conspicuously omitted "sex" from the list of suffrage conditions, forced the movement to reexamine what it was and where it was going. Indeed, the movement struggled to stay alive between 1865 and 1870 amidst disparate ideologies and personality clashes in the ranks.

In arriving at ideological roadblocks, the woman's rights movement was stymied by conditions that all movements inevitably experience. According to Charles Conrad, at some point in a movement's history, idealistic beginnings yield to pragmatic continuances; radical agendas turn conservative as broad platforms narrow and ideological purity prevails. Charles J. Stewart, Craig Allen Smith, and Robert E. Denton, Jr., discuss the pragmatic turn of social movements in terms of crucial functions, explaining that as movements work their way from the task of enthusiastic mobilization to maintenance, they must become more practical and less visionary if they wish to escape oblivion.[21] These scholars echo the advice given by Wendell Phillips to woman's rights leaders before the onset of the Civil War: "Only distinctive movements survive."[22]

As the woman's rights movement lurched into a new decade, many members wanted to become more pragmatic, to narrow its goal to suffrage, and to drop the "competing" and "controversial" issues that composed the larger woman's rights platform, such issues as divorce, the oppressive force of organized religion, the double standard, dress reform, wife abuse, and temperance. But that sentiment was not unanimous. Thus, out of the revisionism emerged two separate factions: the NWSA, committed to fighting for suffrage by way of a federal amendment while simultaneously championing broader woman's rights issues, and the AWSA, exclusively committed to campaigning for suffrage on the state and municipal levels. Personality clashes between the representatives of each organization, particularly Lucy Stone versus Susan B. Anthony, and the uproar over three other notables in the movement, George Francis Train, Victoria Woodhull, and Henry Ward Beecher, accentuated the ideological differences between the two associations.[23]

Rather than magnify these hostilities, the *Journal* strategically elected to treat happenings from the opposing association with respect and objectivity. Two events that threatened to undercut the efforts of the AWSA, the Susan B. Anthony trial and the Beecher-Tilton scandal, illustrate the *Journal*'s unwavering geniality.

When the hoopla surrounding Susan B. Anthony's trial for registering to vote in the 1872 presidential election reached national proportions, and the subsequent efforts to submit a sixteenth amendment to the Constitution became highly visible, the *Journal* dutifully reported the events. Rather than using the opportunity to reiterate the NWSA's "flawed" method of securing enfranchisement and implicitly affirming the AWSA methods by contrast, the *Journal* adopted the policy of giving the trial polite but limited coverage. With strained diplomacy, Lucy Stone described the NWSA's agenda briefly: "Some of the friends of Woman Suffrage have claimed that the passage of the Fourteenth and Fifteenth Amendments secured the ballot to women." Without editorial comment, Stone then summarized the Anthony trial with a terse observation: "On Saturday, the 21st, District-Attorney Crowley entered a *nolle prosesqui* in each of the cases of the fourteen women indicted with Miss Anthony for illegal voting, and the court adjourned sine die."[24] Deliberately resisting an endorsement of Anthony's actions, Stone abandoned her usual role of mobilizing her readers to rally behind a sister's political efforts.

The treatment of the second episode is equally restrained. The Beecher-Tilton scandal that erupted in 1872 had a much more insidious effect on the AWSA and the *Journal*. *Woodhull & Claflin's Weekly*, a racy, often even lurid, chronicle of gossip, quickly became prominent with its sensational story on the presumed love affair between America's most popular minister, Henry Ward Beecher, and the wife of his friend Theodore Tilton. Antisuffragists found the Beecher-Tilton affair a delicious opportunity to associate the suffrage movement with "free love," since Beecher was a past president of the AWSA and Tilton a representative of the NWSA. When the much-derided *Weekly* began to bring discredit on other suffrage newspapers (some press reports even lumped the *Weekly,* the *Journal,* and the *Revolution* in the same category[25]), editors of the *Journal* had grounds for issuing angry rebuttals, especially since Stone believed Stanton had initially leaked the rumor to Victoria Woodhull. But the *Journal* editors elected to adopt the posture of dignified silence on the scandal, claiming that its "will is to keep clear of personalities and discuss principles," not to "endorse or denounce Mrs. Woodhull." Not until 1874, well after the uproar had subsided, did Lucy Stone pen an editorial defending the "victimized" Mrs. Tilton.[26]

Assuming a calm, elevated posture even in the face of damaging events soon gave the paper a reputation for moderation. The paper's symbol of suffrage victories, a dove with an olive branch, accentuated its righteous, dignified, even feminine, reformist posture. Yet the *Journal's* very attitude of diffusing controversy and reducing the hysteria surrounding the suffrage issue prompted more radical supporters to label it as "dull, timid, and uninspiring."[27]

Although the *Journal* maintained diplomatic, albeit strained, relations with its rival association, it did not extend the same courtesies to its rival's mouthpiece, the *Revolution.* The *Journal's* editors knew that the movement was struggling to maintain two competing newspapers. And even though the *Revolution* tottered on financial collapse when the *Journal* made its debut, its editors feared the competition. Consequently, espousing the *Journal's* superiority over the *Revolution* became its first priority. Recognizing the obstacles it faced in being squeezed between competing forces, editors described the *Journal's* place as "a double protest" of "bigoted Conservatism [status quo] on the one hand" and of "destructive Radicalism [the *Revolution*] on the other."[28] The *Woman's Journal* editors were outspoken in linking the "destructive radicalism" of the *Revolution* to the movement's integrity and, ultimately, to its own journalistic endeavor. Henry Blackwell enunciated their objections in the *Journal's* first issue, arguing that "no one can estimate the damage the cause of Woman's enfranchisement has already sustained by the failure of its advocates to limit themselves to the Main Question," and adding that "as advocates of Equal Rights, we protest against loading the good ship 'Woman Suffrage' with a cargo of irrelevant questions."[29]

The *Woman's Journal* found itself not only in the difficult position of espousing the views of a movement within a movement, and of establishing its preeminence over the *Revolution,* but of distinguishing itself as the newspaper of choice from an ever-growing field of newspapers, both prosuffrage and antisuffrage, targeted at women. E. Claire Jerry has observed that 1870 to 1890 were the most prolific years for the suffrage press in the movement's entire history. Thirty-three suffrage papers vied for the attention of potential and fervent woman suffrage supporters.[30] That statistic does not include voices from the periphery, such as the sensational and radical *Woodhull & Claflin's Weekly*, or the mainstream, mildly prosuffragist *Godey's Magazine and Lady's Book*. The saturated suffragist market, together with several antisuffrage magazines such as *True Woman*, made the chances for sustaining a sizable constituency slim.[31]

Finally, like all its rivals, between the years 1870 and 1890, the *Journal* tried to survive a crowded journalistic marketplace as the movement suffered repeated suffrage defeats. The undistinguished zero-to-eight record in suffrage referenda has prompted critics to call it "a black hole," "a period of relative dormancy," "twenty years of constant effort and constant defeat," and "a period of perpetual rebuff."[32] Not until 1890, when Wyoming entered the Union with woman suffrage, did suffrage newspapers begin to outlive the days of ridicule and denunciation and reach the level of respectful attention by the greater populace.[33]

Out of this tumultuous two decades, marked by political denunciation from without and ideological polarization, fragmented constituencies, and personality clashes from within, the *Woman's Journal*, remarkably enough, found a receptive constituency to sustain itself issue after issue for forty-seven uninterrupted years.

Empowering a Powerless Constituency

As a suffrage organ, the *Woman's Journal* fulfilled a far larger purpose than attracting loyal subscribers; it became a vehicle through which the conservative wing of the woman suffrage movement performed necessary functions of an uninstitutionalized collectivity. To understand more fully the significance of the *Journal*, consider how the paper functioned rhetorically for the movement. Movement theorists offer a useful conceptual frame through which to examine the rhetorical tasks facing movements. Stewart, Smith, and Denton, for example, building upon the pioneering work of Eric Hoffer, claim that movements must face five tasks: altering perceptions of society (e.g., transforming perceptions of members' negative self-images and creating we-they distinctions that legitimize the group and delegitimize the opposition); transforming perceptions of history (e.g., deprecating the unsatisfying present by focusing on a promising future or a glorious past); prescribing courses of action (e.g., defending the superiority of reformist tactics); mobilizing for action (e.g., promoting self-sacrifice by molding members into a unified, indestructible core of actors); and sustaining the movement (e.g., justifying setbacks to the committed and remaining visible to the established order).[34]

They also insist that a critic must take into account the rhetorical obstacles that plague individual movements: "Social movements differ from institutionalized collectivities not so much in terms of the functions their persuasive efforts must perform, as in terms of the constraints placed upon the fulfillment of these functions."[35] Thus, before discussing how the *Woman's Journal* altered perceptions of society (in this case, empowering a constituency), one must understand the unusual and difficult problems that beset movement members and hampered its leaders from fulfilling this task.

In her seminal essay on the oxymoronic nature of feminist rhetoric, Karlyn Kohrs Campbell argues that woman's rights rhetors were confronted with four audience constraints.[36] First, a movement composed of individuals with no common characteristic other than gender necessarily made cultivating a unified front a daunting task. Aside from their common femaleness, women were divided from one another by age, education, income, ethnicity, geography, etc. Finding common ground that transcended differences proved difficult. Abigail Scott Duniway captured the seeming hopelessness in mobilizing a nation of women when she wrote that it was easier to harangue state legislators and convince male voters than to organize women.[37] Lamenting the provincialism of women, Julia Ward Howe wrote: "I believe I shall live to see women in New York and some of the other states enfranchised, but not in Massachusetts. I'm sorry, but I believe it will take longer here, because Massachusetts women, as a rule, adhere too strongly to old-time conventions."[38]

Second, if demographic differences were not sufficient to separate women from one another, their lack of publicly shared experience was. Woman's world lay outside the public sphere. Their concerns were individual, not social; private, not public; idiosyncratic, not common. Establishing points of identification required creating a new and radical rhetorical style that could transform individual experiences into socially shared concerns.

Third, women had negative self-concepts. Conrad eloquently describes the oppressive environment in which nineteenth-century women languished: "Robbed of their essential humanness, stripped of their individual identities, and denied the capacity to cope with human existence," he writes, "nineteenth-century feminists experienced a particular kind of fundamental conflict. They were conscious both of the fact that they were fully capable human beings and that their society defined them as incomplete, not-fully human creatures." In short, the existential component of self was incongruent with the socially prescribed component of self.[39] *Woman's Journal* readers recognized this tension as well. Eight years after the AWSA's formation, one *Journal* reader still recognized the need to identify woman's inability to subordinate her socially prescribed self in favor of her new-found enlightened self. "It is surprising to me," she began, "to notice how many women discover a certain sympathy for the cause, who are not identified with it. There is no other subject upon which they have so little of the courage of their own convictions."[40]

Finally, as a consequence of the three obstacles outlined above, women did not view themselves as an audience—persons capable of effecting change. Suffrage rhetors were faced with the prospect of first having to create an audience before they could appeal to one. The *Journal* was forced to devote column space to empowering its readers with such articles as "Woman's Lack of Self-Appreciation" and "Educating Self-Respect"[41] before prescribing courses of action. Creating an audience was, in a real sense, the primary rhetorical task and function of the *Journal*.

To create an audience, the *Journal* relied on what modern scholars have termed consciousness-raising. Consciousness-raising rhetoric is intimate in tone, is inductive in structure, is experiential in evidenciary material, and creates a peer relationship between speaker and reader. Thus, it is a rhetorical adaptation to women's inexperience as public communicators.[42]

This intimate, participatory style of discourse enhanced the efforts of the *Journal's* editors in empowering a powerless constituency in several specific ways. First, editors developed an informed and active readership on politics—a subject traditionally relegated to males only. Second, each editor established his or her own separate constituency in order to fulfill specific needs of individual readers. Third, editors strategically used the paper's regular columns to promote shared experience among women. Fourth, editors continually presented female role models to make progressive womanhood a tangible reality. Finally, editors altered descriptions of the "Antis" in order to make the opposition appear less formidable.

Presidential politics was a subject that generated much controversy and stimulating discussion among *Journal* editors. Readers "overheard" the various points of view expressed by Stone, Higginson, Blackwell, and Howe and eventually contributed their own opinions to the political cauldron.

In its first presidential election of 1872, the *Journal* was uncertain about its role in national politics. On a basic level, debate among its editors revolved around the question of insulation from or integration into the two-party system.[43] While Henry Blackwell outlined the benefits of working inside the established political framework, Mrs. Campbell, then president of the AWSA, wrote in to reiterate the AWSA's "avowed purpose of avoiding political entanglements."[44] Lucy Stone disagreed, arguing that the *Journal* must be involved in national politics. She was pleased that Henry was allowed to write the mildly prosuffrage plank in the Republican platform, which promised "to be mindful of its obligations to the loyal women of America." Shortly thereafter, Stone declared: "Let every woman see to it that the men over whom she can exert an influence vote the Republican ticket." T. W. Higginson, however, remained unconvinced, calling Stone's endorsement "a great blunder," since Ulysses S. Grant did not explicitly endorse woman suffrage.[45] When Mary Livermore, a personal friend of Grant's, and Julia Ward Howe joined Stone in favor of a Republican victory, the move signaled the beginning of a close link between the *Journal* and Republicanism.

Eight years later, the synergy between *Journal* editors and its readers took a radically different form. This time readers took the lead in political endorsements, while editors remained uncommitted. The official line from the *Journal* regarding the presidential contenders was that "woman has nothing to hope from either of the two parties," although the long-standing commitment to the Republican party brought a grudging support of the Republican James Garfield. Readers, however, resisted the editors' perfunctory endorsement of the establishment when the Prohibitionist party, under the leadership of Neal Dow, offered a viable alternative. When Higginson and Stone protested that many suffragists did not believe in Prohibition, readers retorted that their coverage of anti-Prohibitionist suffragists was biased, adding that "it is undoubtedly true that the great mass of Suffragists, and the great mass of women, are in sympathy with this movement."[46] One reader expressed her frustration at the *Journal*'s inability to mobilize its readership behind an acceptable candidate by asking simply: "What shall we do with our consciences if we fail to use our influence for Neal Dow and the Prohibition party?"[47] Yet the *Journal*'s editors believed that their hands were tied in the 1880 presidential election. Although the Republican candidate was a disappointment on the issue of woman suffrage, deserting the party now would make them look fickle and supporting the anti-establishment party would mean losing the support of key suffrage workers.

The *Journal*'s treatment of the presidential elections in 1884 revealed the danger in publicizing opposed viewpoints among an editorial staff. The campaign between Grover Cleveland and James Blaine was a rather dull affair as far as the *Journal*'s editors were concerned until damaging news broke that Cleveland had fathered an illegitimate child. The reaction was swift and denunciatory from Stone and past editor Mary Livermore. Stone was adamant: "Women must be opposed at all cost, to that which is the destruction of the home." Livermore concurred, asserting that "Cleveland is wholly unfit to be the standard-bearer of the American people." Both agreed that the best way for voters to register their outrage over this "moral poverty" was to "stand by the Republican Party." Higginson, on the other hand, strongly objected. The charges of infidelity were "exaggerated," "mere gossip," and "took place fifteen years ago." Most certainly the charge did not "impinge on his *public* character," he emphasized, adding that because each of the candidates favored woman suffrage there was "no reason for making the election an issue in these columns."[48] The controversy between Stone and Higginson over Cleveland's alleged infidelity filled the pages of the *Journal* until election time, entertaining readers with spirited dialogue and activating them to choose sides after serious reflection. After the election, Higginson resigned. The editor who had once attributed the *Journal*'s success to the fact that "the various writers for its pages exercise much freedom of opinion"[49] soured on that tradition. The lively debate on presidential prospects that drew readers into an intellectual environment and made politics an engaging subject was dampened considerably after his departure.

The diversity of opinions that the *Journal* offered on politics was characteristic of the paper's policy to offer distinctive personalities behind its editors' signatures. An attractive dimension of the paper, as Higginson himself recognized, was the ability of each of its four primary editors to carve his or her own distinctive niche as a suffrage voice and develop their own special rapport with admiring *Journal* readers.[50]

Higginson actively encouraged lively interchange between himself and his readers—a practice that no other editor could quite emulate. The emboldened refutations to Higginson's viewpoints served as dramatic proof to other readers that woman could be man's equal argumentatively.

But Higginson's column engendered pleas for practical advice as well as lines of argument. Occasionally, he printed some of these, as he did in the 12 July 1873 issue on a request for lessons in public speaking. "How shall I make myself heard? How shall I learn to express myself? How shall I keep my head clear? Is there any school for debate?" read the pleas for advice from one inquiring reader.[51] No doubt, Higginson elected to print these questions because they so clearly echoed the concerns of other women readers. Such letters as this were a positive sign that members of the movement were growing in confidence and seeking public visibility by requesting forceful, "masculine" social skills from a columnist with whom they had grown comfortable.

Indeed, Higginson often assumed the persona of paternalistic preacher, preparing female readers to be informed public advocates. His subjects included tips on everything from how to speak confidently in public to how to cultivate self-respect, to how to construct a tight rebuttal against the "Antis." Each topic was treated in a pastoral vein of sensitivity and deep conviction. Although he sometimes referred to himself in a self-deprecatory vein as "a pious and painful preacher" who "hammer[s] away at his text,"[52] he elicited more letters from admiring and indignant readers than the other three editors. In his final editorial, T. J. Higginson summed up his contributions to the *Journal* by noting that repeated suffrage defeats gave him an opportunity "to prepare women for suffrage; and it has been in this light that the reader must regard a large part of what I have written during fifteen years."[53]

Higginson's progressive ministerial voice attracted some subscribers; his male counterpart cornered others. Henry Blackwell functioned as the *Journal*'s ambassador to the Massachussets legislature and as a legislative newshound for *Journal* readers. Though his columns were less frequent and not showcased as prominently as others, Blackwell established himself as a link between the paper and the legislative assemblies. His duties to his readers consisted of condensing legislative debates on woman's rights to manageable and interesting proportions, exposing inconsistent voting records of representatives, and composing character sketches of presidential contenders to help readers make informed choices.

Perhaps most importantly, Blackwell worked to bring a sense of vitality and immediacy to his reports, giving his readers front-row seats to the hub of political action. He depicted the scenes of one legislative hearing on statewide suffrage as "exceedingly brilliant and impressive," explaining that "the interest of each session became deeper and more intense" in an assembly "admirably filled" by speakers who "forgot themselves in their subject and by so doing appeared to the best advantage."[54] Blackwell's enlivened and optimistic descriptions of the mundane and seemingly endless congressional hearings on woman suffrage attracted the attention of readers who might otherwise have been discouraged by the dreariness of an unedited transcription.

The columns by Lucy Stone and Julia Ward Howe provided a study in contrast. Stone played the role of taskmaster; Howe assumed the role of cheerleader. Stone used her column to address suffrage activism with tireless urgency, remarkable efficiency, and consistent objectivity. Pleas to initiate or sign a suffrage petition were commonplace. Stone's reporting of her own fact-finding missions, such as exposing sexual inequities in property rights, salary, criminal punishment, and educational opportunities, were conducted with detective-like professionalism. She defied the submissive or shrill feminine way of expressing dissatisfaction; instead, she described grievances in a detached, objective fashion. Stone even characterized herself as the editor "not given to hardness of feeling or to hardness of expression."[55] She, more than any of her associate editors, was primarily responsible for fulfilling the *Journal*'s utilitarian purpose of molding readers into efficient, consecrated workers. Refusing to treat women as delicate creatures, she sometimes shook readers' sensibilities with confrontational words. In 1876, when most of the nation was preparing for the centennial celebration, Stone scolded women for volunteering their time to make the occasion so glorious, calling them "objects of contempt" who unwittingly "glorify the power that smites them."[56] For enthusiastic activists, Stone gave direction as to how they should harness their energies for the cause.

While Stone mobilized the forces, Julia Ward Howe bolstered the faith of the uncommitted. As the "Herald of Glad Tidings," Howe used her column boldly to proclaim the glorious days of a not-too-distant suffrage victory. Strategically, for conservative women, Howe capitalized upon the public's perception of her as a lay preacher and patriotic mother. She waxed eloquent on the righteousness of the woman suffrage cause yet simultaneously advanced the feminine ideal of ministering angel. In fact, Howe used her column to propose what has become a national holiday honoring mothers. Drawing liberally from scripture, Howe appealed to God-fearing readers who desperately needed guidance on how to counter the cry of "heresy" and "atheism" from the Antis. Her column soothed the conscience of traditional Christian readers and buoyed the hope of skeptical and disappointed readers. In short, Howe assumed the *Journal*'s purpose of filling readers with zeal for the cause. The diverse styles of the four distinguished editors proved to be a winning formula for a reform newspaper striving to enlighten and empower its readership.

In addition to offering editorial companions, the *Journal* presented readers with regular columns such as "Foreign Correspondence," which helped to create shared experiences among them. Because each issue featured a diarylike entry from female world travelers or woman's rights activists who followed politics around the globe, readers learned of new worlds and shared at least indirectly in the experience of travel. One typical entry from a woman in England created a virtual experience for readers of Victor Hugo's home and the lecture she heard. In a chatty style, she took readers through each room of his house: "Well, I was ushered into a dark hall, wainscoted and from thence into the dining-room, which was also wainscoted with dark oak handsomely carved. The fireplace was covered in and above to the top of the room with blue patterned tiling. The first thing that attracted my eye was a curious-looking, dark, straight-backed chair at one end of the room, with a chain across the front from each arm in the way a stick is put across a perambulator to prevent a baby from falling forward."[57] Demonstrating a keen understanding of how best to communicate with female readers, this English correspondent used several concrete domestic details to bring Hugo's home to life. Henry Blackwell's minute descriptions of legislative hearings served a similar purpose to that of Foreign Correspondence: creating a sense of immediacy while at the same time expanding intellectual horizons.

The prominent placement of new converts' testimonies in the *Journal* also served to create intimacies and invite participation among its female readership in order to enhance members' self-concept. When the movement could boast a convert from the Antis, the potency of such a confession was far greater. One reader explained her transformation from nonmember to member in these terms: "Educated by the most conservative of parents, I was taught that everything pertaining to man's sphere was especially unfeminine. . . . Woman Suffrage loomed up before me as a nightmare, a figment of some crazed brain. I talked against it. I wrote against it . . . yet secretly I investigated it. . . . I am converted. I never believed in Woman Suffrage before; but I do now."[58] Like a religious conversion, this woman's testimony struck a resounding chord among conservative women and set a striking example for noncommitted women to follow.

The *Journal* also helped create an audience of confident activists by filling its pages with female role models. The regular column "What Women Are Doing" was a compendium of the advancements of individual women across the country. With fifteen to twenty brief entries of women's new positions weekly, the column made readers understand that ordinary women could survive in the male world. Readers learned, for instance, that "Miss Allie H. Jameson has been commissioned as a notary-public at Marshalltown, Iowa," and that "Miss Elizabeth Peebles has been elected clerk of the House in Washington Territory," and that "young lady physicians are putting out their signs in every prominent city in the country."[59] Weekly exposure to real, yet ordinary, women embarking on public careers gave readers ample role models to enlarge their own expectations.

Finally, the *Journal* redefined the image of nonmembers—female Antis—in such a way as to lessen their impact as a threatening force. This strategy was crucial for sustaining readers' confidence in their own abilities to carry out movement goals. As Conrad's study of the *Woman's Journal* reveals, one of its most frequent subjects was to respond to the arguments of antimovement rhetors in such a way as to attract apathetic women.[60] In responding to hostile women, the *Journal* undercut their protestations by attributing their opposition to the intellectual tyranny under which they resided. Quite early, *Journal* editors recognized that a candid and thought-provoking explanation of woman's inferiority was necessary to explain the baffling presence of women against woman suffrage. Quoting from the revered Lucretia Mott, the *Journal* discovered a kind way to dismiss female antisuffragists: "the woman who is satisfied with her inferior condition, averring that she has all the rights that she wants, does but exhibit the enervating effects of the wrongs to which she is subjected."[61] Contrary to popular belief, women unsympathetic to woman suffrage were not happy and comfortable in their traditional sphere; they had been raised, as T. W. Higginson asserted, "in the shadow of intellectual contempt."[62] Consequently, they deserved pity and understanding, not disregard and abuse.

Nonmembers were transformed in the *Journal* from self-assured, satisfied spouses who posed a dangerous counterforce to the cause into frightened and naive souls who clung desperately to antiquated ideas. Higginson further diffused the impact and the seeming novelty of female antisuffragists by comparing them to slaves during the Civil War. "When the Southern slaves were first enlisted as soldiers during our civil war," Higginson recalled, "it was supposed that they would be unwilling to obey those of their own color. It turned out that there was some such reluctance. But it also proved that the gradual process of outgrowing such reluctance was a liberal education in self-respect."[63] Himself a leader of a regiment of African-American soldiers in the Civil War, Higginson's analogy had special force. In refusing to take the arguments of the Antis seriously and characterizing female Antis as deluded beings, the *Journal* reduced the risk of losing members to threatening opposition from their own sex.

Prescribing, Mobilizing, and Maintaining the Movement

In addition to transforming inexperienced public communicators into a membership of capable, assertive actors, the *Journal* helped transform present comforts into grievances and prognostications of suffrage failures into prescriptions for success.

Convincing movement members that an intolerable situation exists is a prerequisite for protest. A satisfied state is tacit support for the established order; a dissatisfied state is a mandate for an uninstitutionalized collectivity. Successful movement rhetors must keep the list of grievances before its members, lest they become lulled by a false sense of security in the here and now. Stone, understanding this intuitively, used the *Journal* throughout her lengthy tenure to articulate gross injustices against women. In its first year, the *Journal* repeatedly legitimized itself as a suffrage organ fighting for the "freedom of woman." Reverberating through its pages was its noble struggle against "social tyranny," restrictions that had "hammered, hindered, limited, and denied" woman her rights and treated her as "a doll or toy, or a pampering plaything . . . compelled to the drudgery of menial service."[64] Sensitive to the prospect that isolated movement victories might signal premature withdrawal by committed activists, Stone preached a guarded optimism: "Many persons suppose that the modifications made in the laws during the last twelve or fifteen years, have done all that is necessary to remove the legal incapacity of married women and to protect their property rights. But an examination of the laws of any State will show that much still remains to be done," she reminded readers.[65]

The difficulty that Stone sometimes encountered in keeping woman's deprived status a pressing issue among readers was especially evident in the national preparation for the centennial celebration. Fearing that woman's rights had become submerged in the clamor of patriotic festivities, Stone unleashed an uncharacteristically passionate plea for sobriety: "Women of the United States, never forget that you are excluded by law from participation in the great question which at this moment agitates the whole country. . . . Oh, woman, the one subjugated class in this great country, the only adult people who are ruled over. Pray for a baptism of fire to reveal to you the depth of the humiliation, the degredation and the unspeakable loss which comes of your unequal position."[66] Stone recognized that exposing the wrongs against women had to be made repeatedly but delicately to motivate active member participation without dampening enthusiasm for suffrage successes. Higginson addressed this dilemma lightheartedly by musing aloud that perhaps espousing grievances was the elixir of life. "What will become of us," he pondered, "if we should wake up, some fine morning, and discover ourselves to be without a grievance?"[67]

While Higginson half-seriously prescribed identifying perpetual states of dissatisfaction, any genuine deprecation of the present, as

Hoffer reminds us, cannot be accomplished without the assured hope of a better future.[68] A rhetorical bathing in gloom and despair will only motivate movement members if they are provided with a glimmer of hope for the cause. As the pillar of faith and bearer of "Good News," Julia Ward Howe cast an aura of invincibility over woman suffrage. Dressing up the movement in the guise of civil religion (reminiscent of her poetic flair in "The Battle Hymn of the Republic"), Howe spoke of a "Grand Army of the Republic of Women," "a new maneuver," "a fresh phalanx in the good fight of faith," and a contest in which "the armor of Paul will become us, the shield and breastplate of strong and shining virtue." In Howe's glorious vision, suffrage was "a prophesy" for which "Divine Providence dispatches us."[69] By transforming despair into hope, Howe rekindled enthusiasm in a movement that witnessed meager victories and primed members for seemingly endless mobilization efforts.

Prescribing, mobilizing, and maintaining courses of action proved to be three interrelated movement functions that the *Journal* helped fulfill specifically for the conservative wing of the movement. As discussed earlier, the *Journal* prescribed narrow, conservative courses of action to reflect the AWSA's agenda. In showcasing AWSA convention news, highlighting the benefits of municipal suffrage, veering away from controversial "extraneous" woman's rights issues, and downplaying action by the NWSA, the *Journal* endorsed the AWSA's methods.

In mobilizing members to carry out the AWSA's preferred methods, *Journal* editors, especially Stone, created a host of opportunities and invited activism with the utmost of urgency. Pleas to become a loyal *Woman's Journal* subscriber, form a local suffrage club, sign suffrage petitions, circulate suffrage tracts, appear at legislative hearings, bake and sew for suffrage bazaars, influence spouses in voting decisions, boycott occasions that aggrandize woman's suppression, and attend AWSA conventions bombarded members incessantly. Stone's mobilization efforts hammered home the news that there was no time to lose. In one typical plea for a gallery of suffragists at city hall, Stone exclaimed: "Whatever else you neglect, do not fail to be present [at the next meeting of the Massachusetts legislature to decide on suffrage measures]. Baking, cooking, making, and mending—let all else go, and be early at the Hall of the Representatives next Wednesday."[70] Delay and procrastination would only prolong the fight, Stone reasoned. Rallying the troops with all the conviction she could muster sustained the visibility of suffrage.

Perhaps the most difficult task of the *Journal* was justifying the movement's dismal record in referenda on state suffrage. The posture adopted by all its editors in the face of defeat was to transcend the circumstances of any one lost battle to focus on the eventual victory. After one suffrage defeat, Julia Ward Howe waxed philosophically: "We see our objects at first like distant mountain tops, which seem near because we see them so definitely and do not see the weary and difficult route which lies between us and them."[71]

To prevent members from dwelling on setbacks, the *Journal* further adopted a policy of giving scant coverage to suffrage defeats and embedding the reports in inconspicuous spaces. When prior issues of the paper had paraded the banner "Vermont and Victory," only to see suffrage go down to defeat in that state, the *Journal* countered with a blurb buried at the bottom of its following issue, which read matter-of-factly: "The Legislature of Vermont lately voted down a measure to give women the right to vote on schools and educational questions by a vote of 123 to 92."[72]

Consistent with its policy of minimizing the significance of repeated drubbings at the polls, *Journal* editors resisted printing their predictions of suffrage failures even when defeat seemed preordained. As the *Journal* correspondent of suffrage activities in Nebraska, Henry Blackwell confided to his wife: "Between ourselves—there is no more hope of carrying woman suffrage in Nebraska than of the millenium coming next year. . . . The prospect is not nearly as good as it was in Kansas in 1869." Yet ever mindful of the importance of maintaining a bouyant optimism for members, Blackwell cautiously added: "Don't publish my predictions as to Nebraska."[73] Adopting strategic silences on bleak suffrage campaigns, devoting sparse coverage to suffrage defeats, and channeling energies to future suffrage successes proved to be a well-orchestrated plan to remain viable as a suffrage organ during a dormant period in the movement's history.

As a suffrage organ, the *Woman's Journal* fulfilled a far larger purpose than attracting loyal subscribers. Most importantly, it created an audience. Despite its readers' immense demographic differences, lack of publicly shared experience, and poor self-images, the *Journal* empowered and unified women by using an intimate, participatory rhetorical style in addressing feminist issues. Second, the *Journal* became a vehicle through which the conservative wing of the woman suffrage movement performed the necessary functions of an uninstitutionalized collectivity: setting movement goals, organizing and dispatching members into efficient lobbying groups, and sustaining hope in the face of repeated suffrage defeats. As a critical frame applied to this suffrage organ, the Stewart, Smith, and Denton functional schema is illuminating. It has allowed for insight beyond the mere cataloging of functions.

Conclusion

The dynamics between the *Woman's Journal* and the special needs of the AWSA, its editors, its readership, its separate constituencies, its competitors, and a resisting public were lively, complex, and fascinating. Far more than a successful business venture, the *Woman's Journal* lived up to its name as "Torchbearer of the Woman Suffrage Cause." As a clearinghouse for suffrage activities everywhere, it broadened intellectual horizons. As a comfort to the insecure and uninitiated, it groomed confident, public communicators. As a guide for the zealous, it molded committed and efficient workers. As a testament to high journalistic standards, it demonstrated sophisticated writing and management skills by women.

Through twenty years of perpetual rebuff, the *Woman's Journal* stood as a beacon of feminist respectability, charting a course of protest between an oppressive status quo and an abrasive radicalism. One aspiring poet, whose genuflections to the "Torchbearer" were featured by the paper, captured the steady assurance and the inspirational tenor of its suffrage message:

> We shall onward go, as the breakers flow,
> In our upward march sublime.
> To the topmost reach of the snowy beach
> We are gaining every day.
> It is surely ours in the coming hours.
> And shall be ours always.[74]

Clara Bewick Colby and the *Woman's Tribune*, 1883–1909

The Free Lance Editor as Movement Leader

E. Claire Jerry

"Equality for All"

Clara Bewick Colby's newspaper, the *Woman's Tribune*, was one of the leading papers of the early woman's rights movement. While journalism historians and experts in suffrage history have recognized its importance, it was also widely praised in its own day. Friends of Bewick Colby lauded it: Olympia Brown called it a "fine and interesting paper" that "filled an important place in the history of the cause."[1] Suffrage leaders welcomed it: May Wright Sewall deemed it "the most ably edited paper devoted to our cause."[2] General circulation newspapers acknowledged its value: the *Tecumseh* (Nebraska) *Republican* pronounced the *Tribune* "one among the ablest and neatest papers published in the state."[3] As this testimony indicates, Clara Bewick Colby and the *Woman's Tribune* played significant roles in the nineteenth-century movement for woman's rights.

Although Bewick Colby was never elected to a national office in the suffrage movement, her friends and enemies alike saw her as "a free lance," an influential figure without organizational ties.[4] In contrast to other affiliated or sponsored papers, the *Tribune* served as her personal outlet and mechanism to influence the movement and to achieve leadership status. The *Woman's Tribune* fulfilled these functions in three interrelated contexts: within the movement, between the paper and the readers, and in Bewick Colby's own life. Because of its distinctive place among suffrage periodicals, a case study of the *Tribune* can enhance an understanding of the roles of editors and their newspapers in social movements.[5]

A much overlooked leadership need in long, ongoing movements is that of a documented history written from the perspective of those within the movement itself.[6] Such a history serves to legitimate the movement as well as to provide a consistent understanding of who and what was important. Bewick Colby used the *Woman's Tribune* to provide this sense of historical community and operated it in an attempt to establish herself as the primary gatekeeper of movement information. This essay will examine the strategies she employed to fill this rhetorical role. Following a brief history of the paper, the essay examines the *Tribune* as a leadership tool in the three contexts of its readers, the movement, and Bewick Colby herself.

History of the *Woman's Tribune*

In May 1883, the members of the Nebraska Woman Suffrage Association voted to begin a newspaper. After Clara Bewick Colby was named editor of the newly formed *Woman's Tribune*, the first issue appeared in August 1883. Bewick Colby was chosen because of her "true editorial instinct" and her "executive ability alike in her domestic and public work."[7] In a letter to fellow suffrage publisher Elizabeth Boynton Harbert, she described her combination of duties: "Where one attends personally to *all* the business including proofreading, make up—[advertising] &c of a paper—goes off to conventions and lectures—and besides tries to keep the domestic wheels running smoothly it is really too much for any mortal."[8] This frenetic activity was, however, to be the norm for Bewick Colby's life for the next quarter century.

After the first year of the *Tribune*, the Nebraska State Woman Suffrage Association, because of declining membership and financial support, withdrew its official backing from the paper, and Bewick Colby became publisher as well as editor.[9] She saw this responsibility as significant for her personal worth, and she took it quite seriously, as she later confided to Boynton Harbert: "I never did anything before that the public would think of twice and I have felt that I must make a success of this [newspaper] or I should never be able to [do] any good in the world."[10]

From 1883 to December 1889, Bewick Colby published the *Tribune* from various newspaper offices in Beatrice. The only exception to Beatrice publication during this period was a brief stint in Washington, D.C. From 27 March to 5 April 1888, Bewick Colby published the *Tribune* as the daily organ of the International Council of Women. Her success with this venture (circulation went as high as 12,500 copies during the council) and her husband's appointment to President Harrison's administration enabled her to move the paper to Washington in 1889. From December 1889 to December 1892, she published in Washington while Congress was in session (November to April), relocating to Beatrice for the remainder of the year (May to October). She explained her reasons for this division:

It is the intention to alternate in this way the offices of publication, believing that by being published at Washington during the sessions of Congress it can better represent all states and also all national legislation which touches the domestic, industrial and political conditions of women; while in its summer work it will still keep its hold upon the liberal and progressive west. It will thus occupy a unique place among the periodicals of the day, and will be indispensable to all those who wish to be informed upon the progress and scope of the "woman movement." (19 October 1889, 272)

Additionally, she used this "unique" operation as an argument for the paper's status as organ of the movement:

The organ of a movement that would be influential must seek an educational and political centre, and it is this necessity that has impelled the TRIBUNE to have its headquarters in Washington during six months of the year, but advantages of location are not all east of the Alleghanies [*sic*] or even the Mississippi. Here we are, midway between the oceans and already the great West is sending its words of greeting to welcome back its own. It is in this West that the great successes of the woman suffrage movement have so far been achieved and others are pressing to accomplishment. The TRIBUNE expects therefore that even its Eastern readers will feel a quickened thrill of interest during its mid-year Western publication. (9 May 1891, 148)

After three years of this "commuting," however, Bewick Colby, feeling the advantages of the Washington location outweighed her Beatrice responsibilities, moved the paper to the capital on a full-time basis from 1893 to 1904.

In 1904, Bewick Colby moved the publication offices of the *Woman's Tribune* to Portland, Oregon, in part because she believed that the next great successes for the movement would be in this region. However, the move marked the end of the paper. Although Bewick Colby and the *Tribune* were not well received by the Oregon suffragists, she seems neither to have planned nor ever fully accepted that the 9 March 1909 issue was the *Tribune's* last. For over a year after the last issue, the "editor" was still soliciting contributions, in the forms of both money and columns; in her mind the paper's suspension from publication was temporary.

The *Woman's Tribune* as a Leadership Tool

Bewick Colby and the *Woman's Tribune* were not just an editor and a newspaper, they were representatives of a special interest. But "representative" was too small a role for this woman. For twenty-six years, Bewick Colby used the *Tribune* to establish her desired role as the authentic voice of the woman suffrage movement and, thus, to become a national leader. By strategically placing her paper as an educational medium, a historical document, and an "in-house news-letter," she fulfilled her purpose in three interrelated contexts: the paper and its readers, the paper within the movement, and the paper in her own life.

The Woman's Tribune *and Its Readers*

In this first context, the *Woman's Tribune* served Bewick Colby's purpose by being a source, a means for women to get something they could not get elsewhere. In accomplishing this, Bewick Colby could solidify her importance to women and the necessity of her paper for them. In other words, she and the paper become indispensable inter-mediaries between the readers and other movement leaders. An examination of the content of the *Woman's Tribune* reveals that it served this purpose for its audience through four functions: creating a self-definition, supplying general knowledge, providing the opportunity for vicarious movement involvement, and educating the total woman.

One important function of the content of the paper was to help the audience define themselves. Bewick Colby not only attempted to reach as many people as possible, she tried to shape their self-images in ways useful to the movement. For example, she tried to give her readers the sense that they were knowledgeable about the value of suffrage newspapers generally and the great importance of the *Tribune* in particular. Having labeled them as "friends of pro-gress," she encouraged them to become "permanent" subscribers (1 November 1883, 1), knowing that thoughtful people would want to "help it to be more useful and to grow better by your patronage" (May 1885, 2). Such knowledgeable individuals would, of course, not be among the group of friends who "forgot their promises" or the well-known suffrage workers who, "fearing to invest a dollar," failed to be good and faithful subscribers (December 1884, 2).

In addition, the editor invited her audience to see themselves as well-informed and thoughtful authorities on woman's rights. Her readers included "persons who are known to be progressive and intelligent, picked men and women of the west . . ." (1 May 1884, 2). The women readers were not only "intelligent enough to appreciate the paper" (October 1884, 2), but they were also "the leading women eminent" in the various fields of endeavor (November 1885, 2). This intellectual acumen enabled the audience to fulfill the final category Bewick Colby created for them, that of guide to the less well informed. Readers were encouraged to invite their friends to subscribe (1 February 1884, 2) and to pay to have the paper sent into homes of the uninitiated, "there to create a sentiment in favor of equal rights and to stimulate to healthy endeavor in all departments of labor and thought" (1 May 1884, 2).

Some women in Bewick Colby's initial audience had needs that seemed to them more immediate and more pressing than their political oppression. To appeal to them, the *Woman's Tribune* had to do more than merely report on the suffrage events of the day. Thomas Clark, social movement critic has observed: "Many supporters of a movement on behalf of an agenda for reform might not be motivated primarily by a desire to attain the benefits of the reforms, but rather may have found in their participation in the movement fulfillment of far more basic psychological needs."[11] Thus, as a second readership function, Bewick Colby had to create this sense of cognitive fulfillment in her readers if they were to see her and her paper as essential to their personal involvement with the movement. She chose to accomplish this goal of supplying knowledge by making the *Tribune*, in part, a general circulation newspaper.

In routine publication, Bewick Colby advanced her concern for news reporting in three ways. First, she reported on general newsworthy events of the day. This included accounts of increasing immigration (e.g., 5 September 1891, 281), activities of political parties (e.g., 19 April 1890, 122), the Patents Office (30 April 1892, 136), and U.S. relations with foreign countries such as Canada (14 October 1893, 173), China (30 March 1894, 65), and Japan (29 December 1894, 197). She covered presidential speeches and summarized congressional debates (e.g., 15 December 1894, 189; 1 January 1884, 1).

A second emphasis in Bewick Colby's news reporting can be classified as a general concern with rights and liberty. For example, she opposed the United States annexation of Hawaii because "ethnologically it will cease to be interesting if the gentle and intelligent Hawaiian is not to be allowed to work out his own destiny" (4 February 1893, 29). She argued strongly in favor of "Hawaii for Hawaiians" (25 February 1893, 41). Bewick Colby had objections to American involvement in Cuba and the Philippines during the Spanish-American War: "Thus, the policy of the administration is for the first time plainly announced. . . . it is to establish sovereignty over these islands to the ruin of everybody that stands in the way" (8 April 1899, 25).

In addition, Bewick Colby's news reporting showed a general orientation toward reform. She took a number of what could be termed "anti-" stands. She came out against opium (12 March 1892, 78), licensing of prostitutes (12 March 1892, 76), press censorship (11 March 1893, 50), spitting (29 April 1893, 79), cigarette advertising (20 May 1893, 89), hunting (19 October 1907, 69), capital punishment (2 May 1896, 45), and vivisection (21 October 1893, 178). Not all reform-oriented articles were negative in tone. Bewick Colby was in favor of and wrote positively about reforms in prisons (e.g., 8 April 1899, 28), reformatories (16 April 1892, 120), and spelling (e.g., 1 October 1892, 182).

The third broad readership function that the *Tribune* served was to be a substitute for the readers' direct involvement in movement activity. In other words, it provided knowledge, information, and experiences of the suffrage movement and of other activities for women who could not participate directly. To fill this role, the *Tribune* had to carry material that explained and vividly described the activities, and it had to reach women who were not being reached by suffrage conventions, speakers, or expositions.

The most important aspect of this function was to make suffrage conventions available to isolated women. Although suffrage news was reported in detail, the mere reporting of suffrage work was not enough. Movement efforts had to be recounted in ways especially meaningful for isolated women; this included covering activities ignored by the general circulation press or reported incompletely. Because of the relative newness of the cause, at the time of *Tribune's* first issue, Nebraska women had been able to attend only one or two state conventions. As the years passed, opportunity for involvement increased. For example, the Nebraska State Woman Suffrage Association held a convention every year except one between 1883 and 1900. In spite of this, many women were still unable to attend because they lacked funds, transportation, interest, or, in many cases, awareness of the event. Thomas Chalmer Coulter, Nebraska historian, described the typical convention in Nebraska:

It would be a mistake to conceive of these conventions as being of an elaborate and lengthy nature, attended by large numbers of interested ladies. A typical convention of the 1880's lasted, at the most, two days and was of the simplest possible description. Taking the Lincoln convention of 1885 as an example, we find that fewer than one hundred delegates attended the gathering. . . . It is sad to note that the press failed to devote more space to the event than a plain announcement of its occurrence and program required. Reports of the content of addresses and of resolutions passed are conspicuous by their absence. It might be mentioned in passing that even such a brief notice as this was an improvement on the treatment received by the York convention of the previous year, a convention passed by in utter silence by the York newspapers and mentioned only in a single-line comment by the big urban dailies of the state.[12]

In contrast, the *Woman's Tribune* reported on both events, including speech excerpts, reprints of the resolutions passed, and lists of elected officers (1 February 1884, 2; February 1885, 1). Thus, not only were most women unable to attend the conventions, their only contact with them was through announcements and reports in the *Tribune*.

Nebraska convention news was not the only type of suffrage reporting that was important to the *Tribune's* isolated readers. The national focus of the paper also enabled them to experience the movement outside their state boundaries. Bewick Colby noted: "The especial need of women in remote places taking a suffrage paper is shown by a letter recently received at the TRIBUNE office. The writer had had a sample copy of the TRIBUNE sent nearly two years ago, and this 'hoarded with miserly care,' gave her the address where to send for information when she was distressed by the local news that Elizabeth Cady Stanton was dead, and that Susan B. Anthony had gone insane" (18 January 1893, 19). The editor took pleasure in telling this woman the "true" state of affairs. She also added information as to what Cady Stanton and Anthony were doing currently for the movement.

National coverage was not limited to reports of activities; a more personal note was occasionally injected for women who might never meet suffrage leaders. The most prominent instance of this was Bewick Colby's account of the sixteenth convention of the National Woman Suffrage Association, which included columns with detailed descriptions of both physical and vocal characteristics of convention speakers. For example, she painted her close friend and fellow suffrage editor Elizabeth Boynton Harbert as

a tall, graceful, rather slender lady, of middle age. She has delicate features, and a fine and intellectual face. Her waving gray hair, drawn low over the temples and coiled at the back of the neck, formed a fitting frame for the delicate face, and made her dark eyes more noticeable. Mrs. Harbert stood behind a small reading desk and read a carefully prepared address from manuscript. The reading was animated, and the reader's eyes were upon the audience oftener than upon the paper. She made no gestures. Her voice was pleasant and the enunication [sic] clear and distinct, but the tones were too even and monotonous. (1 April 1884, 1)

The editor was determined to demonstrate to her subscribers that their leaders were capable of representing them. As the Boynton Harbert picture demonstrated, for Bewick Colby speaking aptitude was a primary indicator of ability. She featured the style of Helen Gougar:

She is an impassioned speaker, and was not dependent upon either a written speech or manuscript notes. Her gestures were frequent as she stepped back and forth at the front of the platform, but the movements seemed all necessary to emphasize the words she spoke. They were not forced. Mrs. Cougar [sic] has more of the effective stump speaker about her than any of the other ladies of the convention. Her speech was abundantly illustrated by stories, funny and pathetic, and her appeals to the emotions of her audience met with a ready response. (1 April 1884, 1)

Significantly, this particular description highlighted that a woman suffrage leader was capable of rhetorical adaptation and could, therefore, speak in a way acceptable to any audience, male or female.

In addition to the recounting of suffrage conventions, speeches from most woman's congresses, congressional hearings on suffrage, and prominent social gatherings were also included in the *Tribune*. For example, Bewick Colby reprinted speeches given before the Association for the Advancement of Women, Chautauquas, the Woman's Christian Temperance Union, and national and international woman's congresses. Speeches from national fairs and expositions were another popular feature. This coverage was clearly intended for the woman who could not experience these events for herself: "Those who visit the Exposition for themselves will be the more interested to have the birds [sic] eye view of another which will deepen their own impression; and those who cannot attend will be glad to have the TRIBUNE notes of whatever is new and particularly valuable" (6 May 1893, 82). To make her accounts of the Lewis and Clark Exposition in 1904 even more accessible, Bewick Colby added pen and ink drawings of the major buildings.[13]

As another key in her presentation of her special call to leadership, Bewick Colby stressed the fact that she was more mobile and had much more access to the major events of the day than did most of her readers. She also underscored that her personal exposure to leaders, speeches, arguments, and educational activities had been instrumental in launching and maintaining her career and her commitment to her cause. In an attempt to foster such commitment in others less fortunate (and thus less able to lead), she used her paper to bring to them what they could not obtain for themselves—a day-to-day appreciation of and involvement in the movement.

The *Tribune*'s final readership function was education. Bewick

Colby attempted to educate her readers by providing information about domestic projects, nontraditional opportunities for women, and leisure activities. Information useful in the home was covered in long-running columns such as "Home Hints," "Hygiene and Medical Progress," and "Health, Beauty, and Dress." Nontraditional opportunities were most typically described in reports of women successful in fields such as education, music, city government, religion, art, science, medicine, the theater, and journalism. Colleges and medical schools that admitted women ran advertisements in the *Tribune*. As women made inroads into "unusual" occupations such as gold mining, exploration, dry-cleaning, river piloting, and agriculture, Bewick Colby encouraged others to follow. Finally, true to her pledge to cover women "in all their varied interests" (1 January 1884, 1), Bewick Colby discussed a range of topics designed to broaden women's experience of the world. She wrote about music study, current literature, lyric poetry, and sports.

By far the most common way in which she attempted to expand her readers' horizons was through travelogues. Traveling herself on suffrage business or for personal reasons, she wrote about what she saw. In the early years of the paper, she provided information about both suffrage and scenery in Oregon, Wyoming, Louisiana, and Kansas. Later on she wrote about Iowa, the Black Hills of the Dakotas, and "Dixie." In the last decade of the *Tribune*, she added an international flavor, writing of her travels in England and Holland.

Diversity, which was the watchword of the *Woman's Tribune*, made it unique among reform newspapers.[14] Because she recognized that women did not and could not live by political rights alone, Bewick Colby strove to give her paper variety and practical utility. As her readership changed to a more cosmopolitan group with more leisure, the need for this type of reporting diminished. This development was undoubtedly frustrating for her, because, as Olympia Brown observed: "she wanted to help everybody and instruct everybody. Unfortunately many people do not wish to be instructed and some cannot be helped."[15] Moreover, as she expanded news and educational reporting in the *Tribune*, she was chastised by her friends and allies. For example, Susan B. Anthony wrote: "You must realize that the Tribune, as managed of late years, carries but very little in it for even the most earnest suffrage woman. All that you put in it about the mysteries of Eastern religions, the reform dress, etc., etc., you could just as well get into the daily papers and it would go to a great many more people who really need it. Our suffrage women get enough of all that in their ordinary papers, and don't wish to pay a separate woman's paper merely to have that kind of reading."[16] Of course, Anthony's reasons played directly into the vision Bewick

Colby had for her paper. Only Olympia Brown saw the virtues of this approach as well as its weaknesses: "Undoubtedly this very versatility and variety unfitted the Tribune to be an organ of the National-American Association while it made it a most interesting and profitable family paper, in which Woman's Suffrage was commended to many by the very fact that it was made interesting by being associated with other subjects."[17] Even if her associates disapproved, the choice Bewick Colby made to emphasize news and educational issues beyond suffrage was strategic and intentional. This approach was intended to make her not just a suffrage leader, but a personal leader as well. She wanted her newspaper to become a part of all facets of her readers' experience, to touch them where and as they lived. Diversity was one of her primary keys to importance.

The Woman's Tribune *as Organ of the Woman Suffrage Movement*

Advertising itself as a woman suffrage newspaper and nationally recognized as such,[18] the *Tribune* first and foremost had to fulfill the purpose of being an organ for the movement it purported to represent. If this status could be achieved, the *Tribune* would become key in establishing allegiance to the movement itself and to the paper's leading role in the movement. Bewick Colby accomplished this in three ways: she reported on state, national, and international suffrage activities; she focused on movement successes; and she used the paper as a repository for historical record, highlighting movement leaders and stressing their relationship with the *Tribune*.

Three trends emerged in Bewick Colby's coverage of suffrage activity. State suffrage work appeared most frequently during the first and last periods of the *Tribune*, i.e., the years in which the paper was published in Nebraska and in Oregon. National suffrage reporting was most prominent during the years Bewick Colby published in Washington, D.C. International activity, which began to appear regularly during the Washington period, continued for the remainder of the paper's career. While these shifts reflected corresponding changes in the movement and in Bewick Colby's life, they were tactically related to her constant purpose of being the authentic voice of the suffrage movement. For example, states covered in the early period appear to have been chosen strategically. Because they were often areas of greater population (e.g., New York and the District of Columbia), they presented a larger base for potential subscribers. They were also areas of important suffrage activity (e.g., Kansas), which demonstrated to the national leadership that the *Tribune* recognized key issues and was capable of covering national concerns.

As Bewick Colby's spheres of interest and influence expanded, so did her coverage of suffrage activities. Her personal and professional move to the nation's capital presented her with an even wider field. As she became more widely recognized as one of Susan B. Anthony's "girls" or "lieutenants,"[19] greater coverage of Anthony's organization, the National Woman Suffrage Association (NWSA), was both appropriate and useful for maintaining her national image. As she became more involved in committee work and as national activity grew, extensive reporting of the national organization's activities was both natural and necessary for a paper desiring acceptance as its official organ. For example, she encouraged membership in the NWSA (March 1886, 2); she invited comments on Anthony's draft of volume two of the *History of Woman Suffrage* (August 1884, 2); and in the first three years of the paper, she gave "reports of all important features of suffrage conventions" (November 1886, 2). Moreover, the gradual increase in international coverage paralleled Bewick Colby's own intensified involvement with worldwide suffrage and women's concerns. These ties further strengthened the editor's image as a leader of not only national but international stature.

As another part of her goal of having the *Tribune* serve as an organ for the movement, Bewick Colby emphasized suffrage success and progress, highlighting the role played by the *Woman's Tribune* in these achievements. This reporting bias manifested itself in a positive tone, which took several forms. First, successful suffrage campaigns and their benefits were covered extensively; failures and drawbacks received few columns and almost always were regarded optimistically. Only a few successful suffrage campaigns emerged to be reported during the tenure of the *Tribune*, but these few received ample coverage. Wyoming was the most prominent example (filling one issue almost completely), followed by stories about Colorado and Idaho. Even failures emerged positively, as in this conclusion about defeat in South Dakota: "every vote cast for it is that much of a victory over ancient custom, prejudice and conservatism gained by education and agitation" (31 December 1898, 97).

In addition, suffrage work such as conventions and publishing were reported in glowing, highly laudatory terms. For example, an 1893 series of meetings in New York was described in lofty words: "The Conventions in the State of New York in December were but the tuning of the instrument in the master's hand the grand march of progress which is now to be played . . ." (6 January 1894, 2). Bewick Colby showered equal praise on the role newspapers played in the movement. Even though she was herself an orator, Bewick Colby always maintained, at least in the pages of the *Tribune*, that publishing was superior to lecturing activity. She posited this claim as early as March 1885: "The spoken word has its power for the day, but for building up a new line of thought in the popular heart there must be the written word, which shall be quietly digested and made part of the reader's own thought. Then the change in belief comes irresistibly . . ." (2). She repeatedly argued that newspapers were more enduring than speeches and that they could be used passively to engage nonbelievers in the movement: "But while the lecture amuses and interests for an hour or two, often the many cares and interests of our complex life sweep away the impression immediately, while the paper read in quiet moments gradually makes conviction, and the reader instead of being transitorily influenced by the opinion of another, builds up opinions of his [sic] own from the logic of events, a faith that cannot be shaken" (November 1886, 2). Over and over, this editor praised newspapers in general as "the best way to help the suffrage cause in any community" (6 May 1893, 82). She even asserted that "the progress and possibility of all suffrage work depend upon their existence and push" (7 January 1893, 2). Of course, Bewick Colby was happy to provide the *Tribune* as the foremost example of these useful suffrage tools (e.g., 17 July 1899, 46), and she printed praise from other papers that supported her claim. For example, she included from the *Eugene* (Oregon) *Register*: "If it is true, as a beautiful woman remarked to me the other evening, that 'the printed word has so much more authority than the spoken,' then the suffragists have an effective aid in the coming campaign in the Woman's Tribune, of which Clara Colby is the editor" (6 January 1906, 3).

This praise of the *Tribune* as but one representative of good publishing work was typical of references to the role of the *Tribune* in the movement, which were written with pride and confidence. For example, the first three volumes of the paper were filled with supporting testimony from other suffrage leaders. Helen Gougar, a suffrage publisher from Indiana, wrote that the *Tribune* was a "medium of communication so important to the furthering of our cause" and praised Bewick Colby, saying that she had "demonstrated her ability as pre-eminently that of an editor, and we may all safely abide in her" (January 1886, 2). Recognized national leaders such as Elizabeth Cady Stanton and Susan B. Anthony supplied several statements of support, further bolstering Bewick Colby's claim to national importance. Letters and speeches by Cady Stanton appeared regularly in the *Tribune* almost from the beginning. Bewick Colby also made her connection to Cady Stanton explicit: "These [readers] will now be glad to learn that Mrs. Stanton authorizes the TRIBUNE to announce her name as one of its regular contributors" (April 1885, 2).

Finally, Bewick Colby played upon the self-esteem of her readers to bolster her own suffrage authority; she was, after all, their elected representative doing what they had judged her most fit to do (1 January 1884, 1).

A third way in which Bewick Colby served as an organ for the movement was by using the *Woman's Tribune* as a repository for suffrage history. Several emphases emerged. First, Bewick Colby highlighted major moments in the movement's past. From the paper's beginning, Bewick Colby consciously chose material with a historical goal in mind. For example, in the opening issue of the third volume, she celebrated the fact that the *Tribune* had "given reports which make it of permanent historical value" (November 1885, 2). Although suffrage history was the primary focus, the record was not limited to suffrage alone: "EVERY intelligent woman ought to have the DAILY WOMAN'S TRIBUNE. It will be of great present interest and in the future will be of historical value. It will be an epitome of all that has been done for women in the past forty years, and all that she is doing to-day. The best thought of the leading women of the nation will be contained in it" (17 March 1888, 1). Bewick Colby was optimistic that her concern with recordkeeping would eventually be rewarded. She wrote in 1897 that, along with *Woman's Words, Revolution,* and *Ballot Box,* "Some day the volumes of the TRIBUNE will be conned [*sic*] with the same curious interest and will offer a review of the progress of the movement which will have a definite historic value" (21 July, 58).

Bewick Colby's emphasis on the history of "the past forty years" demonstrated the importance she and the movement placed on the 1848 Seneca Falls Convention. The *Tribune* included many references to early woman's rights conventions.[20] The first of these was the lengthy review of Seneca Falls in the 27 March 1888 issue. The fortieth anniversary of the first national woman's rights convention, held in Worcester, Massachusetts, was celebrated with a convention in Boston; Bewick Colby covered the new and recalled the old (31 January 1891, 32). As the years went by and fewer and fewer women could claim personal exposure to the great events and figures of the past, convention history received additional attention from suffragists and more space in the *Tribune.* For example, in response to the tendency of some women to forget important bits of suffrage history, Bewick Colby wrote short columns to remind them of its significance (29 September 1894, 166; 28 July 1906, 58). Finally, as she had remembered conventions on their fortieth and fiftieth, Bewick Colby commemorated Seneca Falls one last time, on the occasion of its sixtieth anniversary (13 June 1908, 26; 28 November 1908, 54).

In a similar manner, Bewick Colby recalled the history of the leaders of the suffrage movement.[21] Her reports of the significance of leaders in the movement's past fell into two categories: stories of key suffrage events in famous women's lives and obituaries. The best examples of the former were the records of Susan B. Anthony, Elizabeth Cady Stanton, and Bewick Colby herself. For example, Bewick Colby felt justified publishing Cady Stanton's autobiography: "WHEN the 'Woman Movement' shall have been crowned with complete success how eagerly will these reminiscences of Mrs. Stanton's be read. Great historic interest attaches to those who have led in any of the great struggles for human freedom and those who dared to strike for justice for woman will be doubly honored, for their foes were not a foreign foe but of their own household" (29 June 1889, 204). In addition, Bewick Colby retold the "famous trial of Miss Anthony" (1 February 1890, 36), as well as frequently recalling the impression Anthony had made while on her lecture tours (e.g., April 1885, 2).[22] An account of her own background in the movement enabled Bewick Colby to draw several of these strands together. In the 17 February 1894 issue of the *Tribune*, she combined convention history, a well-known movement leader, and herself into one brief story with historical significance:

The first time I saw her [Lucy Stone] was in 1880 in Boston, when she spoke to my paper on "Farmers' Wives," given before A.A.W. . . . Then by invitation of Lucy Stone I went down to the Worcester convention, that wonderful thirtieth anniversary, where were gathered so many of the old-time agitators who never again met on earth, and this was my memorable initiation into suffrage work. Urged by Mrs. Stone to speak I said I never had spoken at a suffrage meeting and I knew I never should, but I wanted to voice my gratitude as a young woman for the freedom and opportunities that the labors of these had gained for this generation. (34)

Such records would later serve to enhance Bewick Colby's perception of herself as a movement leader.

The use of the paper as historical repository, particularly in reference to leaders and their past, was closely related to the last way in which the *Tribune* fulfilled the suffrage purpose for the movement. The coverage of the present-day activities of suffrage leaders not only kept the readers informed about what their administration was doing for them, but it also demonstrated the close relationship between the *Tribune* and the movement vanguard. The best and most important examples of this are found in the numerous columns related to and authored by Susan B. Anthony and Elizabeth Cady Stanton. For instance, Anthony was contributing to the paper as early as October 1884. Cady Stanton's earliest column was an open letter about the role of women in Christianity and Mormonism (January 1885, 1). The first *Tribune* reprint of a Cady Stanton speech was in March 1885 (1). Coverage of national leaders was limited during the early years of the paper (1883–89) because this was the period of emphasis on Nebraska activities; nonetheless, seven Cady Stanton speeches were reprinted in full or in part during this time.[23]

Reports of the activities of national leaders expanded during the *Tribune*'s years in Washington, D.C. (1889–1904). For example, no fewer than four Anthony and nineteen Cady Stanton speeches were reprinted during this period. These included speeches at national suffrage conventions, before other women's groups, to state legislatures and the United States Congress, and at social gatherings. Essays and letters were prominent features; Cady Stanton alone authored at least twenty-five. Of the letters Bewick Colby printed, some were written for publication, some were originally private correspondence. An unusual example of the latter was a letter in which Cady Stanton complained about the quality of Bewick Colby's proofreading (1 November 1890, 252); more typically, the editor took advantage of every opportunity to publish private letters in which these leaders praised her work. Finally, a substantial amount of space was devoted to the publication of Cady Stanton's "Reminiscences," a collection that would later appear as the autobiography *Eighty Years and More*. These were issued as seventy-one numbers between 6 April 1889 and 9 July 1892 and covered Cady Stanton's life up to the final date of publication. These "Reminiscences" were particularly important for demonstrating the relationship between Bewick Colby and this national leader. Not only did she print them, but the *Tribune* editor was apparently the inspiration behind the writing of them. Cady Stanton said of Bewick Colby's influence: "In Omaha I began my reminiscences at Mrs. Colby's suggestion, and at the point of the bayonet she has kept me at them ever since, until now I have a painful sense of guilt if I allow a week to pass without sending her a budget. For whatever weariness or pleasure the readers of the TRIBUNE have experienced in perusing these chapters, they may blame or praise Mrs. Colby" (7 December 1895, 150).[24] The special tie was furthered by Cady Stanton's subscription support, which Bewick Colby capitalized upon as early as 1885: "These [readers] will be glad to learn that Mrs. Stanton authorizes the TRIBUNE to announce her name as one of its regular contributors" (April, 2). In 1888, Cady Stanton wrote for *Tribune* publication a letter that closed: "I consider it the best suffrage paper ever published" (19 May, 3). The editor took pride in the fact that "THE WOMAN'S TRIBUNE is the only suffrage paper to which Mrs. Stanton contributes," and she regularly used this claim in her advertising (e.g., 7

December 1889, 296). Bewick Colby summarized this relationship by stressing their interdependence:

Gladly does the TRIBUNE devote its space to record the honors that the world has laid on the head of this revered leader. Mrs. Stanton has always been a warm friend of the WOMAN'S TRIBUNE and has contributed to its columns enough valuable material to have given character and dignity to any magazine. Perhaps the TRIBUNE has been equally helpful to her in furnishing a forum for the untrammeled presentation of her convictions, and especially in having been the means of bringing her to the point of writing her reminiscences which have drawn the hearts of women towards her in love where otherwise they might have felt only gratitude and admiration. (7 December 1895, 150)

Bewick Colby continued to exploit her relationship with Cady Stanton in the years following her death. For example, she would reprint her speeches, saying: "The TRIBUNE is glad to reproduce in this issue a stirring appeal to women by Mrs. Stanton which was published in this paper some years ago. In these strong words she, being dead, yet speaks to the women of today in words that have the ring of immortal truth in them" (10 January 1903, 2). Although Anthony never received the space or adulation the *Tribune* gave to Cady Stanton, Bewick Colby also emphasized the personal nature of her relationship to this leader. For example, in reporting on "The Anthony Reunion" in 1897, Bewick Colby made it clear that she had been one of the fortunate few persons outside the family who had been invited to attend (7 August, 61).

Bewick Colby's concern with movement history and movement leaders was consistent with her stated purpose of being a suffrage organ, more specifically of being the organ of the NWSA. The history she featured was that of NWSA, not American Woman Suffrage Association, leaders. The early conventions she commemorated, while technically belonging to the movement as a whole, were closely associated with Anthony and Cady Stanton. Her personal relationship with these two leaders served to highlight the images Bewick Colby had conceived: the *Tribune* as authentic voice of the movement and herself as a movement leader. For example, she stressed that Cady Stanton had chosen to publish her "Reminiscences" in the *Tribune* because its readers formed her "sympathetic circle" (1 December 1888, 4). Moreover, whenever possible, Bewick Colby attempted to use movement history as an argument in support of suffrage. For instance, in her 1891 presidential address to the Nebraska State Woman Suffrage Association, she reviewed the history of the organization as support for why its work should be continued (21 November 1891, 306). This use of historical record was designed to guarantee the importance of the *Woman's Tribune* to the suffrage movement, not just in the present but throughout posterity.

For Bewick Colby to be perceived as important in the movement, her paper had to serve the movement's needs. The three means she used to accomplish this were both appropriate to her and, at the same time, quite strategic. Because she was basically independent, in that she held no nationally elected office, she could, and did, cover all the bases—local, national, and international. This coverage enabled her to draw upon a broad base of support and strengthened her claim that she was the best representative of the entire movement. Her emphasis on movement successes, while strategically intended to motivate her audience, was consistent with her overall idealistic approach to reform. Finally, her portrayal of movement leaders as personal friends and avid supporters allowed her, at the very least, to back in their reflected glory. Thus, the choices Bewick Colby made in regard to her suffrage purpose were strategically designed to promote herself and her paper while still meeting the needs of the movement.

The Woman's Tribune *as the Editor's Tool*

In spite of her constant attempts to meet the needs of readers and to become the organ of the suffrage movement, Bewick Colby never accepted what must have seemed obvious to everyone else—her paper was always "number two," and she was a leader in search of someone to lead. The evidence in the *Tribune* does not suggest that Bewick Colby ever stopped believing either in the causes she served or in her own importance to those causes. She established two roles for herself, one as a journalist, the other as suffrage leader. In terms of the former, Bewick Colby saw herself and had to sell herself as editor, *the* editor of the *Tribune*. For example, as editor she wrote "all articles not otherwise accredited" (August 1883, 2:1). She also stressed that as editor she edited alone and managed alone (1 November 1883, 1) and that she alone was financially responsible for the paper (December 1884, 2). Finally, although willing to admit that she lacked experience for the tremendous tasks that faced her (1 November 1883, 1), Bewick Colby proclaimed that, as editor, she had the necessary courage "for the effort that must still be put forth . . ." (November 1885, 2).

The second role that Bewick Colby assumed was that of movement leader, with the *Tribune* figuring as the movement's authentic voice. For example, she used the *Tribune* to demonstrate that she deserved leadership because of her ability to fight obstacles and withstand failure. Some of the paper's (and, by extension, the movement's) problems were endemic to the movement and were not attributable to Bewick Colby directly. However, there were a number of other factors indicating difficulties to which Bewick Colby directly contributed. First, her style of administration was probably a major factor in her inability to be elected to national office. Bewick Colby's approach to her first experience with broad-based leadership, her tenure as Nebraska state president, was responsible, according to Daniel Fus, Nebraska suffrage historian, for the lack of suffrage progress that state experienced:

Her fourteen-year term of office marked this period of the Nebraska movement as the most inactive, ineffective, disorganized, and directionless in its history, a fact largely attributable to Mrs. Colby herself. . . . Mrs. Colby's style of leadership and her inability to fulfill these goals [of full, immediate suffrage] in the manner she choose [sic] virtually paralyzed the movement. Municipal suffrage required working with the biennial legislature, a task which . . . she attempted to accomplish almost single-handedly. She seemed unaware of or unwilling to organize and crystallize the opinion of Nebraska suffragists in a sustained effort. . . . [She was] deficient as an organizer and administrator. . . .[25]

These administrative failings reappeared in the way she ran the *Tribune*, for instance, in her careless bookkeeping and her incomplete subscription lists.

Bewick Colby stubbornly chose to follow her own course not only at the state level but at the national level as well. Susan B. Anthony regularly chastised her for obstinately adhering to positions that prevented her from achieving and being successful in positions of power.[26] Much of this stubbornness was related to Bewick Colby's unwillingness to compromise the *Tribune*'s status; even when faced with schisms in the movement, she would not acknowledge the claim of the *Woman's Journal* as the official movement organ. By insisting on the acceptance of her views, she created the impression that she was a poor candidate for national office. In other words, Bewick Colby consciously chose to pursue courses and adopt rhetorical positions that she initiated and believed in, whether or not they were the best means of achieving the goal.

This notion of conscious choice provides a context for many of Bewick Colby's apparent failures. For instance, she probably could have merged the work of the *Tribune* with that of the *Woman's Journal* rather than competing with it for so many years. She could have joined forces with the National American Woman Suffrage Association's push for federal suffrage rather than single-handedly lobbying for congressional legislation. She could have thrown her lot in with established regional leaders rather than attempting to undermine their authority with her own, as in Oregon when she battled Scott Duniway for state control. She could have done all these things to further the cause, but she chose not to. Throughout her professional life, Bewick Colby simply and repeatedly refused to adapt; her activity was to be all on her own terms or not at all. She consciously assumed the status of "free lance" movement leader; that status was not thrust on her by others. The result of these choices was, on the face of it, failure and defeat. The *Tribune* was never an official movement organ, and it folded before suffrage was achieved. Bewick Colby was not lauded as a major movement leader, and the *Tribune* did not become the primary record and voice of the movement.

Nonetheless, in terms of Bewick Colby's professional life, the *Tribune* lasted for twenty-six years, the second-longest span for all movement papers and the longest one for papers without national support. Unlike most other suffrage publications, it had a national circulation and a national perspective; at its peak, it reached more readers than any other paper representing its cause. Through the pages of this newspaper, Bewick Colby took suffrage issues, arguments, and activities to women who were too isolated to participate in the movement directly. By combining suffrage with other issues, most particularly general news, she enabled suffrage to reach individuals who were not interested in a narrow reform paper; this targeted audience, most importantly, included men. Bewick Colby never lost sight of the larger context within which suffrage for American women was contained. Throughout the paper's life, she reported on a wide range of woman's rights topics, and she saw American rights within the scope of rights for women worldwide. Bewick Colby herself embodied the kind of woman the movement sought to create—independent, assertive, committed, serious-minded. As editor and publisher, she exemplified an unparalleled "role-model" style of leadership.

Moreover, she succeeded in her desired aim to be a documentary leader as well. The *Tribune* served, and continues to serve, as a unique archival record. Not only did the paper preserve a record of speeches, events, and figures unrepresented elsewhere, it also chronicled the ideology and rhetorical strategies of a movement as they unfolded, rather than in historical retrospect. Although the *Tribune* was never officially the movement's voice, for "many women" it was "the only source of information and sole authority on the subject of Woman's Suffrage."[27]

8

The *Woman's Column*, 1888–1904

Extending the Suffrage Community

Marsha L. Vanderford

> "... a printed slip made up from our Notes & News
> Concerning Women"

On 28 May 1882, Alice Stone Blackwell wrote to her cousin Kitty Barry, describing one of many prowoman suffrage projects devised by her father, Henry Blackwell: "Papa has struck out another brilliant idea. He wrote a letter in mother's name and sent it to almost every newspaper in New England, offering to furnish them weekly with a column of news-items about women, if they would publish it. Between 100 and 200 papers have accepted the offer, including some influential weeklies; so we get out the column weekly—a printed slip made up from our Notes & News Concerning Women—and have it sent to them."[1] The news column was one of many strategies to promote woman's rights that was implemented by the Blackwell family, whose efforts spanned the protracted campaign that culminated in the Nineteenth Amendment to the Constitution. Six years later, the mailing was formalized into a weekly four-page subscription journal called the *Woman's Column* sponsored by the American Woman Suffrage Association (AWSA).[2]

Publication Background

The *Column* was considered a supplement to the *Woman's Journal*, the official organ of the AWSA.[3] In this capacity, the *Column* reflected the liberal wing of the woman suffrage campaign, which dominated the movement at the end of the nineteenth century. Liberalism, according to Rossiter, reflects a belief that society can be improved substantially without violating traditional values or destroying established institutions.[4] The AWSA embraced suffrage as a single goal designed to improve significantly woman's lot and her society as a whole.[5] The organization had historically eschewed broader rights for women, rights that threatened marriage, the church, and sexual mores.[6] Rather than reject and confront existing agencies, the AWSA maintained ties with political parties and worked cooperatively with other reform groups.[7] Lucy Stone, the AWSA's primary spokesperson, recruited many upper- and middle-class, professional, and club women to the association by avoiding the radical goals and methods chosen by the National Woman Suffrage Association (NWSA).

Adopting radicalism as a political ideology, the NWSA was dedicated to a plan for thorough change and advocated the destruction of established institutions.[8] The NWSA's leaders, Elizabeth Cady Stanton and Susan B. Anthony, saw suffrage as just one part of a broad plan to provide complete equality and opportunity for the full development of all women.[9] In order to reach those goals, Cady Stanton and Anthony attacked many traditional values and institutions, including marriage, the church, sexual double standards, and the "cardinal virtues" defining women. Cutting ties with the Republican party and the Abolitionists over the passage of the Fourteenth and Fifteenth Amendments, the NWSA's leaders insisted upon the primacy of woman's equality above all other reforms.[10] In pursuing its goals, the NWSA became associated with issues and individuals considered shocking and threatening to the American public: birth control, sex education, divorce, and cooperative economics.[11]

When the AWSA and NWSA united in 1890, the *Column* served, alongside the *Woman's Journal*, as an organ of the newly formed National American Woman Suffrage Association (NAWSA). By the time of the merger, the NWSA had grown less radical, turning its focus to the single goal of suffrage. The NAWSA's typical members were generally conformists, women "who agreed with their middle-class contemporaries on every issue but suffrage."[12] Thus, the long-awaited reconciliation did not affect the *Column's* liberal voice.

Although originally developed to provide newspaper editors with suffrage materials and other news related to women's issues, the *Column* clearly had the additional purposes of serving as a vehicle for "missionary work," that is, to convert new believers, and as a communication channel between subscribers already converted to the cause (1 January 1898). Similar to many other suffrage periodicals, the *Column* was a subscription newspaper but was distributed widely for proselytizing purposes. Complimentary copies were sent to educators, ministers, politicians, and other influential citizens. For example, in 1888, hundreds of copies of the *Column* were sent to the Ohio Centennial Exposition, and in 1892 and 1893, the NAWSA sent fifteen hundred to prominent Alabamians.[13] The *Column* also served as a rhetorical resource in various local, state, and national suffrage campaigns. In 1890, for example, Lucy Stone, then president of the AWSA, donated ninety-five thousand copies to the suffrage campaign in South Dakota.[14]

Alice Stone Blackwell served as the editor of the *Column* from 1888 to 1904.[15] Literally a second-generation feminist, daughter of Lucy Stone and Henry Blackwell, Alice Stone Blackwell adopted her parents' liberal approach: maintaining ties with various reform groups; attracting middle-class, educated converts; and dissociating suffrage from politically volatile issues.[16] Her parents' ideology did not, however prevent Stone Blackwell from making friends with young women in the NWSA, placing her in the forefront of reconciliation efforts between the two organizations. Historians credit Blackwell with being a primary force in accomplishing the merger of the liberal and radical wings of the movement in 1890.[17]

The *Column* was published from 1888 through 1904 at 3 Park Street, Boston, Massachusetts. Compared to other suffrage newspapers, it enjoyed a long run; its fourteen-year publication period was almost double the average life of its sister journals.[18] A weekly from 1888 to 1898 and a bimonthly from 1898 to 1904, the *Woman's Column* was typically four pages long, except between 2 March 1895, and 1 January 1898, when the journal ran eight pages per issue.

A major attraction of the *Woman's Column* for subscribers was its cost. From 1888 to 1895, the *Column* was published weekly at a rate of twenty-five cents per year. When the *Column* increased its pages from four to eight per issue in 1895, subscription rates jumped to fifty cents per year. Blackwell justified the increase as necessary due to high publication costs (2 March 1895). Three years later, suffering from declining subscriptions, she restored the twenty-five-cent rate, reduced the journal to a four-page edition, and published it on a bimonthly basis (1 January 1898). Even at its highest rate, the *Column* was a bargain. Sister journals charged subscription rates of one to three dollars per year during the nineteenth century and three to six dollars per year after the turn of the century.[19]

As a result of modest subscription rates, the *Column* may have been distributed in greater numbers than any other suffrage periodical. In a letter to Blackwell, one reader explained, "I find more [people] are willing to take the *Column* as it comes nearer the reach of their pocket book than the Journal."[20] The *Column*'s price also allowed some suffragists to purchase extra subscriptions to be sent to friends and prominent public figures. In April 1891, the *Column* reported that a reader in Illinois purchased enough subscriptions for every member of the Illinois State Legislature. One Kansas subscriber supported thirty-one subscriptions sent to clergymen and professors (4 April 1891). Blackwell commented, "*The Woman's Column* is flourishing, and its subscription list increases in a sort of geometric progression. Once started, it grows faster and faster. There seems to be an almost unlimited field for it" (4 April 1891).

The *Column's* primary target audience was comprised of white, middle-class, rather conservative women who were promising potential suffrage converts. By 1888, a growing number of these women had been liberated from time-consuming household tasks by an influx of inexpensive immigrant house servants and a growing number of time-saving household appliances. Suddenly acquiring free time and leisure, these women had formed thousands of local, regional, and national organizations devoted to entertainment, self-improvement, and social reform.[21] Within these organizations, women "were participating in the life of their day and assuming leadership in social welfare."[22] In addition, increasing numbers of women were college educated and unhappy with the limited activities traditionally considered appropriate for middle-class women.[23] This audience had the time, means, and leadership abilities needed to make suffrage a reality. Moreover, their dedication to social improvement provided a convenient rationale for their entrance into the public sphere.

One function of the *Column* was to harness the energy and resources of these women to the suffrage cause. The recruitment of new converts was essential for the survival of suffrage at the turn of the century when state and local referenda on woman suffrage were continually proposed and defeated. Middle-class women were natural targets for conversion. Many had already committed themselves to public activity but perceived woman suffrage as too radical to support, associating it with a threat to marriage and the family.[24] Many social club women were conservative, satisfied with woman's place in society, and suspicious of change.[25] Others were liberals with different reform targets than suffrage: temperance, child labor reform, gambling, or prostitution.[26] Such liberal reformers found woman's moral voice a natural and necessary part of these causes.[27] Yet many social reform activists maintained conservative views of women—satisfied with her political status and invested in traditional beliefs in her pure nature and domestic sphere of interest.[28] The *Woman's Column* attempted to attract middle-class converts to the suffrage movement, dissociating it from radical positions and people and associating it with traditional values, images, institutions, and individuals.

Format and Content

The *Woman's Column* followed no set format and included no regular features.[29] As a summary of ideas and events surrounding women's rights, the paper predominantly consisted of excerpts from speeches, newspaper reports, and journal articles concerning suffrage, women's advances, and social reforms. Editorial passages often introduced or commented upon the content of the material quoted from other sources. Much of the paper was dedicated to one-paragraph—often one-sentence—descriptions of individual and group activities. The accounts ran continuously, without visual interruption. Frequently, a dozen or more short reports occupied an entire column or more of the newspaper.

The *Column*'s format encouraged readers to attend to a variety of issues. The articles and excerpts were mixed together, frequently without headings or titles to orient the reader to particular issues or club news. A typical page from 11 August 1900 included a review of a speech by William Jennings Bryan, a report on suffrage reform in New Zealand, a description of schoolgirl carpenters in Chicago, the victory of a fifteen-year-old girl in a school speech contest, the story of a ten-year-old "business woman," and a report on the activities of the Independent Women Voters of Boston. In order to find articles of special interest, the reader had to sift through news of all kinds, including suffrage. The resulting exposure to suffrage arguments and activities had the potential to convert women who read the *Column* for club news and general information on social reforms.

Civic and Reform Issues

In addition to suffrage activity and pro-woman suffrage arguments, the *Column* devoted a significant amount of attention to other issues of interest to middle-class women. Intended to reach "hundreds of thousands of readers who would not take a paper devoted specifically to this reform [woman suffrage]," the *Column* appealed to potential converts by carrying news of clubs and events already accepted by the target audience.[30] By the turn of the century, thousands of women belonged to civic, social, reform, and career clubs. The Women's Christian Temperance Union (WCTU), for example, established branches in every state and included over two hundred thousand women among its members. By 1890, many of the two hundred fifty thousand women who held teaching positions nationally belonged to educational organizations.[31] By focusing on the women's clubs and their agendas, the *Column* became a reform journal, like other women's newspapers, a part of a "crusade for freedom of the American woman and the betterment of American society."[32] Similar in this regard to the *Revolution*, the *Column* included larger issues of social injustice and women's rights: the regulation of vice, the working conditions of women and children, inequities suffered by women within marriage, and access for women to higher education and career opportunities. Unlike the *Revolution*, the *Column* approached these issues from a liberal, rather than a radical, position.

By covering news about prostitution, the *Column* trod into delicate territory usually sidestepped by conservative women. However, the paper's position on this sensitive subject did not threaten traditional religious values. Noting the implementation of vice ordinances in the Philippines, the *Column* criticized the United States government for implicitly approving of prostitution by providing regulations on prostitutes and health safeguards for tempted soldiers stationed there. Closer to home, the *Column* lauded the work of such women as Donaldine Cameron, who "waged a war relentless and vigorous" against prostitution in San Francisco's Chinatown and urged similar action against white slavery rings on the East Coast (3 September 1904; 29 November 1902).

The newspaper also turned readers' attention to deplorable working conditions in factories and shops where women and children were employed. For example, in 1890, the *Column* noted that of the two thousand white children working in Georgia's cotton factories, only seventeen could read or write and that the lowest number of hours worked by any of the children was sixty-eight per week (18 January 1890). The reports were not designed to rally workers' support for reform; instead, the reports noted undesirable conditions in relationship to club activities and legislative reforms that *Column* readers could influence, join, or emulate. In the Georgia example, Stone Blackwell implied that woman suffrage would correct the unjust labor practices; therefore "it would appear from this that women in Georgia need to have a voice in legislation" (18 January 1890). Reform issues related more directly to middle-class women were also discussed, especially the injustices suffered by women under inequitable marriage laws. The *Column* reported child custody problems in which husbands removed children from maternal care against the mothers' will and legal decisions that required working women to pay for debts incurred by drunken spouses. The newspaper followed closely the changing laws on women's property and inheritance rights. Throughout its discussion of these issues, the *Column*'s treatment of marital issues was moderate. The newspaper did not advocate divorce or suggest that single life would be preferable to marriage for women. Instead, the *Column* reprinted articles and speeches that reflected a liberal reform stance, the improvement of women's status within marriage, an accepted and desirable institution.

Extensive coverage was given to various civic clubs that endeavored to correct social problems. The *Column* frequently reported the actions of groups such as the Women's Christian Association of Cincinnati, the Woman's Alliance of Chicago, and the New Century Club of Wilmington, which pursued better housing and employment conditions for working girls (3 January 1891; 4 September 1897). Other organizations, including the New York Women's Association, the Ladies Health Protective Association, and the New Orleans Woman's League for Sewage and Drainage, were praised for achieving improved health conditions in their communities (4 September 1897; 22 April 1899). The *Column* also lauded the efforts of women's groups fighting vice in their cities and towns: the Phyllis Wheatley Club protested the establishment of a "vice preserve" in Buffalo, and the Woman's Club of Ouray, Colorado "wag[ed] war against the gamblers in that town" (22 April 1899; 19 April 1902). The dates, times, and topics of classes and lectures devoted to women's self-improvement also appeared in the *Column* (e.g., 4 September 1897; 7 January 1893; 22 April 1899).

More prominently featured were the activities and accomplishments of national organizations devoted to reform and women's rights, including the Young Women's Christian Association (YWCA), the General Federation of Women's Clubs, and the WCTU. The YWCA notices frequently announced classes and conferences for young working women (8 February 1890). *Column* reports on the General Federation generally included schedules of its annual conventions and narrations of its proceedings (e.g., 1 January 1898; 27 July 1901). The *Column* also provided abundant coverage of the WCTU in its various branches, including Australia and Canada: announcements of new chapters and publications, discussions of temperance strategies, and personal information about the WCTU leaders (e.g., 1 February 1890; 2 January 1892; 2 January 1897).

Beyond covering news of women working for reform, the *Column* celebrated the already accomplished goals that enhanced women's rights. Advancement in higher education was a frequent and celebrated topic within the *Column*'s pages. Regular reports included the establishment of new women's colleges and degree programs; firsts for women in medical, legal, and agricultural studies; the implementation of scholarship programs for women; and the successes of girls in academic competition with boys. The *Column* noted with pride that women had overturned the most obstinate barriers in higher education, even "stiff old Harvard and Yale themselves admit women to post graduate courses" (14 January 1899).

Advancements in women's career opportunities were reported alongside achievements in higher education. The *Column* noted the successes of women around the world as they were admitted to the bar. The ordination of women as Protestant ministers was routinely reported, as were the appointments of women physicians to public hospitals and high medical academic ranks. Beyond these three highly visible career paths, the newspaper provided evidence of progress in a variety of occupational fields. For example, the *Column* reported the first woman to serve as president of a railroad company, the successful businesses of female real estate agents, and the election of women to municipal offices (22 February 1890; 3 January 1891).

The *Column* also served as a source of news about professional organizations, appealing to increasing numbers of educated and skilled women workers. For example, in 1896, the Teachers Club of Chicago was reported to be investigating the cause of the "restless and unruly child" and had resolved to establish a school for "incorrigible children" (23 May 1896). The *Column* also provided news for business women by printing the meeting schedule of the National Association of Business Women Convention (27 July 1901). In addition, the newspaper frequently praised the activities of nurses' organizations such as the visiting nurses of Henry Street Settlement, which provided medical treatment for children whose parents could not afford health care (14 March 1903).

By devoting substantial amounts of space to issues besides suffrage, the *Column* paralleled a strategy found in the *Woman's Tribune,* whose editor believed that "'features of [the *Tribune*] . . . which do not directly pertain to suffrage . . . have brought in most words of approval.'" She explained that "'not devoting the paper wholly to the reform for which it stands first'" was "'most acceptable to the majority of its readers.'"[33] Discussion of reform issues and club news provided an initial reason for many middle-class women to read the *Column,* but perusing it could, potentially, convert them to the suffrage cause.

The *Column* and Suffrage Issues

Clearly the *Column* covered topics of interest to its target audience, but its underlying editorial focus was on suffrage, which it effectively and continuously linked to other reform issues. To understand its stance on suffrage, one must first examine its rationale for supporting suffrage and then its treatment of suffrage topics.

The editorial philosophy of the *Column* reflected a traditional analysis of woman's nature as pious and pure, representing her virtuous nature as a civilizing force within the community. Appealing to moderate readers, the *Column* predominantly argued for suffrage from expediency.[34] The newspaper primarily represented the enfranchisement of women as a means to the moral improvement of the community.[35] Such causal arguments were typical of the suffrage movement at the turn of the century.[36] Specifically, the *Column* contended that woman's special virtuous nature, when empowered with the franchise, would reduce the corruptions of a male-dominated society. Typical of the *Column*'s stance were arguments that women would work to end war, elect superior political officials, and curtail vice. For example, Blackwell drew upon the traditional belief in basic differences between men and women to argue that woman suffrage would decrease chances for war. In a response to Edward Atkinson, who predicted the end of armed conflict during the twentieth century, she indicated that Atkinson "should appreciate the need of woman suffrage as the indispensable means to the end he seeks." She claimed that women understood most clearly the "cruelty, folly, and wastefulness of war" because they had given "birth to the soldier at the peril of their lives" and could "realize more fully than man the value of human life" (6 January 1894). Woman's maternal natures, combined with male aggressiveness, were recognized as the reasons men alone could not deter violence: "A political society of men alone, from which women are excluded, cannot maintain permanent peace, because male human beings have in excess the belligerent instinct, which needs to be moderated by the humaner instinct of women" (22 September 1894).

A reprint of a speech by Julia Ward Howe provided the link between women's votes and improved government officials: "I am not one of those who promise that the advent of woman in the political arena will right every wrong; but I do believe that where women have voted so far, they have shown a disposition to choose the best candidates, outside of party lines" (4 April 1891). Reinforcing Ward Howe, Blackwell indicated, "Let the great mass of good mothers, wives and sisters have a voice in choosing our representatives, and a higher class of men will be chosen" (29 April 1893).

More broadly, the *Column* linked woman suffrage to the accomplishment of great social reforms, especially to the restriction of vices: "If all these women held in their hands the ballot, and made themselves a power for good, what could they not do? They could close the saloons, the gambling houses and the brothels" (27 July 1901). The *Column* provided numerous examples of how women's influence had restricted immorality. In 1890, the *Column* reported that women's votes had closed the "dram" shops in Howard County, Missouri, citing women's votes and the WCTU as determining factors in the decision (18 January 1890). A report from Chicago made the same argument regarding gambling:

"Gambling has flourished . . . under the sanction of the mayor and chief of police of the city of Chicago." How would it be if the mothers of Chicago could help elect the city government? It cannot be imagined that mothers, whose children are the very apple of their eye, would deliberately vote for those who would dig pitfalls for the feet of their children. Wendell Phillips said years ago: "The suffrage of women has much to do with the government of great cities." (8 February 1890)

Expediency arguments that linked woman suffrage to social reforms appealed to a growing number of middle-class Americans accepting a Progressive philosophy in which government became responsible for social welfare. The *Column* portrayed the political activism of woman's moral nature as a necessary force in the accomplishment of that goal.[37]

When not advocating woman suffrage based upon expediency arguments, the *Column*'s focus was primarily refutational. Blackwell printed excerpts of antisuffrage arguments from a variety of sources. Following each attack, editorial comments or reprinted material rebutted the opponent's charges. Several times during the publication of the *Column*, Blackwell developed special editions and sections of the paper featuring answers to antisuffrage arguments with which suffragists were commonly challenged (e.g., 10 January 1903; 25 January 1890; 14 May 1904). A focus on refutation served two purposes; it provided ready-made answers for suffragists faced with antisuffrage arguments, and it helped to convert those readers who came to the paper seeking other news.

Antisuffrage arguments that were frequently published in the *Column* included: (1) women would not vote if given the franchise; (2) women have indirect influence without the vote; (3) women should be protected against the burden of voting; (4) voting would unsex women; (5) society and the family would suffer if women vote; and (6) women are not mentally or emotionally fit to vote. Blackwell's succinct answers to these arguments in special refutational editions of the *Column* are typical of her counterarguments found throughout the *Column*'s publication:

(1) Women would not vote if given the franchise.

This common charge was supported by examples of low turnout by women voters in states and territories where women had school and municipal suffrage. The editor's typical response was to argue from a literal analogy: although men, in similar "low interest" elections, did not vote in large numbers, no one had used that as evidence to argue that men's right to vote should be withdrawn. In addition, Blackwell frequently noted that the proportion of women voting in these elections was equal to, if not greater than, the male vote (10 January 1903).

(2) Women have indirect political influence without the vote.

Opponents to women's suffrage argued that husbands and sons represented the interests of women citizens. Opponents also noted that women wielded moral influence in the political arena by teaching their sons ethical principles upon which they later voted as adults. Blackwell noted the lack of proportional representation raised by this system. A man with many female relatives had one vote to speak for them all; a bachelor had only himself to represent. She argued further that women's special nature was fundamentally different from men's and, therefore, could not be represented by men. Finally, the *Column* deemed the indirect route to political influence "needlessly long and hard" (10 January 1903).

(3) Women should be protected against the burden of voting.

This argument was divided into two parts: women's complete attention was necessary to fulfill their household duties, and they required protection from the "dirty pool of politics." The *Column* responded to the time issue by comparing the time necessary for women to vote with the time women wasted on trivialities. In addition, Blackwell indicated that women already invested time in political involvement: reading newspapers, joining political clubs, and attending speeches. Responding to the need for protection from the turbulence of political life, the *Column* appealed to traditional beliefs in woman as a moralizing force. The paper argued that woman's presence in the political arena would improve its atmosphere. The newspaper provided evidence from states and territories that had granted women the franchise. According to the *Column*, men conducted themselves with appropriate decorum in political meetings and at the polls where women were enfranchised. In addition, Blackwell further argued that voting was a right and not a burden from which to be protected.

(4) Voting would unsex women.

The *Column* accepted the belief that inherent differences existed between men and women but responded that these were not caused by, nor could they be changed by, the vote. Blackwell called upon examples of woman suffrage states and countries that demonstrated that women maintained their feminine traits despite exercise of the franchise.

(5) Society and the family would suffer if women vote.

This argument addressed fears that woman suffrage would increase divorce and decrease female interest in home and family. Opponents argued that diminished interest in domestic duties would result in an increase in juvenile delinquency, an epidemic of malnourished children, the infusion of sex into politics, and the ultimate deterioration of society. The *Column* reassured readers that suffrage did not threaten marriage, refuting the divorce issue in several ways. First, the paper noted that in states where women voted, the divorce rate was no higher, and often lower, than in states where women were denied suffrage. Second, it noted that husbands and wives disagreed about many important ideas, including more volatile issues, such as religion, without being led to divorce. Third, the *Column* placed trust in the good sense of married couples who could "agree to disagree" and still remain married (25 January 1890).

Answering the allegation that women would abandon home for politics, the *Column* argued that women had not deserted the hearth in states where suffrage had been passed; even the most ardent suffragists were still primarily interested in the maintenance and enrichment of home and family. Reinforcing the female virtue of domesticity, the *Column* argued that the franchise should be seen as a means for women to protect their families. Woman suffrage would increase women's influence over community health and sanitary standards that affected the well-being of children and husbands (24 January 1903).

(6) Women are not emotionally or mentally fit to vote.

The *Column* agreed that women were emotional and visionary but argued that men also shared these characteristics. According to the *Column*, an emotional, visionary spirit had been the underlying motivation for every important and compassionate act of American history. The *Column* further refuted the claim that women were mentally unfit to exercise the ballot by providing statistics that girls were receiving more education than boys in every state (10 January 1903). In addition, the newspaper provided ample data that women were mentally capable of interacting with men in traditional male forums: women had achieved advanced degrees, demonstrated business skills, and managed complex reform campaigns.

Whether arguing for suffrage from expediency or refuting anti-suffrage arguments, the *Column* utilized four important strategies to win middle-class women to suffrage: relying upon the use of testimony on behalf of woman's rights from sources held in high esteem by conservative audiences; developing a positive, upbeat voice that emphasized progress within established institutions; avoiding alienation of potential converts by employing rationality, gentility, and humor in refutation of antisuffrage arguments; and linking woman suffrage to the goals espoused by accepted women's social and reform organizations.

Blackwell did not rely upon a single editorial voice to speak for suffrage. Instead, she often used sources respected by conservative audiences to make editorial points or refute opponents. For example, when supporting the claim that woman suffrage would increase chances of world peace, Blackwell employed a story from Otto von Bismarck, first chancellor of the German Empire, which blamed war upon male temperament:

[French Marshall Vaillant] said to me [Bismarck], "We shall cross bayonets some day."

"Very well, if you like. But, if you please, why?"

"Because we are cocks, and one cock does not like to hear another crow louder than himself. At Sadowa you crowed too loud." (22 September 1894)

Reflecting the traditional belief in inherent differences between men and women, the *Column* commented that " 'crowing' is an accomplishment confined solely to the male bird. According to Bismarck, it caused the Franco-Prussian war, with all its horrors" (22 September 1894).

The *Column* regularly printed woman suffrage endorsements from clergymen, politicians, and religious and political institutions. For example, when the California Republican party convention adopted a woman suffrage plank in 1896, the *Column* gave extensive coverage to the process that culminated in the success (23 May 1896). Especially celebrated were endorsements from politicians in states that had already achieved limited suffrage for women. Kansas Congressman Simpson was quoted as stating that "municipal suffrage for woman, which already prevails in Kansas, has proved such a success that it is working in aid of the broader suffrage now proposed" (6 January 1894). The *Column* also included support from foreign authorities. Prosuffrage resolutions from British Cardinal Archbishop Vaughn and the National Union of Conservative Associations from Scotland were among the growing evidence of international acceptance of woman suffrage (23 May 1896; 3 January 1891).

The *Column* accumulated impressive documentation of support for suffrage. This evidence was necessary to convert readers who would not associate themselves with radical issues. Thus, the *Column* appealed to women who did not have the "courage of the Grimké sisters and Lucretia Mott in the pioneer days" of the movement.[38] The *Column* made woman suffrage acceptable to conservative women.

The *Column* was also attractive to middle-class audiences because it avoided a strident and critical attitude. Although many problems and injustices were acknowledged, the tone of the paper was predominantly positive. Unlike the *Revolution*, which was problem oriented, the *Column* was similar in tone to the *Woman's Journal*, noting progress made and emphasizing solutions.[39] Corrupt governments, child labor abuses, and asylum reform were not covered in extensive detail. For example, the abusive treatment of women prisoners in mental asylums was rarely mentioned in the newspaper, but solutions to the problem were continuously monitored, including the number of women physicians and police matrons who were appointed to the mental facilities (e.g., 25 January 1890; 8 February 1890). The *Column* focused upon the progress being made to solve injustices already understood by the reform-oriented reader.

A focus on solutions gave the *Column* an optimistic perspective in which, gradually, social ills were confronted and defeated. Even when a goal of the women's movement was not fulfilled, the *Column* interpreted the event as progress. Typical was an 1897 report that a woman's license vote referendum had been defeated by 108 to 125 in Massachusetts. The *Woman's Column* turned the event into a victory by relating that "last year it was defeated by a vote . . . of 93–116. This is a gain, though not so marked a gain as is shown in the vote on full suffrage, which went from practically zero last year to 74 to 107 this year." The *Column* encouraged readers to perceive woman suffrage as an inevitable part of ongoing progress and reform: "We are not 'there' yet, but we are getting there all the same" (20 March 1897). By incorporating the cause into the natural course of social advances, the newspaper denied readers' reservations that suffrage was a radical proposition.

The *Column's* positive tone was reinforced by a benevolent and rational approach to antisuffrage advocates. Rather than berating and vilifying opponents, Blackwell refuted arguments through unemotional reasoning based upon verifiable evidence. For example, responding to the claim that women were mentally unprepared to vote, Blackwell stated:

Statistics published by the National Bureau of Education show that the high schools of every State in the Union are graduating more girls than boys. . . .

The whole number of boys in attendance at public high schools in the United States in 1898 was 189,187; of girls 260,413. Because of the growing tendency to take boys out of school early in order to put them into business, girls are getting more schooling than boys. Equal suffrage would increase the proportion of voters who have received more than a merely elementary education. (10 January 1903)

Often the editor approached opponents' claims with a humorous, gentle form of ridicule—poking fun at illogical positions. Typical was the response to Professor Harry Thurston Peck of Columbia University. Peck had written in *Cosmopolitan Magazine* that if "women are admitted to the highest education, they will lower the standard of scholarship, and will be unsexed." Turning the tables on the professor, Blackwell remarked:

Far from lowering the standard, women have taken rather more than their share of the prizes in the universities where they study on equal terms with men. Prof. Peck disposes of this inconvenient fact by the ingenious theory that the women reported to have thus distinguished themselves were really "very commonplace girls," but that the professors were so influenced by their femininity as to award them honors which they had not earned over the heads of the more deserving men. If this were so, it would be not so much an argument against the fitness of women for higher education as an argument against the fitness of some men to be college professors. (14 January 1899)

Absence of vilification and the *Column*'s informative focus created a moderate tone to the journal, making it suitable for distribution to the general public. Letters to the editor describe the *Column* as so "quiet and Quaker-like, that it convinces people before they are aware of it" (14 October 1893). The newspaper did not reflect the philosophical stance of the *Una* nor the radical persuasive strategies of the *Revolution*. It was fundamentally informative.[40] It provided no basis of alienation for conservative readers or for antisuffrage opponents. The facts and excerpts printed were allowed to speak for themselves, often eliciting no editorial comment upon their content.

A final strategy demonstrated that the goals sought by social reform and self-improvement groups could be gained through the enfranchisement of women. The *Column* reflected the restrained ideology of turn-of-the-century feminists for whom enfranchisement became a "panacea" for other social reforms.[41] Hence, the goals already accepted by a wide population of women involved in the YWCA, the WCTU, the ladies reading circles, and local community groups were causally connected to the ballot: restriction of vice (prostitution, gambling, and drinking), improvement of community health conditions, restriction of abuse toward women and children, and the expansion of women's interests and influence. Addressing the goals of clubs devoted to self-improvement, the *Column* argued that the franchise would have a marked effect on women themselves: "The ballot is necessary for woman's own development, that it may do for her what it has already done for man. It incites inquiry into the questions one will be called upon to help decide. Thus one is drawn out of his own narrow channel into a world wide knowledge and sympathy. The ballot is a means of culture, which we all want" (3 January 1891). The *Column* tapped the "new reform stirrings" felt by thousands of club members and argued that solutions could be found only by women's participation in politics.[42]

In addition to arguments for suffrage, the *Column* included extensive coverage of suffrage campaigns around the world, but especially in the United States. The newspaper paid special attention to suffrage legislation, ranging from detailed coverage of partisan opinion in local referenda, to wide-ranging national and international status reports. Chronologies of suffrage progress in the legislatures frequently appeared in the *Column*. A typical article listed woman suffrage gains between 1845 and 1893, counting twenty-one states where women had achieved school suffrage, two states and two countries where women had achieved municipal suffrage, and two states and one country that had achieved full suffrage for women (7 April 1894). Typical of the detailed accounts was a reprinted report from Kansas in 1894. The author explained a change in the political situation when the German American League failed to unite in support of the Republican party against a suffrage amendment. The reprint stated that "'the people are more and more rallying to our measure,'" noting that a Senator Ingalls, formerly against the amendment was now "on the fence" arguing that woman suffrage "'would be a good thing for the state but not for the women'" (22 September 1894). The explanation is typical of the *Column*'s attention to factors underlying the potential success or failure of various suffrage amendments.

The *Column* offered readers not only campaign news but also an avenue through which to influence such assemblies as suffrage club activities. The scheduled meetings and projects of local groups were published, and readers were encouraged to participate. For example, when the Equal Suffrage Club of Portland (Maine) was fund-raising, the *Column* advertised tickets for an "entertainment" to be presented by the club, a mock hearing before the Maine Legislature in support of suffrage (22 April 1899). Political action taken by suffrage groups was another important element of the *Column*'s suffrage coverage. Typical was a 1900 report that the Independent Women Voters of Boston had met, organized, and developed a list of suitable nominees for members of the Boston school board (11 August 1900).

State suffrage activities were covered extensively, including schedules of state conventions. In 1896, for example, the *Column* advertised the times, dates, and speakers of an upcoming congress of the Oregon State Equal Suffrage Association (23 May 1896). Proceedings of the state conventions, including resolutions, speeches, and entertainments, were frequently reported so that those who had not attended could keep informed. Typical was a *Column* reprint of Laura Clay's address to the Kentucky Equal Rights Association at its annual meeting in 1891 (3 January 1891). Most frequently included were advertisements and summaries of the fortnightly meetings of the Massachusetts Woman's Suffrage Association (e.g., 22 April 1899).

The *Column* highlighted regional and national suffrage organization activities. When the New England Woman Suffrage Association held its annual conference and festival, the *Column* provided a half-page blocked advertisement for the event, listing place, dates, and participants (23 May 1896). Conferences of the NAWSA were announced by the newspaper far in advance, including information concerning railroad routes, hotel rates, topics, speakers, and convention booth information. Reviews of speakers, resolutions, and entertainments were printed following the conventions (e.g., 15 June 1901).

Rhetorical Functions

In its coverage of suffrage news and social reform, the *Woman's Column* fulfilled two important rhetorical functions for the woman suffrage cause. It converted new members by creating an image of women that encouraged readers to see themselves as capable of political action. Concurrently, the newspaper reinforced suffrage activists' dedication to the movement by creating a sense of community designed to empower movement members.

The Conversion Function: The Creation of a New Woman

One of the *Column*'s primary functions was to provide a new image of woman, one that effectively refuted traditional visions of women as unfit to participate in the political arena. Readers' perceptions of themselves had to transcend traditional limitations in order to empower readers as political activists and voters. Edwin Black has indicated that rhetoric creates a "second persona"—"a model of what the rhetor would have his real auditor become."[43] The newspaper provided readers with a series of stories about women who had succeeded in careers and social reforms. From these stories emerged collective images of a new woman that served as "cues" for how readers were to perceive woman's place within society.[44] The ideology suggested by the role models encouraged women to perceive themselves as strong, intelligent, motivated, and competitive within formerly male arenas. The new woman was deserving of the vote, fully capable of exercising the franchise, and had the ability to participate in a political campaign for woman suffrage.

The *Column*'s pages were filled with images of strong and fearless women. Those who waged war against prostitution and gambling demonstrated for readers that women could stand up to political corruption. Other stories provided evidence that women had the physical stamina and bravery to participate in the world outside the home. Postmistresses rode hundreds of miles through isolated areas without fear to perform their duties (2 January 1892). An American teacher defied local hostilities and the Argentine frontier to establish a normal school (27 July 1901). The *Column* also recounted the heroism of a woman who risked her life to flag down a train bound for a broken bridge (27 July 1901).

Women's mental capacities were also celebrated. Exposed to news of women's progress in higher education, medicine, law, and the church, readers were encouraged to conclude that women were intelligent and capable of understanding complex issues necessary to participate in political life. The *Column*'s stories frequently implied that women were better prepared intellectually than men for these tasks. According to the newspaper, women frequently outstripped male academic performance. In 1896, the *Column* reported that "more than two-thirds of the outgoing [Radcliffe] class were graduated with honor—a percentage far surpassing that of Harvard College" (27 June 1896).

Stories of women's success in traditionally male occupations created an image of women as capable of competing with men and as competent outside the home. For example, the newspaper recounted the success of Clara Locke's application for a captain's license, in which the examiner had "declared that he had never examined a man who answered his questions so correctly" (3 January 1891). Another report compared the careful and prudent management practices of female prison administrators with their careless male counterparts (25 January 1890).

The new woman emerging from the *Column*'s reports refuted the conservative image of woman as politically incompetent. The *Column* maintained, however, a careful balance between the transformed vision of women and the reader's ability to identify with the new images. The *Column*'s new woman retained enough traditional virtues to avoid alienating those who maintained attachment to the ideal of "true womanhood." In particular, the newspaper reaffirmed traditional beliefs in the female virtue of domesticity as a way of associating the new woman with the *Column* reader. The newspaper emphasized that the professional and politically active woman was still concerned about home and family. She was often married, had children, and was interested in feminine beauty.

The *Column*'s role models were frequently identified as firmly connected to their families. For example, Anna Pratt, one of the earliest female botanists, was introduced in the *Column* as "happily married to Mr. John Peerless" (18 January 1890). In another story, the journal noted that archaeologist Madame Dieulafoy had discovered the remains of the palace of Darius while in the company of her husband (11 August 1900). The *Column* praised the wise woman voter of Colorado whose "children's . . . garments are as carefully patched, and [whose] . . . tables as plentifully supplied" as if she were not politically active (19 March 1904).

Nor was the transformed woman lacking in beauty and grace. In 1904, the *Column* described the adventurous Miss Ada L. A. Murcutt, who "once traveled for 1,000 miles across the heart of Australia on horseback with only one man as an escort." While interviewing Miss Murcutt, Henry Blackwell indicated that she was quite feminine, sitting "in her room . . . sewing a bit of lace on a collar" (3 September 1904). A similar description reassured the reader of the appropriate feminine attributes of a woman member of the Colorado Legislature. The *Column* reported that during the last session of the legislature, Mrs. Heartz was presented with a Easter bonnet as a token of her colleagues' esteem: "Mrs. Heartz promptly put it on, and then the applause shook the walls. . . . [Anyone] who fears that women would cease to care for pretty clothes if they were given the ballot might also be reassured by the fact that after nine years of equal suffrage in Colorado, the object chosen as the most acceptable gift to be presented to the only lady member of the Legislature was an Easter bonnet" (19 April 1902). The *Column* reassured those readers who feared that political activity might "unsex" them.

The *Column* often provided a traditional sphere for the new woman's achievements. Those who had ventured into the male world of business were often described as doing so within a feminine environment. For example, in 1890, the *Column* reported that three women had created successful businesses by expanding their domestic skills. One had created and sold a new candy made from olive trees, another ran an embroidery shop, and the third woman sold mincemeat and plum pudding (8 February 1890; 22 February 1890). The *Column* noted that Mrs. Taylor's pudding business had attracted "as much business as she can attend to, and all without the necessity of leaving her home" (8 February 1890). The transformed woman was often successful in a male world but kept one foot firmly planted in the female sphere.

The *Column* encouraged identification of conservative women by agreeing that the home was the appropriate sphere for women's activities but represented the sphere as ever widening.[45] Women's political activity was represented as an extension of her role within the home. Describing society as an enlarged household, the *Column* argued that women had a stake in political activity because they could no longer keep their families safe and children educated without having a voice in a government that increasingly influenced the general quality of life. The *Column* indicated that, having the franchise, the voting woman in Colorado was learning that "she can reach out from her own hearthstone . . . and help alleviate misery, remove evil, and make cleaner and purer places for other mothers' children, as well as her own" (19 March 1904).

According to the *Column*, women already possessed the knowledge necessary for political involvement. Domestic skills were transferable to the political arena:

A good housekeeper tolerates no dark corners in her domain for the accumulation of dust and germs. Air and light and brush and broom are her preventative against vermin and disease. Shall she not look as well to the ways of her larger household, employing the same methods. . . . The trouble is that we have had "bachelors quarters" so long [in politics], and the sole occupant has been so intent on his armament and . . . his money-gathering . . . that he could not be expected to . . . care for his cupboards and cellars. (22 September 1894)

The focus on educated, well-bred, family women as role models encouraged identification of middle-class readers. Few references were made to working-class women. Such a strategy was important in converting conservative audiences. During the last decades of the nineteenth century, middle-class Americans associated working-class issues with organized labor, and organized labor, in turn, with social strife and anarchy. The strikes of textile, mining, and railroad workers loomed large and negatively in the minds of affluent Americans who identified with capitalism and management.[46] The *Woman's Column* coverage reflected the dissociation of upper- and middle-class Americans from the working class at the turn of the century. The suffrage issue divided society along economic, educational, occupational, and racial lines. According to Joseph Gusfield, when political issues are split along plural demographic lines, the intensity of feeling associated with the issue is heightened.[47]

Sustaining the Movement: Empowering Members

At the same time that the *Column* recruited new members, the newspaper functioned to sustain the suffrage campaign, maintaining optimism among suffrage activists and reassuring them about the inevitability of success.[48] Bolstering confidence and energy in active suffragists was tremendously important at the turn of the century. Very little progress was made on behalf of woman suffrage at the national level during the years of the *Column*'s publication; nonetheless, an enormous amount of energy was necessary for coordinating the activities of a variety of suffrage associations, organizing and implementing suffrage campaigns at the state and national level, and educating the public.[49] The need for sustained activity and the potential for discouragement were great.

One of the important functions of rhetoric designed to sustain hope in movement members is its ability to make advocates believe that they can effect change.[50] In the case of nineteenth-century suffragists, the empowerment issue was particularly acute. Acting in individual communities, dispersed geographically, suffragists required a sense of community as a foundation of power.[51]

The *Column* played an important role in providing the movement with a sense of unity. Its publication followed two decades of fragmentation within the suffrage movement, a period in which the AWSA and NWSA competed for the loyalties of suffragists, and a wide variety of suffrage strategies and issues were debated and criticized within the movement. Preceding the formal unification of the NWSA and AWSA by two years, the *Column* unified the efforts of the two organizations by printing news of individuals and activities formerly divided into opposing camps. Once adamant enemies, Lucy Stone and Elizabeth Cady Stanton were both celebrated as heroines within the pages of the *Column*. As editor, Blackwell took an inclusive position. Issues once the territory of the NWSA—for example, prostitution, working conditions, and divorce—appeared in the *Column*, but discussion of those issues reflected the AWSA's liberal values. Rather than compete with or criticize other women's journals, Blackwell advertised them and reprinted their articles. Within the *Column*'s pages could be found the times and schedules of a wide variety of events reflecting a plethora of women's interests and issues.

Beyond the development of a unified front, the *Woman's Column* created the image of an active and interactive community of suffragists. The newspaper served as a vehicle through which individuals and clubs could interact with the suffrage community. The newspaper served as a network for isolated suffragists, as a national and international bulletin board for sharing suffrage news and asking for help. For example, the Massachusetts Woman Suffrage Association frequently used the *Column* as a means through which to obtain items to be sold in its "Country Store" fund-raising booth, and Lucy Stone used the newspaper to prescribe effective means of employing local media for the suffrage cause (1 February 1890; 15 February 1890; 3 January 1891).

Full of practical information and positive news, the *Column* told the reader who to ask, where to go, how to do it, what to say, and where to get materials. The advice shared in the *Column* ranged from guidelines for compiling suffrage leaflets to suggested fund-raising projects (2 January 1892; 18 January 1890). Blackwell provided rhetorical resources for suffrage groups, printing speeches that could be used as the source of argumentation, developing special refutational editions of the *Column*, and advertising brochures on suffrage issues.

In addition to suggesting group strategies, the *Column* empowered individual suffragists by connecting them to other believers and by offering suggestions for individual action. One subscriber wrote a letter to the *Column* suggesting that, although she could not support suffrage in a public forum, she could share her campaign tactic as an example for others who were homebound:

In my front parlour hangs a large, beautiful picture of dear Lucy Stone. It looks down upon me as I enter the door from the hall. Every little while a guest will look at the face and say, with much interest, "Your mother?" I answer, "Yes, my suffrage mother."

Then often follows a conversation about this beautiful picture and the transplanted life it represents. I tell her of the long, unselfish life given to the cause of justice and right, and of the early abuse and struggles it encountered. She listens with a growing interest. Then she looks upon the lovely picture again and says: "What a sweet face she kept through it all," and as my chance caller departs I feel sure that Lucy Stone has made one more impression for truth and righteousness.

I would like to suggest that every lover of this noble woman and her cause, place her large picture on the wall, where it will speak daily. . . . (1 January 1898)

The *Column* assured the reader that she was not alone in her struggle for justice and that help was available. The newspaper contributed to a sense of community for the suffragist, and it assured her that the community was substantial and growing. Readers of the *Woman's Column* could conclude from reports of suffrage clubs and campaign progress that a great number of people actively supported suffrage. In addition, the inclusion of powerful legitimators (politicians and clergymen) as members of the suffrage community provided the reader with a perception that important and influential agents were joining the movement, increasing the force she perceived surrounded her.

The *Column* furnished ample evidence of a growing suffrage movement, noting increasing support of one of America's most well-established institutions, the press. The *Column* frequently reported endorsements from daily newspapers: the Aiken *Journal and Review* praised woman suffrage efforts in South Carolina; the Waltham, Massachusetts, *Evening News* "pronounced the anti-suffrage movement 'a mistake and a stumbling block in the march of ages'"; the Australian *Herald* called for woman's suffrage in Victoria; and the New York *Daily Press* satirized antisuffrage arguments (6 January 1894; 4 September 1897; 3 September 1904). The *Column* indicated that during the campaign for woman suffrage in 1896 in California "not one prominent newspaper in the entire State has taken a stand in opposition to woman suffrage. . . . The city dailies have reported the meetings with the greatest fairness and have allotted ample space [to the issues]" (23 May 1896).

The acceptance of suffrage by major newspapers assured suffragists that the movement had gained impressive strengths and resources, allowing it to reach a broader audience than lectures, pamphlets, and petitions could attain.[52] The reader perceived that the suffrage network was enlarged tremendously by the addition of the mainstream press as a vehicle for suffrage news. The endorsements also attracted potential converts, proving that although "woman suffrage was not yet generally accepted . . . it was no longer considered the province of eccentrics and crack pots."[53]

Conclusion

The *Column* was a part of a force leading the women's movement toward pragmatic goals. It addressed middle-class readers and continued the recruitment of conservative and liberal women began by Lucy Stone and the AWSA during the 1870s. To this end, the newspaper attracted readers by including women's club news, linking suffrage to the accomplishment of great social reforms, employing testimony from respected sources, relying upon factual and gentle forms of refutation, and providing role models that incorporated and transcended traditional views of women. In addition, the newspaper empowered suffragists by developing a sense of community, a power base that reassured activists of the inevitability of success. In a letter to the editor, Mrs. Virginia D. Young explained the *Column's* effect: "I was glad to find many strong suffragists in Marion among its brightest women, and this gain I attributed to the visits of that good little 'Boston Pippin,' the *Woman's Column!* Some of my friends, who only tolerated my views two years ago, can now beat me arguing in favor of my favorite 'fad'—woman suffrage. To have got in this entering wedge, in so conservative a place as Marion . . . is encouraging" (27 May 1893).

The *Farmer's Wife*, 1891–1894

Raising a Prairie Consciousness

Thomas R. Burkholder

"Equal Rights to All, Special Privilege to None"

"For 52 years," writes Lynne Masel-Walters, "the suffrage press served as mirror and molder of the feminist struggle. . . . The publications were significant factors in determining the direction the movement would take on its ragged course toward enfranchisement."[1] On the national level, this task was performed by major publications such as the *Woman's Tribune*, the *Woman's Journal*, and the *Revolution*. Published and edited by nationally known suffrage leaders, these newspapers exerted a major rhetorical influence in the movement.[2]

As Martha Solomon observes in the introduction to this volume, various writers have examined the rhetorical dimensions of social movements.[3] Those scholars agree that persuasion serves a variety of crucial functions within movements generally. For instance, Herbert W. Simons identifies those functions or "rhetorical requirements" as: the need to "attract, maintain and mold workers (i.e., followers) into an efficiently organized unit"; the need to "secure adoption of their product by the larger structure" of society; and the need to "react to resistance generated by the larger structure."[4] Charles Stewart, Craig Smith, and Robert E. Denton, Jr., built upon the work of Simons and others to refine those rhetorical functions of movements. They conclude that movements seek rhetorically to transform perceptions of history, transform perceptions of society, prescribe courses of action, mobilize followers for action, and sustain the movement.[5] In fulfilling those functions, the nineteenth-century woman's rights press encountered a distinctive rhetorical problem.

With regard to the woman's movement generally, Karlyn Kohrs Campbell describes that rhetorical problem, saying, "Feminism is characterized by the tension between a concept defining potential members—womanhood—and a concept defining its goals—personhood."[6] In response, rhetors within the movement developed a distinctive rhetorical style and strategy, "consciousness raising." That style and strategy, Campbell concludes, "is central to feminist rhetoric because of the obstacles presented by women audiences. An audience is composed of agents of change, persons capable of acting to implement the rhetor's goals. Women are not audiences because they do not see themselves as agents of change."[7] Before women could see themselves as agents of change, they needed to achieve a common identity. They needed to become aware of shared experiences, which could in turn motivate action to reach a common goal—personhood. Through consciousness-raising, common identity and, ultimately, motivation to act could be achieved. Consciousness-raising, Campbell argues, is a rhetorical style and strategy signaled by: "personal tone, speaking as a peer, relying on examples, testimony, and enactment as evidence, inductive structure, and efforts to stimulate audience participation."[8] Elements of consciousness-raising were present in the nineteenth-century woman's rights press.

Unfortunately, the mainstream press gave only slight attention to working-class women. Masel-Walters comments that while the "problems of the working women were discussed in the journals . . . rarely was the focus on the factory operative, the domestic employee, or the home-bound piece worker." Instead, articles in mainstream journals "centered around woman in the more genteel, higher status occupations of greater acceptability to the middle-class, such as medicine, teaching, the fine arts and business administration."[9] Because Masel-Walters did not comment on the representation of farm women in those journals, the implication is that farm women were virtually ignored. However, another woman's rights press was alive and kicking on the prairie. Farm women were its primary audience, and it developed its own approach to consciousness-raising. One of those newspapers was the *Farmer's Wife*, published monthly in Topeka, Kansas, between July 1891 and October 1894.

Only one scholar, historian Marilyn Dell Brady, has examined that publication.[10] Brady's essay is an excellent, comprehensive, historical account of the *Farmer's Wife*. But while it includes a variety of excerpts from articles and speeches published in that newspaper,

Brady makes no effort to identify, analyze, and illuminate the rhetorical strategies employed by those writers and speakers. In fact, she calls those rhetorical efforts "somewhat confused and contradictory attempts to interweave private and public concerns for women and to envision women, as mothers, holding powerful positions in both their families and in society at large."[11] However, detailed rhetorical analysis of those articles and speeches reveals sophisticated use of consciousness-raising strategies, natural rights arguments, and expediency arguments that were particularly well adapted to women on the Kansas prairie.

Background of the *Farmer's Wife*

The *Farmer's Wife* was edited by Emma D. Pack, and the publisher was her husband, Ira. Emma Pack was born in New York and raised on a dairy farm in Pennsylvania. In 1871, she married Ira Pack and moved to Iowa. There, according to an article in the *American Nonconformist*, "she soon became connected with the Grange movement. . . . She has been connected with newspaper and magazine work either as contributor or proprietor, since her girlhood."[12] In 1879, the couple moved to Topeka, where both continued their careers in journalism. As Brady explains: "From 1884 to 1890, Ira Pack had published the *City And Farm Record*, a Topeka paper devoted to real estate and land sales. . . . Meanwhile, Emma Pack was editing *Villa Range: Ladies Home Journal*, Topeka, which consisted largely of reprinted fiction, fashion news, and domestic advice."[13]

By 1890, Ira Pack had become associated with the Farmer's Alliance and Industrial Union, the forerunner of the People's party. Within a year, the Packs terminated publication of both their newspapers and merged their operations into the *Farmer's Wife*. According to Brady, "Ira edited the first three issues before turning the duties over to Emma, who continued to edit the paper for its three-year existence."[14] Under the leadership of Emma and Ira Pack, the direction in which the *Farmer's Wife* hoped to move the public was never in doubt. Appearing boldly on the masthead was the motto "Equal Rights to All, Special Privilege to None!" In this turbulent final decade of the nineteenth century, the publication was not only a voice for woman's rights, but for Kansas Populism as well.

Analysis of the speeches, essays, and articles that appeared in this Kansas newspaper provides an interesting and useful case study of the early woman's rights press in the West. National attention was focused on the woman suffrage movement in Kansas from the time of statehood. Leaders of the movement attended the earliest state constitutional conventions and, in vain, urged inclusion of a suffrage provision. The unsuccessful referendum campaign of 1867 brought major prosuffrage figures to the state. Eleanor Flexner reports that Lucy Stone, Henry Blackwell, Olympia Brown, Susan B. Anthony, and Elizabeth Cady Stanton campaigned throughout the state in support of the 1867 referendum.[15] But as the campaign of 1894 approached, Kansas suffragists urged representatives of the national organizations to stay out of the state unless invited. Their fear was that the presence of "outsiders" in 1867 had alienated some male voters who might otherwise have supported the referendum.[16] The national leaders obliged, and in 1894, Kansas women fought their own fight. In that divisive campaign, the People's party endorsed woman suffrage and joined Kansas suffragists in their crusade. Because the *Farmer's Wife* spoke for both suffrage and Populism, it exemplified that effort to raise a purely prairie consciousness in support of the amendment.

Content of the *Farmer's Wife*

Those who contributed to the newspaper were a diverse lot. They included Annie L. Diggs and Mary Elizabeth Lease, both nationally known Populist orators from Kansas, as well as Mary A. Livermore and Frances Willard, both national leaders of the Women's Christian Temperance Union (WCTU). But many of those writers were obscure representatives of the woman's movement and Populism at the "grassroots." Indeed, Brady discovered that "over half of the approximately thirty women whose original articles and poems appeared in the *Farmer's Wife* could not be identified, making generalizations about the contributors and their motivations hazardous."[17] Generalizations regarding circulation would be even more hazardous. Statistics on publication and distribution are unavailable. The fact that the *Farmer's Wife* carried articles and essays from nationally known figures might indicate that it aspired to be a national publication. However, the paper itself provides no evidence that readership approached that level.[18]

The nature of the material that appeared in the newspaper is somewhat easier to assess. The publication consistently followed an eight-page, five-column format. Typically, page one carried one or two poems, usually written specifically for the *Farmer's Wife*, which addressed issues of general concern for farm women: the rigors of woman's life on the prairie, equal suffrage, woman's political and economic status, and Prohibition. The first page also consistently presented one or two long articles, covering two to three columns, also written for the *Farmer's Wife* and addressing similar issues. The second page usually consisted of numerous short articles of interest to members of the Farmers' Alliance. Page three often carried announcements and reports of the meetings of such organizations as the WCTU, the National Women's Alliance, and the Farmers' Alliance and Industrial Union. The "Topics of the Times" section presented short articles of interest to Farmers' Alliance members, frequently reprinted from other newspapers.

Subsequent pages were devoted to sections that varied from issue to issue. Their titles and order also varied, and like the contributors, the articles, essays, poems, letters, and speeches presented there were diverse. The "Home and Farm" section carried material of a domestic nature; many of these articles were clearly aimed at women living on prairie farms. Writers frequently discussed topics as varied as building milking stools, making dolls from flour sacks, and constructing a "model" rat trap. Advice columns addressed such subjects as rural housekeeping, cleaning eggs before sale, storing potatoes, and raising livestock. Perhaps curiously, other efforts often seemed far removed from the interests and lives of farm women. "The Ladies' Corner," which became "Mother and Daughter" in later issues, reprinted serialized fiction for both women and children from eastern newspapers. Also featured were articles on the latest fashions, travel, and entertaining. While Brady suggests that these articles might have provided "a welcome element of novelty for rural women,"[19] novelty was not their only function. These articles stood in stark contrast to the hard lives of farm women on the prairie, and that contrast provided a foundation for the political material that appeared in the *Farmer's Wife*.

Consistent with the early woman's rights press in general, the *Farmer's Wife* sought to identify and attract potential members to the movement. But the aim was to gain support not for woman suffrage alone, but for the People's party as well. Thus, the rhetoric in the *Farmer's Wife* represented a unique blending of woman's rights and Populist issues and a distinctive form of consciousness-raising, which were particularly well adapted to its primary audience, prairie farm women.

Raising a Prairie Consciousness

Frequently alone, isolated both geographically and intellectually, and largely ignored by the established woman's rights press, farm women lacked the common identity necessary to see themselves as potentially effective agents of change and to envision themselves as active members of the movement. But various writers in the *Farmer's Wife* helped build that identity. To do so, Frances I. Garside exploited the contrast between her prairie sisters and city women: "The women who live in cities can form no estimate of the work done day after day by the farmer's wife on the frontier," she said. Implicit in her statement was an understanding of life on the frontier. Adopting the persona of a peer of woman on the farm, Garside depicted woman's life on the prairie as a litany of backbreaking toil without end:

The milk is to be strained and put away, crocks scalded, butter churned, and the dishes and chamber work still wait. Dinner and supper and afternoon work take up her day. Then in their turns throughout the week there is washing, ironing, baking every other day, scrubbing, sweeping, sewing and mending. In harvest time she will have as many as fourteen to cook for and does it all alone. It is seldom that a farmer feels that he can afford to hire help in the kitchen. She has the vegetable garden to see to. To brighten the dreariness of her life she has close to the seldom opened front door a bed of half starved looking flowers—old fashioned coxcomb, four-o'clocks, grass pinks and a few other cheerful looking plants that will thrive under neglect. She makes everything that her family wears except hats and shoes. She has no time to think of rest or self.[20]

The picture of woman's life on the frontier farm painted by Garside was full of great anguish. "It is in most cases her lot to welcome a new baby every other year, and the only time when help is employed to assist her is for a period of two or three weeks when the little stranger arrives," she said. "The births of the babies are about all that vary the monotony of her life. Occasionally death calls and takes from her tired arms a little life and leaves in its place an added pain in her heart. She is old and tired out at thirty."[21] Thus "speaking pain," Garside made universal the sorrow prairie women had believed they suffered alone.

Progress itself seemed to pass farm women by. In another issue of the *Farmer's Wife*, Fannie McCormick lamented: "New machinery has done much to lighten and lessen the work of men on the farm ... but machinery has as yet wrought but little benefit to farmers' wives. Dishwashing, cooking, scrubbing and ironing, like perpetual motion, seem to be beyond the skill of inventors," she said. "Women's work on the farm is constant, unceasing toil—a never-ending, recurring round of duties, 'world without end.'"[22] Because these circumstances were neither imaginary nor unique, Garside, McCormick, and other writers helped build a common identity among farm women. Personal in tone, filled with examples, and written from the viewpoint of women familiar with the plight of woman on the frontier farm, that is, from the viewpoint of peers, their writing constituted a distinctive form of consciousness-raising.

Through essays, articles, and letters that appeared in the *Farmer's Wife*, farm women discovered that their suffering was shared by countless others. Moreover, they learned that their plight was distinct from that of their sisters in eastern cities. That common identity was essential for farm women to see themselves as potentially effective actors within the suffrage and Populist movements. Only when individual women recognized that their plight was common, that they were oppressed generally rather than as individuals, could they begin to see themselves as a group capable of acting in their own behalf. Thus motivated, their action was directed toward one major goal: achieving woman suffrage as a means of improving the condition of their class, their families, and themselves.

Like those in the eastern press, many arguments for suffrage that appeared in the *Farmer's Wife* were based upon a theory of natural rights. All humans, it was argued, were granted by God certain "inalienable rights." In line with that philosophy, governments existed only through the consent of the governed. All people had the right to participate in government, that is, the right to vote. Such participation, suffragists argued, was the right of women as well as men.[23] In the *Farmer's Wife*, that philosophy was reinforced by the Populist commitment to "equal rights for all, special privilege for none."

In a speech delivered at Rossville, Kansas, on 4 July 1893 and reprinted in the *Farmer's Wife*, Bina A. Otis, wife of Kansas Populist Congressman John G. Otis, implored her sisters to "join hands and unitedly ask the legal voters to grant us our natural rights."[24] In her address delivered at the Kansas State Fair in September of that same year, Otis called the franchise "a privilege that we believe is our inalienable right under a republican form of government."[25] Mrs. Crumb of Osage County told the Women's Progressive Political League gathered in Topeka: "Perhaps our most important message should be a warning to you, brothers, that just once more we ask you to restore to us our privilege so long withheld, and invest woman with her inalienable right of suffrage."[26] And M. Katherine Gernen, of Russell, argued that suffrage was not something to be "granted," but rather, "a right which the Declaration of Independence and the Constitution recognizes."[27] As a human being and an American citizen, these women argued, woman as well as man had the natural right to self-governance. That right demanded suffrage. Thus, action to ensure woman suffrage was in line with the finest American ideals.

But natural rights theory was only the foundation of the suffrage argument found in the *Farmer's Wife*. The argument itself was often from expediency rather than from theory. Prairie women advocated suffrage as a means of protecting their homes and their families and as a means of establishing Prohibition. At the often less-than-gentle prodding of writers in the *Farmer's Wife*, they began to see themselves as potential agents of change, if only woman suffrage could be achieved. Their rhetorical efforts were not "confused and contradictory," as Brady suggests. Rather, their arguments extended woman's traditional, private role as protector of home and family into the public realm.

Significantly, many of the pragmatic arguments for suffrage linked woman's campaign for voting rights with traditional Populist issues. The appeals were aimed directly at farm women, who were frequently party members. Again drawing a distinction between these women and their eastern sisters, McCormick argued: "The women on the farms are intelligent as a class. They work, and read and think. They devote what leisure time they have to reading, instead of fashionable dress and society calls. Consequently they are well informed on the leading topics of the day; and many a woman now living on a Kansas farm, in her girlhood attended the best schools in the east. Yet these women are disfranchised."[28] For readers of the *Farmer's Wife*, the "leading topics of the day" were the issues of concern for the People's party, the Populists: the perceived oppression and deprivation of western farmers at the hands of eastern bankers, industrialists, railroaders, and politicians. McCormick and others argued that women should be given the vote in order to increase support for the party at the polls: "We must . . . storm the forts of these monopolies at the ballot box," she said. "The producers will besiege them on one side and the consumers they will have robbed on the other, and they will meet in the center of their works, and the astonished plutocrats will surrender without ceremony."[29] The issue, opposition to trusts and monopolies, was traditionally Populist. But effective opposition, McCormick argued, could come only with the support of active, enfranchised woman.

Contributors to the *Farmer's Wife* regarded suffrage as essential in achieving Populist goals. In her article entitled "Woman's Opportunity," Nettie S. Nutt argued:

Woman's opportunity now stands before her, and if every advocate of female suffrage would join issues with every great political reform element, enrolling the nation's toilers under its banner, woman's triumph would bless even this generation, bringing in its train the overthrow of many other powerful evils. Then let not woman undervalue the power and influence of organization, but under the banner of the Woman's Alliance join hands throughout the length and breadth of the land, bringing victory by making our power felt as industrial and political forces.[30]

Arguments from expediency appeared in the mainstream suffrage press as well, but the union of woman suffrage and the issues of Populism in the *Farmer's Wife* was distinctive. It enabled the farm woman at last to see herself as capable of improving the condition of her class, her family, and herself.

While woman suffrage was the primary issue, woman's rights rhetoric in the *Farmer's Wife* addressed other concerns as well. Most were traditionally Populist issues, approached from woman's perspective. One of those issues was education. In an article which appeared in the September 1891 issue, national WCTU leader Mary A. Livermore argued that education was necessary for woman whether or not she was enfranchised: "If women were never to vote in America, they will always be the mothers of voters. For mothers to abjectly renounce all hold upon their sons when they arrive at the voting age, and to scornfully refuse to acquire the information that would enable them wisely to advise them at critical periods, is to win the contempt of the young men."[31] In another essay, Nutt infused the same position with Populist philosophy: "Teach [the mothers] the principles of equality and justice, and they will transmit them to their sons, and . . . equality and justice will find their way into the laws enacted by those sons."[32] These arguments justified woman's right to education by once again extending her private, traditional role of rearing her children into the public arena.

Perhaps the most innovative effort in the *Farmer's Wife* to link education, woman's traditional interests, and Populism was the attempt to establish a "home kindergarten" for farm children. In 1891, Emily E. Lathrop and her husband proposed that farm women educate their children at home on "the relation of labor and industry to education and development of the individual and the society." Urging the paper to publish a series of "home lessons," they encouraged farm mothers to "instruct a class weekly . . . in an easy course of thought as will early plant in [children's] minds the true purpose of life's labor."[33] The lessons consisted of a series of questions and answers upon which mothers were to drill their children. For example:

Question: Has the earth always had a home and food and a right to life for every kind of living creature?
Answer: Yes; every living thing has had a right by birth and creation to its own kind of food and home for existence and growth.
Question: Then would it be right to keep these creatures away from their homes and food?

Answer: No; we would be robbers to take the nest and food from the birds, or the home and clothes and food from people.[34]

True to Populist ideology, the lesson stressed the natural rights of producers of wealth to enjoy the fruit of their labor and condemned those who would live at the producers' expense. Many would have called it not a "lesson" but political indoctrination:

Question: What kind of people are those who live upon the labor of others? Answer: There are two kinds; one who are ignorant, vile savages, and lazy, poor vagabonds; and the other, who are learned, greedy, civilized, and idle, rich hypocrites; neither of whom add anything to the comforts of mankind, but make the burden heavy for good laboring people to bear.[35]

No further lessons for the Lathrop's home kindergarten appeared after the January 1892 issue of the *Farmer's Wife*. But one can easily imagine their first efforts being taught and retaught by the light of countless oil lamps, in farmhouses spread across the Kansas prairie. The home kindergarten offered woman on the farm an opportunity to act, in her own home and in her traditional role, in a manner consistent with the goals of the People's party. Such efforts helped to raise in farmers' wives a consciousness of their role as women, mothers, and teachers on the prairie.

Labor reform was another issue on the Populist agenda. In the *Farmer's Wife*, labor concerns were linked with one of woman's traditional roles, protection of her children. In urging women to become more active in politics, Frances F. Allen argued: "Mothers, what assurance have you that the dear little ones you feed and nurture so tenderly today, will not help swell the number of hungry ones in the years to come, unless something is done to wrest the power from the merciless few who can give or withhold at will."[36] Male Populist discourse was traditionally confrontational. Allen placed herself squarely within that tradition:

Better heed the moaning of the wind and the swaying of the trees, than wait in fancied security till the fury of the cyclone is upon you. Better to turn aside the course of the little rippling stream while it is yet in your power, than to wait till it is a mighty, rushing torrent, carrying destruction in its path. Better it is to quench the little spark before a great flame is kindled that will be all-destroying. And better, far better, to decide the conflict between labor and capital with ballots instead of bullets, before it is too late.[37]

Thus, Allen and other writers in the *Farmer's Wife* proved themselves to be rhetors no less forceful than their Populist brothers. "The connecting theme that does appear throughout the paper," writes Brady, "is an image of women exercising power both in their homes and in their communities. For the contributors to the *Farmer's Wife*, as for other women activists of the era," she continues, "the problems that both women and society faced were to be overcome by women assuming power in both the private world of the family and the public world of politics."[38]

The aim of these essays and articles was to raise a collective consciousness of woman's general oppression, to develop a sense of common identity, and ultimately to motivate action for social change. Women on the prairie had envisioned themselves as alone, isolated both geographically and intellectually, and without power to improve the condition of their class, their families, and themselves. The women whose speeches and articles appeared in the *Farmer's Wife* sought to create an alternative rhetorical vision of woman empowered to act, in her traditional role as mother as well as in the political arena, to effect social change.

To credit the *Farmer's Wife* alone with attracting significant numbers of Kansas farm women to the suffrage and Populist movements is problematic. Surely other factors also served that function. But those women did become active participants. Brady concludes that "women were reported as serving as local officers in Alliance organizations and speaking at Alliance meetings throughout Kansas. Accounts and letters of women who were traveling as lectures for the Alliance cause were printed regularly in the *Farmer's Wife*."[39] And Elizabeth N. Barr, herself a member of the Kansas Farmers' Alliance, explained that "[Alliance] women with skins tanned to parchment by the hot winds, with bony hands of toil and clad in faded calico, could talk in meeting, and could talk right straight to the point."[40] That the *Farmer's Wife* helped those women first to envision themselves in such roles, and then actually to enact them, seems certain.

Another indication of the effectiveness of those efforts was the appearance of debunking strategies in the *Farmer's Wife*. Self-assured and active in the campaign, women set out to poke fun at their opponents. At times, man's arguments and man himself were held up to ridicule and scorn. On the editorial page of the June 1894 issue, a supposed letter to the editor entitled "An Eye-Opener" appeared over the signature of one "Zacharian Hardhack." It was a sarcastic, hilarious parody of the opponents of suffrage and feminism:

Dear Sur:—My woman she sampled a hull lot o' papers til she finally settled down 'pon yourn as bein' the most practical, so I let her hev the money fer to git it rite along, an' I hev been readin' of late the wimmins talks, which 'pears to me as sumwhat nonsensical—nothin' to be wondered at, howsomever, for it sint, an' never kin be, wimmins spear to rite for the papers, an' they allus make a mess on't if they try. But I've been thinkin' o' givin' in a few o' my ideas, which I'm sure'll prove a sort o' eye opener to these misguided sistern. I, for one'd just like to go back to the good old days when wimmin knowed their place.[41]

Juxtaposed against the rhetoric of Allen, Garside, McCormick, and the others, and even against Lathrop's home kindergarten, old Zacharian's ideas were "eye-opening" indeed!

Conclusion

Efforts of Kansas woman's rights advocates to gather support for woman suffrage were partly successful. The state legislature placed a suffrage referendum on the ballot for the 1894 election. In June of that year, the People's party of Kansas drafted a platform plank supporting the amendment. That action sparked a flurry of prosuffrage activity in the *Farmer's Wife*. But Populist victories in the elections of 1890 and 1892 in Kansas had been accomplished through cooperation or "fusion" between Populists and Democrats, for whom woman suffrage was anathema. When the Populists declared for woman suffrage in 1894, the Democrats walked out of the coalition. As a result, Kansas Republicans swept nearly every race, and the woman suffrage amendment was rejected. With that defeat, the *Farmer's Wife* ceased publication.

Nevertheless, the *Farmer's Wife* stands as an interesting and illustrative case study of the effort of farm women to gain equal rights in the nineteenth century. Their efforts to raise a prairie consciousness represented a distinct application of consciousness-raising strategies. Through the articles, essays, speeches, and letters published in the *Farmer's Wife*, woman herself became proof of the claims she raised. She enacted the role that was her primary aim: personhood. She became an advocate, capable as any man. She argued for woman suffrage and woman's rights. By linking her natural rights as a person and a citizen to the cause of Populism, she produced discourse unique to the woman's rights movement on the prairie. The *Farmer's Wife* filled a gap left by the mainstream suffrage press. Both argued for suffrage and woman's rights. But the *Farmer's Wife* adapted those arguments to the particular needs of frontier farm women.

The *Woman's Exponent*, 1872–1914

Champion for "The Rights of the Women of Zion, and the Rights of the Women of All Nations"

Tarla Rai Peterson

> Woman feels her servitude, her degradation, and she is determined
> to assert her rights, to attain to an equality with man, and to train
> herself to fill any position and place of trust and honor as
> appropriately and with as much dignity as her brother man. . . .
> Her highest motive is, that she may be recognized as a
> responsible being, capable of judging for and maintaining herself.
> (1 July 1877, 20)

From 1872 to 1914, the *Woman's Exponent* agitated for woman's right to "be recognized as a responsible being." The paper sought to accomplish this task by replacing the four cardinal feminine virtues of piety, purity, submissiveness, and domesticity with a triumvirate: piety, purity, and independence. To accomplish this, the *Exponent* argued that piety and purity were incompatible with submissiveness, and only inconsequentially related to domesticity. Because they were Mormons, most *Exponent* readers were simultaneously involved in two social movements, and their experiences in one movement increased their self-perception as potential activists in the other. Their allegiance to the Mormon religion had led to virtual expulsion from American society, while their practice of plural marriage had inculcated the principle of civil disobedience into their lives. Thus, the *Exponent* had only to articulate what Mormon women already believed: neither piety nor purity would be obtained by submissiveness. Once this connection had been severed, readers were encouraged to become "real," instead of "true," women by joining the ranks of the suffragists. The paper's rhetoric encouraged Mormon women to view themselves as heroines whose collective participation in the public sphere could produce a new society.

Beginnings

The idea for a Utah woman's paper was conceived in 1871, when Edward L. Sloan, editor of the Salt Lake *Herald*, suggested establishing a woman's column, edited by a woman, in the *Herald*. When the staff opposed Sloan's idea, he decided to originate a separate woman's paper, which he named the *Woman's Exponent*. Sloan asked Louisa Lula Green, a frequent *Herald* contributor, to edit the paper.[1] Green established the *Exponent* as an eight-page journal of articles, poems, stories, letters, reports, and editorials, a general format that was retained throughout the paper's existence. The *Woman's Exponent* had only two editors: Louisa Green Richards (married Levi W. Richards in 1873), from 1872 to 1877; and Emmeline Woodward Wells, from 1877 to 1914. In October 1873, Cornelia H. Horne was listed as business manager, and a female "Committee of Consultation" was formed. In November of 1875, Cornelia Horne's name was dropped, and Emmeline B. Woodward Wells appeared as associate editor. Two years later, Woodward Wells became editor and, over the years, publisher, business manager, and owner.[2]

Because no papers regarding the business affairs of the *Exponent* are known to have survived, circulation is difficult to ascertain. Readership was somewhat larger than circulation would indicate because copies were shared within polygamous families, and it was discussed in woman's meetings.[3] In 1880, Woodward Wells wrote that only five hundred new subscribers would bring solvency to the paper (1 June 1880, 4). Inducements to subscribers included a sewing machine for each club or one hundred names (15 April 1873, 172). In 1885, the *American Newspaper Directory* estimated its circulation between five hundred and one thousand, and in 1888, the *Pacific States Newspaper Directory* listed it at four thousand. Although the paper may not have reached the four thousand mark, its circulation did peak during the late 1880s.[4] In 1899, Woodward Wells wrote that in order for the paper to continue, at least one-tenth of the thirty thousand members of the Relief Society (the benevolent society to which female members of the Mormon Church, as well as a few other Utah women, belonged) must subscribe with cash payments (1 January 1899, 84). Although she continued to publish the *Exponent* for another fifteen years, the once biweekly publication gradually reduced its issue. The final volume, covering an eighteen-month period (September 1912 to February 1914) contained only thirteen issues.[5] Despite its relatively small circulation, the paper was well known throughout the Utah Territory and reached a readership in other parts of the country through its exchanges with non-Utah papers.

A prospectus announcing the new woman's paper stated that the *Exponent* would discuss "every subject interesting and valuable to women, . . . defend the right, inculcate sound principles and disseminate useful knowledge." It would also facilitate the work of the woman's Relief Society. Because Utah women had been granted suffrage in 1870, Sloan assumed the *Exponent* would not focus on "that pet subject with most woman's papers."[6] However, the first issue inaugurated an advocacy for woman suffrage that continued throughout the paper's existence. Finally, the *Exponent* would enable Mormon women, who had been "grossly misrepresented through the press," to express their point of view. For "who are so able to speak for the women of Utah as the women of Utah themselves? . . . For these reasons . . . the publication of the *Woman's Exponent*, a journal owned by, controlled by, and edited by Utah ladies has been commenced" (1 June 1872, 8).

While enjoying harmonious relations with the Mormon ecclesiastic hierarchy, the paper was printed at the *Herald* offices rather than at the offices of the church-owned *Deseret Weekly*. It was produced independently by women, with long-term employees limited to women typesetters. Moreover, it was financially sustained by subscriptions and occasional share purchases by interested women.[7] Women also provided financial assistance in order to initiate publication. Louisa Green wrote of an unusual cake that was served at a surprise party given by one Salt Lake City woman's group: "When I cut the 'Cake' . . . some of the sisters kept cautioning me against cutting too far into the center. But being in utter ignorance of their meaning I cut too far and to my surprise the greenbacks began to stick out, and the sisters who were watching my delight crowded them back; and I desisted in astonishment."[8] The cake, which had been filled with cash, rather than cake batter, represented the group's fund-raising efforts.

"To Speak for the Women of Utah"

The *Exponent* systematically urged both men and women to view woman as "a responsible being, capable of judging for and maintaining herself." Woodward Wells wrote that "we have grown tired, as

Mrs. Stanton pertinently remarks, of being classed with idiots, luna-tics, and criminals" (1 March 1880, 146). This perspective led both to an advocacy for expanding woman's spheres, and a defense of the Mormon woman's "right" to practice plural marriage, a fundamen-tal tenet of her faith.

Determined to offer "every subject interesting and valuable to women," the *Exponent* included an assortment of materials, unified in their attention to "women's issues." A major portion of each is-sue was devoted to letters from readers, articles (including poetry) from correspondents, and minutes or reports from the Mormon Relief Societies and Retrenchment Associations (young woman's social reform organizations). Typical topics were suffrage, equal op-portunity for women, polygamy, family life, home manufacturing, religious doctrine, nature, travel, and notable women. In addition, most issues contained at least two editorials advocating the ex-pansion of "woman's sphere," with the most common topics being suffrage, polygamy, woman's education, and woman's career oppor-tunities. Politics, social reform, and Christian virtues appeared oc-casionally. Reprints of articles from other publications, most often the *Woman's Journal*, filled several columns. News events, es-pecially those concerning women and their advancement in non-traditional roles, were reported with liberal doses of editorial comment. Household hints, recipes, or brief anecdotes were occa-sionally used as fillers, and the back page consisted mostly of adver-tisements.[9]

The *Exponent* identified with the woman's movement but gave woman's rights an unusual theological twist. Green Richards imme-diately imbued it with a sense of mission that established its unique character. In 1877, she claimed that the *Exponent* "not only finds its way into the homes of the people of this Territory, but it has gone as a glad messenger of salvation to some of the most remote quarters of the globe" (1 June 1877, 4; 15 May 1881, 188). Woodward Wells, who replaced Green Richards in 1877, wrote that women could record the "work of reformation" in the columns of the *Exponent*.

The *Exponent*'s editorial stance derived largely from the experi-ences of Emmeline B. Woodward Wells, who edited the paper for thirty-seven years. Her commitment to woman's "right to choose for herself" stemmed largely from her own experiences.[10] Wood-ward Wells, who joined the Mormon church at age fourteen, was deserted by her first husband, became a plural wife at age seventeen, and eventually came to depend on the *Exponent* as the primary source of income for herself and her five daughters. In 1883, she recorded in her diary, "I have been trying very hard to get some ad-vertisements to help out my paper. . . . It is quite necessary that I should make an extra exertion to keep up or I shall not be able to live in the manner we do now."[11] The forced independence Woodward Wells experienced strengthened her conviction that women should prepare themselves to be self-sustaining, emotionally as well as economically, by enlarging their spheres of experience. In her valedictory editorial, the eighty-four-year-old Woodward Wells wrote, "We love women and would ever strive to uplift and help them attain their ideas."[12] She used the *Woman's Exponent* as an outlet for her desire to advance the cause of woman's independence.

The *Exponent's* simultaneous promotion of polygamy and suffrage as woman's "rights" reflected the concerns of both its editor and readership. According to the *Exponent*, woman's position as an adult member of American society should guarantee her freedom to practice her religion and to select her political representatives. Utah women had been granted suffrage in 1870, two years before the *Exponent* commenced publication. Rather than seeking initial enfranchisement, most *Exponent* readers first fought a losing battle to prevent disfranchisement, then struggled to regain that lost right. By 1872, polygamy and woman's suffrage were hopelessly entangled, for congressional antipolygamy bills invariably included a clause removing suffrage from Utah women. The Utah "woman question" was difficult for suffragists to answer, for while most woman's rights advocates outside Utah considered polygamy demeaning to women, they were loath to support measures intended to strip Utah women of their suffrage.

Both *Exponent* editors assumed that their readers would "lead the van in the questions which are being agitated among the sex," for unlike other woman's journals, the *Exponent* would be "actuated by the spirit of a religion embodying all the grandest and holiest principles that have ever been revealed from heaven" (1 June 1877, 4; 1 June 1878, 4). This sense of religious mission infused every issue. For example, Green Richards responded to requests to desist writing about polygamy because "it is offensive," and "not a fitting subject for a woman's pen, it is too indelicate," by proclaiming that "sincerity and conviction" bade her continue (1 May 1876, 181).

The paper was primarily exhortative, avoiding sentimentality and romance. It owed "its origin to the exigencies of the 'Mormon' faith, to its enlarged conceptions of 'woman's mission,' and practical development of woman's work. . . . No love-sick heroines or heroes there, with suggestive sentiment and highly colored obtrusiveness."[13] The paper's moralistic and didactic tone comported well with the lofty mission envisioned by its editors.

Editorials, articles, and even poetry presented woman suffrage as a moral issue that all intelligent beings would support. Arguments against woman suffrage and other expansions of woman's sphere were often satirized. "Do-gooders" were told that most plural wives had no desire to be freed from their "bondage," and columns were devoted to explaining polygamy's relative advantages when compared to most monogamous situations. Should these arguments fall on deaf ears, *Exponent* authors pled with antipolygamy agitators to consider that women had far more to lose than men if polygamous marriages were invalidated.

Throughout its history, the journal emphasized its value to its readers; both editors constantly reminded Utah women about the benefits deriving from a woman's paper. Editorials argued that the *Exponent* facilitated the progress of woman's work in Utah, provided a channel of communication with other women, and kept Utah women posted on various woman's organizations. They also claimed that the *Exponent* was a woman's industry that deserved support through both literary contributions and subscriptions.[14]

The editors argued that it was imperative for Mormon women to support the organ that enabled them to answer attacks directed against polygamy. Green Richards told readers that the *Exponent* gave them "a power that was being felt far and wide" (1 June 1877, 4). In 1896, Woodward Wells wrote that "the prestige the *Exponent* has given the women of the Church in the outside world is little realized; it has broken down mountains of prejudice" (1 and 15 November 1896, 68). "Through its columns the sisters . . . have spoken to the world, as they could not have done in any other way, . . . giving evidence of their liberty of thought and action, and their religious sincerity" (15 May 1880, 188).

The *Exponent* also became an organ for disseminating Relief Society news and instruction. Relief Society presidents were urged to subscribe and to solicit subscriptions in their geographical areas. The *Exponent* advocated and reported Relief Society projects, including home nursing and midwifery courses, the Deseret Hospital, sericulture, grain purchase and storage, and the Woman's Commission Store (an outlet for the sale of home-manufactured products).[15] Eliza R. Snow, influential "president of all the female Relief Societies," also supported the paper and publicly urged women to subscribe.[16]

Finally, Woodward Wells continually reiterated the value of the *Exponent* as a history of Utah women. She claimed that the *"Woman's Exponent* [would] furnish good material for future historians . . . not only concerning woman's work, industrial and educational, but the lives of the women" (July 1911, 4). Woodward Wells wrote indignantly that "judging from [history], one would suppose [women's] lives were insignificant and their opinions worthless."

The *Exponent* would correct this error, ensuring that "historians of the present age will find it very embarrassing to ignore woman" (1 March 1888, 148).

Because of its value to women and its function for the Mormon community, sustaining the paper was a duty as well as a privilege. Woodward Wells asserted that women who failed to subscribe "were in many respects blind to their own best and highest interest" (1 and 15 July 1893, 4). After receiving a request to provide copies of the *Exponent* for the 1900 World Exposition at Paris, she expressed the hope that "the sisters will not feel after this that the *Exponent* is of little or no consequence" (15 August 1898, 29).

The Function of the *Exponent* for Its Audience

Because of the *Exponent*'s close ties to the Mormon community, understanding its function for its readers requires consideration of its roles both in relation to its audience as church women and as suffrage supporters. For the most part, its readers shared a deep commitment to each other and an awareness of themselves as independent agents. Contrary to what one might expect, Mormon women needed less empowering than their non-Mormon counterparts, for Mormon women participated in religious decision making and activity more directly than most Victorian women. Their involvement in building a frontier "kingdom" led to concern with many women's issues and, ultimately, to promotion of woman suffrage. Because Mormon women were not conceptually submissive to males, replacing the "true" woman's submissiveness with the "real" woman's independence did not represent a radical departure from cultural norms.

Mormon women's perceptions of their role contrasted sharply with those of their contemporaries. First, although current Mormon doctrine limits priesthood to males, the women who read the *Exponent* were, both ideologically and practically, coparticipants in priesthood authority. In 1878, Sarah M. Kimball, who had initiated the organization of the Relief Society, told her sisters that when Mormon women had asked church president Joseph Smith to bestow institutional legitimacy upon a woman's organization, he responded "that he was glad to have the opportunity of organizing the women, as part of the priesthood belonged to them."[17] The sisters later invited Smith to advise them regarding woman's role in healing the sick (a formal priesthood function): "Regarding the female laying on hands he further remarked there could be no devil in it if God gave his sanction by healing, that there could be no more sin in any female laying hands on the sick than in wetting the face with water."[18] Frequent testimonials "to the healing of the sick by the administrations of the sisters" in meeting minutes, diaries, and letters attest that women regularly participated in such activities.[19]

Moreover, Mormon women had been legitimized in seeking equality with men by a singular interpretation of Eve's fall. While Mormonism shares with other Christian fundamentalist religions the notion that woman became inferior to man by virtue of her fall in the Garden of Eden, Woodward Wells argued that since woman *became* inferior to man in the Garden, she had to have been created as his equal. The *Exponent* promulgated a concomitant doctrine that woman could effectuate her own redemption, thus returning to a state of equality with man, by obedience to divine law. Polygamy was one such divine law, and women, as well as men, experienced emotional conversions to "the principle."[20] Polygamy was therefore viewed as part of the "new era [that] has been ushered in, mainly through the exertions of self-made women, acted upon by an influence many comprehended not, which was working for the redemption [of women] from under the curse" (1 March 1881, 148).

Finally, early Mormon woman's rights activists saw woman's roles as wife, mother, citizen, and individual bound within the same framework of eternal order that bound man as husband, father, citizen, and individual. Thus, it was no more radical to advocate the development of woman to her highest potential than to advocate the same for man. More importantly, the distinctions between male and female spheres typical of Victorian America were impractical in polygamous Mormon society. Women retained title to property when they married; men who could afford to provide individual homes for their wives often transferred each dwelling's title to the wife. By the 1880s, vigorous prosecution of those who violated antipolygamy legislation had encouraged the development of an elaborate "underground" for Mormons who participated in plural marriage. With their husbands in hiding from federal marshals, women had assumed political control of many Utah communities. The experiential base of women who dominated the territory's medical profession (physicians as well as midwives) and served as teachers, writers, lawyers, and business managers provided *Exponent* readers with an unusually broad perspective on woman's sphere.[21]

The Exponent *and Plural Marriage*

Central to the Mormon faith, and particularly important to women, polygamy became a vital issue for the *Exponent* and its readers. For the devout Mormon woman, celestial (plural) marriage symbolized divine law, whereby she could achieve self-redemption. Thus, her animosity toward those who interfered with her agency in this matter assumed Promethean dimensions. From its public avowal in 1852, social and political pressure against plural marriage steadily mounted. In 1882, the Utah Commission was created to ensure prosecution of polygamists. The final antipolygamy law, the Edmunds-Tucker Act of 1887, disfranchised all who had ever practiced polygamy. Thus, Mormons, and especially Mormon women, faced a critical period during the decade of the 1880s. Not until 1890, when Wilford Woodruff, president of the Mormon Church, issued the "Manifesto" suspending plural marriage, did the *Exponent's* support of the practice cease.[22]

The *Exponent* vigorously defended plural marriage on the editorial page and in letters from Utah women. Woodward Wells editorialized about polygamy's divine origin, its constitutionality, its biblical precedence, its social value, its emancipating structure, and its elevating influence on society. She wrote that plural marriage gave women "more time for thought, for mental culture, more freedom of action, a broader field of labor, and inculcated liberality and generosity" (15 August 1876, 44).

While the *Exponent* never denied the supremacy of man as head of the household, woman was described as a partner rather than a subservient and passive possession. It argued for woman's emancipation from unjustified restraints within the traditional monogamous relationship, by restructuring power and position within the marriage institution. Woodward Wells visualized a marital partnership where "each partner granted to the other the same freedom of thought, feeling and expression" (15 February 1878, 140). Although non-Mormon woman's rights activists disagreed, *Exponent* authors maintained that plural marriage represented an innovation that gave unprecedented advantage to women. "Plural marriage," one wrote, "makes woman more the companion and much less the subordinate than any other form of marriage" (1 September 1877, 54). Letters from readers presented a more militant defense of the Mormon woman's right to judge for herself. One reader warned potential philanthropists: "When men talk of helping 'Mormon' women to free themselves from thralldom and oppression, they talk the veriest nonsense. 'Mormon' women do not need their aid: with the same courage and fortitude, which helped them to brave the wilderness and desert . . . they are still endowed; their courage does not falter, and they are not easily intimidated" (1 February 1881, 182). Another letter, signed by "Sarah M." (probably Sarah M. Kimball, a leading Utah suffragist and Mormon religious leader), demonstrates the unusual mixture of religious fervor and satire found in many *Exponent* articles. Sarah first ridiculed the intelligence of those who supported antipolygamy legislation, then pled with them for mercy, and finally prophesied their eventual destruction:

So the deed is done, the Edmund's [sic] bill has received the royal signature. And our doom is sealed . . . by our wonderful wise legislators. . . . Have we not suffered enough in being driven from our homes into the desert, that they must still follow us and hunt us down as they do wild savage beasts, who are not fit to dwell upon this beautiful earth. Have we not a right to the air we breathe? . . . Let us stand firm and unflinching to the cause we have espoused . . . and although the wicked may rage and struggle to overthrow this work, their plans will be thwarted, and the arm paralysed [sic] that fights against the people of God. Our course is onward and upward, and no power on earth can prevail against us. (15 April 1882, 171)

Antipolygamy laws simply represented a continuation of the persecutions Sarah had survived in Illinois and Missouri. Although she and other Mormon women would continue to endure, the *Exponent* ensured that they would no longer suffer alone or in silence.

As legal prosecutions of polygamists escalated, the *Exponent* chronicled arrests, trials, and incarcerations of leading Mormon males. Women's arrests were reported in vivid detail. In 1885, an article listed the names of female "political prisoners," two with infants, who were serving in the Utah penitentiary for refusing to testify against their husbands (15 July 1885, 28).

When Belle Harris and her baby were imprisoned for refusing to testify, letters of indignation came from throughout the territory and beyond. A monogamous wife by the name of "Mary" wrote:

I am brim full [sic] of contempt and disgust . . . and if you can find or imagine any words which can more fully express my contempt consider them said. Don't talk about the Spanish Inquisition or the Star Chamber after this abuse of an innocent woman. . . . [Federal officials] drag women and babes from their homes and put them in prison without trial of any kind, because they refuse to answer impudent questions; . . . [These officials state that] we mean to pop all women into the Penitentiary who have children in the marriage relation that we don't approve of; we will confiscate all your property we desire; . . . we will degrade your children; . . . we will heap insult on insult upon you until you revolt, then we will call on the military to exterminate you; mobs have killed your prophets, your men, women and children before, and may do so again. . . . We are going to get rid of you now. (1 August 1883, 38)

Mary then added a warning to the offending officials that "the cup of sorrow you are pressing to the lips of the Latter-day Saints [Mormons] you shall drain to the dregs, for . . . the measure you give you shall receive."

These women organized protest meetings throughout Utah, culminating in the spring of 1886 at a "great mass meeting, held in the theatre," in Salt Lake City. The meeting's proclaimed intent, to "protest against the tyranny and indecency of Federal Officials in Utah, and against their own disfranchisement without cause," illustrates the constant interconnection between polygamy and woman suffrage in Utah. Women from throughout Utah attended the meeting, which was reported (both favorably and unfavorably) by the regional press. The female participants informed "gentiles" that plural wives would not "sit quietly down, like slaves, and see our rights taken from us, our characters maligned and insults heaped upon us, all because of religion, the free exercise of which is guaranteed to us by the glorious Constitution."[23] The *Exponent*'s detailed coverage of such meetings attempted to assure outsiders that the "victims" of polygamy needed no assistance. Rather, they demanded the right to make their own judgments and accepted the responsibility of living with the consequences of those judgments.

The *Exponent*'s defense against the antipolygamy crusade spread a mantle of martyrdom over plural wives, which projected a self-image of valiant heroism. Rather than slaves of an archaic system, Mormon women became political activists invested with a sense of divine approbation. Thus, the *Exponent*'s rhetoric, although failing to sustain polygamy, created for Mormon women a heroic self-image that helped them survive the temporary disfranchisement, continued social stigmatization, and permanent dissolution of legal family ties that accompanied its demise.

The Exponent *and Other Women's Issues*

This sense of mission carried over into other aspects of woman's rights and responsibilities. The *Exponent* advocated advanced education as a duty incumbent upon all women, because it was the best means for developing one's latent capacities. An educated woman was better able to judge for herself when faced with the expanding array of options she would find available in the future. Education was essential both for a mother to act intelligently within her own home and for a woman to influence society positively. Through the education of women, the "entire world could realize a higher civilization" ("Progress of Women in the Last Seventy Years," February 1912, 44).

Though exercising care not to denigrate traditionally established roles for women, Woodward Wells continually urged women who chose to devote themselves to the roles of mother and wife to be more than a "toy," a "painted doll," or a "household deity" (1 November 1874, 82). The *Exponent* argued that since many of the world's evils resulted from weakness in the home: "In the name of justice, reason, and common sense, woman should be fortified and strengthened by every possible advantage that she may be adequately and thoroughly fitted not only to grace the drawing room, and manage every department of her household but to perform with skill and wisdom the arduous and elaborate work of molding and fashioning the fabric of which society is to be woven" ("Progress of Women in the Last Seventy Years," February 1912, 44). Another article explained that traditional life choices were counterproductive for some women: "If there be some woman in whom the love of learning extinguishes all other love, then the heaven-appointed sphere of that woman is not the nursery. It may be the library, the laboratory, the observatory" (1 April 1873, 163). Thus, although domesticity remained a viable alternative, it was neither a sufficient nor necessary requirement for woman.

The *Exponent* responded in mock humility to statements that woman's small brain made education too strenuous by explaining that "as we belong to that unfortunate class whose brain is deficient in weight, we would like to ask the learned philosopher whether the superior intellect consists in the quantity or quality." Readers were asked to "compare the reign of [Queen Victoria] with that of the kings who preceded her, and see if her success . . . will not encourage those who are deficient in weight of intellect to cultivate that organ, the brain" (15 January 1884, 121). The paper argued that although women had been forced to contend with more hindrances than men in developing their abilities, removing these obstacles would prove their capability and benefit all humanity.

Readers were repeatedly reassured that by expanding their education they would neither lose their feminine charm nor limit themselves to spinsterhood. In fact, their marriages would be more fulfilling, for "the wife who can talk intelligently with her husband . . . may keep him at home occasionally." Additionally, men who were desirable as husbands preferred an intelligent spouse. Women were exhorted to seek such men, for "as for men loving women more who know very little, who are submissive and inferior, who have no positive opinions of their own, why they are certainly inferior men, and it is not that class of men that strong minded women would choose for husbands, so they need give themselves no uneasiness on the subject at all" (1 December 1883, 100).

The *Exponent* also advocated woman's right to choose employment even when financial support from her husband or father was available. Woodward Wells reveled in the possibility of "intelligent, cultivated women" stepping into avenues of employment and "actually earning money of their own" (15 May 1883, 188). Although the economics of Utah life dictated that most people's employment responded directly to immediate economic needs, Woodward Wells dreamed of a time when women's professions would transcend the bounds of economic necessity.

For such transcendence to occur, Woodward Wells wrote, woman must "have access to every avenue of employment. [However,] Custom has said that woman must only earn a living by a few circumscribed modes of employment" (1 June 1872, 2). To enlarge the sphere of professional options considered by its readers, articles detailing the achievements of women as doctors, lawyers, educators, politicians, journalists, and artists and in other nondomestic roles filled the pages of the *Exponent*. Editorials decrying the prejudice that intimidated other women from following similar professions pointed out that this was not only detrimental to woman, but to the whole of society. They argued that "a monarchy may prescribe women in her rights, and perhaps survive, but a republic cannot afford to let half its intellect and morality lie fallow" (1 March 1880, 146). One article suggested that the best means of determining which professions were appropriate for women was to "give them their choice. . . . If there are branches of knowledge improper for women to learn or duties unfit to perform, they will know it a thousand times better than men" (1 April 1873, 163). Women who devoted their lives to "domestic" pursuits were only featured if their "fierce independence" led to incarceration as political prisoners. Thus, domesticity, although harmless, became an insignificant characteristic of womanhood.

In the *Exponent*'s first issue, Woodward Wells began arguing that men and women should receive equal renumeration for labor performed or service rendered. She wrote that custom "says that if a woman does as much work as a man, and does it as well, she must not receive equal pay for it, and herein a wrong is inflicted upon her by the deprivation of a right to which she is justly entitled" (1 June 1873, 2). One tongue-in-cheek article suggested that women become gardeners, because "a peck of peas has a certain market value not depending upon the hands which raised them. . . . A man who would sell a beet is not obliged to put on a label, 'raised by a man, ten cents,' and upon another, 'raised by a woman, four cents'" (15 March 1874, 155). The article then provided practical information on how to set up a gardening business.

In 1879, Woodward Wells expressed guarded optimism regarding possible improvement in the area of equal compensation for work done. Plural wives often assumed the economic responsibility for their homes, as well as operating and managing farms, retail establishments, hospitals, and other businesses throughout Utah. Given this exposure, the *Exponent* conjectured that "as women become more conversant with business matters and step out of the kitchen now and then . . . these evils [inequities between compensation for men and women] which exist today may in a great measure be eradicated" (1 October 1879, 68).

The *Exponent*'s statements regarding the debilitating results of unjust compensation extended beyond local concerns. In 1902, Woodward Wells published excerpts of a University of Chicago graduate student's study on the deplorable conditions and starvation wages imposed upon women and immigrants working in the garment factories (15 May 1902, 108). The paper agitated for "woman's" issues, such as support for public education, minimum wage laws, woman and child labor laws, extension of property rights to women, and legitimization of children from polygamous marriages.

The Exponent *and the National Suffrage Movement*

Besides providing a focus for the opinions and activities of Utah women, the *Exponent* also kept them apprised of national developments of the woman's movement, which focused increasingly on suffrage. By 1872, when the *Exponent* began publication, the woman's rights movement had separated into two factions. Although Woodward Wells, her paper, and her people were rejected by the more conservative American Woman Suffrage Association (AWSA), the *Exponent* regularly used material from the *Woman's Journal* and reported on Lucy Stone's public appearances. Woodward Wells attempted to familiarize her readers with women such as Susan B. Anthony, Elizabeth Cady Stanton, and the Reverend Anna Shaw by writing life sketches as well as reporting their activities relating to woman suffrage.

The *Exponent* became increasingly involved with national women's organizations through Woodward Wells's participation in the National Woman's Suffrage Association (NWSA). In January 1878, she sent a petition supporting adoption of a woman suffrage amendment to Washington. Her efforts in securing thirteen thousand signatures from enfranchised women were acknowledged by Sarah Andrews Spencer, secretary of the NWSA.[24] In 1879, when she represented Utah women at the NWSA convention in Washington, D.C., the *Exponent* devoted several issues to the convention. Nine articles and four editorials regarding suffrage and other "woman's issues" discussed at the convention were supplemented by human interest stories about the participants.

The NWSA conventions were occasions for suffragists to lobby Congress for an equal suffrage amendment and to support Utah women against congressional measures to disfranchise them through antipolygamy legislation. Although Anthony and Cady Stanton's willingness to accept Mormon women won Woodward Wells's unqualified allegiance, more conservative woman's rights activists expressed anger and disbelief. When leaders of the AWSA criticized the NWSA for allowing Mormon women to attend their convention, Cady Stanton retorted that "if George Q. Cannon can sit in the Congress of the United States without compromising that body on the question of Polygamy . . . I should think Mormon women might sit on our platform without making us responsible for their religious faith" (15 May 1879, 240). Thus, in the *Exponent*, suffrage and polygamy were inextricably linked and arguments in behalf of one carried overtones of the other.

After 1879, Woodward Wells regularly attended meetings and presented reports from Utah for the NWSA, the International Council of Women, and National Council of Women. In 1891, she represented Utah at the National Council of Women, and in 1902, she became the first western woman to hold an executive office in the council.[25] All the details of these gatherings were reported in the *Exponent*. Woodward Wells's experiences in the national women's organizations reinforced her conviction that women were capable of altering social tradition and thus effecting the work of reformation. She wrote: "Women can teach publicly on the platform, not only commonplace matters . . . but also can expound doctrine and principle. Evidently superior women are becoming lights to the world; they are no longer hid away in a corner knitting or darning stockings . . . but they stand up and proclaim great moral and spiritual truths" (1 May 1891, 164).

Although the *Exponent* took the "woman question" seriously, some levity can be found in articles combining support for woman suffrage and polygamy. For example: "The Rev. J. D. Fulton regards polygamy as far more scriptural than woman suffrage; and the agitation of the latter, he alleges, causes a great decrease in the number of boy babies. This is a serious matter; for if the theory be correct, the agitation will have to be stopped by granting the right of suffrage to the women or polygamy may become compulsory in another generation or so" (15 March 1873, 161). In reply to congressmen who justified disfranchising Utah women because they had shown "weakness" in failing to vote against polygamy, one article stated:

If these same women would cast the ballot for the men who come here and call them fools, ignorant dupes, and their children a name one does not like to soil the paper with, then, I suppose, they would be counted brave and intelligent. . . . So far from relinquishing their own right to vote . . . they are all the time working in the interests of equal political rights for all women; and furthermore, have interceded with the Legislature to so revise the Statutes of Utah as to make women eligible to office. . . . We trust this will not wound the sensitive feelings of Mr. Cassidy [Congressional representative from Nevada]. (1 December 1888, 100)

After the abandonment of polygamy opened the way for Utah statehood, the *Exponent* endorsed woman suffrage in the Utah State Convention. The success of the Utah Woman Suffrage Association in obtaining affirmative commitments from most delegates and woman suffrage planks on all party platforms was due largely to the efforts of Woodward Wells, president of the Utah Woman Suffrage Association, and her associates. The *Exponent* chronicled their efforts in detail.

As the energies and strategies of the woman's movement outside of Utah focused more on the single issue of suffrage, it quite expectedly assumed dimensions of unlimited power and possibility. The *Exponent* never succumbed to the illusion that suffrage would ameliorate all of the ills of society or open every door to women. Instead, Woodward Wells saw the apathy of woman and the power of tradition as the two greatest restraints on her freedom. She wrote that without constant vigilance on the part of woman, the ballot was merely a "shadow without the substance" (1 March 1880, 146; 1 July 1882, 17, 18). The *Exponent* suggested that women vote as a block, run for public office (and support woman candidates), and demand social improvements.

Rather than an end in itself, suffrage was the means whereby woman could "exert an instrumentality in all departments" (15 February 1880, 140). The *Exponent* repeatedly urged women to exercise their right to vote frequently and responsibly. When Utah women were reenfranchised in 1897, the paper's masthead was changed to "The Ballot in the Hands of the Women of Utah Should be a Power to Better the Home, the State, and the Nation."

Conclusion

To a significant extent, the *Exponent* provided a power base from and through which female leadership in Utah functioned. Mormon women had found submissiveness to be incompatible with the values of piety and purity. Because their piety demanded that they develop independence, the *Exponent*'s call for an enlargement of woman's sphere filled an important developmental need.

Woodward Wells's personal diary illustrates the progress from a sense of isolation and weakness to a sense of emancipation and collective strength that many of these women experienced. For years, her diary included entries similar to the following excerpt written in 1874: "O if my husband could only love me even a little and not seem so perfectly indifferent to any sensation of that kind. . . . He is surrounded by love on every side, and I am cast out. O my poor aching heart, where shall it rest its burdens. . . . My heart is bleeding almost . . . and I have no one to go to for comfort or shelter, no strong arm to lean upon."[26] During the early 1880s, the loneliness was gradually replaced with other sensations. Her time was overfilled with work on the *Exponent*, organizing various women's groups, travel, and speaking at funerals, parties, and suffrage gatherings. She wrote in 1888 of an occasion when she provided her home as a place of refuge from federal marshals in order for "the most genial of [her] associates," Romania B. Pratt, to spend a night with her husband, Charles W. Penrose. However, the evening was disturbed when Romania, a physician, was called out to care for a patient. In 1890, she found it difficult to devote time to her husband when he visited, because she "had to wait on so many people. . . . [She was also] trying to get off [her] mail and rush the girls up with the other paper."[27] One can assume that other stalwarts shared Woodward Wells's early sense of isolation. However, the *Exponent*, as self-appointed representative of independent women provided unflagging support for their endeavors.

The cause espoused by the *Exponent* centered around piety, and although its rhetorical messages were similar to those of the national proponents of woman's rights, motivations derived from different sources. The rhetorical challenge faced by a woman's paper published in Utah Territory's cultural milieu was to discover a means for celebrating female independence without denigrating female domesticity. The *Exponent* neutralized the four "cardinal virtues" defining woman's roles by articulating the incompatibility of piety and purity with submissiveness and then providing independence as a replacement for submissiveness. Given the new construct of independence, it made little sense to restrict woman's options by demanding that she demonstrate domesticity.

The *Exponent*'s strategy of associating piety with independence succeeded largely because it drew upon cultural resources unique to the Mormon community. These resources included woman's legitimization as man's equal in both religious and secular settings. Mormon women performed religious ordinances for the spiritual and temporal edification of other church members. They also wielded direct political and economic control in their communities. The paper, as a mainstream organ of Mormon culture, became a legitimate representative of Mormon women.

Because expanding woman's sphere was described as a service to all humanity, the *Exponent* emphasized integration when discussing the relationship between men and women, explaining: "Women have not asked for suffrage because of place or power, but that they may be acknowledged as being an equal in the work and business of the great world in which all must live and take part. . . . This great work can never be done well by one half of the human family; it is the opinion of all who think deeply that men and women must do the work together and unitedly" (15 September and 1 October 1897, 196). An article arguing for woman's right to choose employment from "among whatever legitimate courses present themselves" closed simply by stating that "men and women were not made to dwell separate, but in the society of each other." Rather than expressing hostility toward the other "half of the human family," the *Woman's Exponent* hoped to enlist them in her cause—"That [woman] may be recognized as a responsible being, capable of judging for and maintaining herself" (15 May 1873, 187).

The *Woman's Exponent* provides a rare example of an alliance between traditionalism and woman's rights activism. Advocating the unusual combination of polygamy and woman suffrage as basic "rights" provided the *Exponent* with difficult rhetorical constraints. On the one hand, its defence of Mormon plural marriage, a practice that non-Mormons described as debasing to women, appeared to confirm male domination in society. On the other hand, it advocated radical expansion of woman's political and economic spheres. Although the editors' insistent championing of a widely repudiated marriage system may have attenuated their argument for placing woman on equal political footing with men, it filled an important function. Women who first defended polygamy, and then established support networks for families of "reformed" polygamists, viewed themselves as more than victims of circumstance. By refusing to testify in court, going to prison, and defending their marriage system in various public forums, these women became each others heroines. Their discourse created images of valorous women who rescued their communities, schools, husbands, and children. These women identified with their sisters, turning the traditional tale of brave men protecting fragile women on its head. The *Exponent* empowered its readers by creating the (perhaps overly optimistic) expectation that woman's status would ultimately be determined by her own acts.

11

Evolving Rhetorical Strategies/ Evolving Identities

Linda Steiner

The reliance of American woman's rights advocates on their own periodicals for organizing and sustaining an entire social movement is clearly articulated in the introduction to this volume. The preceding chapters trace how journals published by women activists mixed various kinds of symbolic materials in order to attract and convert women readers and to bring them together as a community. Articles, editorials, and even fiction and poetry helped women to recognize their common oppression and the obstacles they confronted on account of their gender.

As Kohrs Campbell has observed, consciousness-raising was a primary rhetorical strategy for generating a sense of community within the woman's movement; she shows how this worked in speeches, debates, and public discussions.[1] Rhetors had a crucial role in helping women come to recognize their common problems, the educational and professional barriers they faced as women, and the mounting restrictions on their social and political activity. Furthermore, speakers could enact on the platform the "new woman" who could replace the "true woman" ideal. So aware were Anna Howard Shaw and other movement leaders of this task that they carefully chose both dress and hairstyle to demonstrate how the new woman could be different without appearing abrasive or "unwomanly."

The nineteenth-century woman's rights publications were also necessary, given that "new women" then had relatively few opportunities to meet in person, to see what these new women actually looked like. Local, state, and even national organizations sponsored speaking tours, meetings, and conventions, but these were hardly enough to support an emergent political movement, much less a cultural community just beginning to form itself. These publications dramatized what it was like to be a woman's rights activist and reassured readers they were not alone in taking on this identity. As such, their lives took on significance and purpose.

As different as their approaches and content were, these journals knit their readers into a cohesive community; they turned women who were widely dispersed and disparate in situation into sisters. In short, these periodicals engaged women in consciousness-raising and consciousness-changing, both individually and collectively. Readers testified in print that their publications transformed both their understanding of themselves as individuals and of women as a group. Readers marveled at how, in and by reading their own communications, they entered a whole new social landscape and committed themselves to a new way of being.

In discussing the functions that social movements must perform, Stewart, Smith, and Denton clarify the link between consciousness-raising and social action. Proponents of change must alter the self-perceptions of their followers, they explain, and must prescribe how to accomplish the goals they specify.[2] They conclude:

Social movements must attempt to alter self-perceptions of target audiences so that supporters and potential supporters come to believe in their self-worth and ability to bring about urgent change. Efforts such as replacing old labels attached to groups by their oppressors are designed to instill feelings of pride and power, to help audiences to discover themselves as substantial human beings. . . . Social movements often hope that self-discovery may result in a new "personal identity" and in the realization of "a people." Self-discovery is an important means of creating "we-they" distinctions and a basis of group identification through a sense of shared fate.[3]

As Edwin Black has insightfully noted, discourse not only conveys an image of the rhetor, what literary scholars call the persona of the author, but it also implies an auditor or reader who shares the rhetor's ideology. "The critic can see in the auditor implied by the discourse a model of what the rhetor would have his [sic] real auditor become."[4] Although Black focuses on this "second persona" to facilitate the critic's making moral judgments about discourse, the concept also describes the receiver's counterpart of enactment. Perceiving the implied characteristics of such an ideal receiver helps readers or listeners form new self-concepts. In this sense, creating a "second persona" is the obverse of consciousness-raising.

Woman's rights editors and publishers well understood the prescriptive elements of their descriptions of new women, at least of white, middle-class women. Pricking a sense of the dreariness and marginality of an older way of life achieves little unless audience members develop a sense of themselves as having purpose, responsibilities, abilities. Stimulating an awareness of shared difficulties and past oppression may even discourage audience members unless they develop an alternative image of themselves as agents of change. Woman's rights editors and their readers, then, together constructed the new women they would become.

The following discussion will try to elucidate several models that suffrage journals offered to women. A close reading suggests that the definition of the new woman was neither static nor monolithic but varied across space and over time. Editors and readers were often uncomfortable with the idea of criticizing other women; some opposed any open criticism of sister activists, especially when in full view of hostile antisuffragists. Nonetheless, outcroppings of open conflict within the suffrage movement suggest that opposing conceptions of the new woman were often explicitly contrasted. I argue that at least three distinct ideal types emerged in the woman's movement journals: a sensible woman, a strong-minded woman, and a responsible woman.

Recognizing this concern with establishing a new and more satisfying identity also helps explain the concern with suffrage. It explains why, united as activists were on such issues as suffrage, there were contradictory notions of why women ought to be enfranchised and of what they would do with the vote. As Kohrs Campbell emphasizes, once enfranchised, few women voted, and they tended not to vote as a bloc.[5] I argue that at the center of the debates over and within the suffrage movement was essentially and primarily a debate over how much and what kind of respect and honor the new woman deserved. Although the amendment did not engender a unified movement toward achieving fuller equality for women, it did symbolically and publicly mark—at the national level—the status of the version of new woman that had attracted the greatest number of adherents by the early twentieth century.

Again, the primary arena in which these new definitions were forged, articulated, and legitimized was necessarily the woman's rights press. Editors "tried out" several versions, sometimes hesitantly, sometimes aggressively. Writers and readers proposed and rejected, amended and refined, various conceptions of how a new woman talked and dressed, how she conducted her domestic and public life, how she judged others' actions, how she made decisions, and even how she named herself. The publications explained and justified different vocabularies, different rituals and symbols, different histories and futures, different villains and heroines, different political and personal strategies. One *Woman's Journal* writer aptly described suffrage periodicals as "our own camping ground . . . where we may indulge in private rehearsals and scan our own mistakes with a critical eye, the truest wisdom being not to 'pass our imperfections by.' "[6]

The Background of the Quest for a New Identity

If the quest for identity is, as Black says, a modern pilgrimage, woman's rights advocates were modern.[7] Certainly they were reacting to the challenges of modernity. They faced large-scale social, economic, political, and cultural upheavals that undermined the basis of social identity, which heretofore had been fairly stable, at least for middle-class women. The analysis presented here of the evolving definitions of and for a new woman depends, therefore, on a brief review of some of these nineteenth-century upheavals. First, population growth, due both to natural increases and then especially to immigration, eased the earlier problem of scarcity of labor, making women's nondomestic work decreasingly necessary. Both informal and institutionalized codes emerged in ways that began to differentiate proper and improper work roles for women. More critically, as factories increasingly depended on lower-class and immigrant people's (including, incidentally, women's) work, and as industrial technologies and products efficiently provided consumer goods, middle-class women were left without meaningful productive work. And the increasing separation of workplace and home required by the industrial model made informal training and involvement in work more difficult for women. Relative to men, then, women lost responsibility and status, a process Ann Douglas calls "disestablishment."[8]

Furthermore, while urbanization profoundly transformed American cultural life as a whole, it had peculiar impact on middle-class women. Already confined to the domestic sphere and confined to responsibilities that were more psychological and emotional than productive, middle-class women were now limited to smaller, more insular homes. Since in the urban context, large families were more a burden than a resource, they bore fewer children.

Finally, secularism, self-reliance, and self-improvement, as well as achievement marked by monetary reward, were being widely and loudly heralded as part of the emergent "modern" American culture. But these values were available exclusively to men. Certainly the egalitarian rhetoric about extension of the ballot did not apply to women. In sum, then, women were excluded from the values and achievements most celebrated and glorified by the culture; the economic activities and even many of the domestic responsibilities that had once provided the grounds for a meaningful identity became superfluous or trivial. At a time of intense political, social, and economic ferment, with exciting developments in science, religion, and philosophy, middle-class women were becoming all too aware of their increasing marginality. For some women, the dominant national rhetoric about women's special status as consumers, as upholders of morality and civility, and as mothers (the cult of "true womanhood") was pitifully insufficient consolation. No wonder that an early woman's rights activist asserted in the *Lily* that "there is a demand now for a new type of womanhood."[9] The rest of this chapter will be devoted to highlighting the various types of new womanhood suggested and celebrated in the *Lily* and the woman's rights papers discussed in previous chapters; other suffrage papers published at the time will be briefly mentioned.

The Sensible Woman as Reformer: The *Lily* and the *Una*

Hinck's chapter shows that as the *Lily*'s focus moved from temperance to woman's rights, the image of the ideal woman changed from one whose primary virtues are benevolence, piety, and nurturance to one capable of responsible action and intelligent analysis. Precisely because of its ambivalent relationship to the male-dominated temperance movement, especially at the early stages of its publication, the *Lily* lacked a clear picture of the woman for whom it spoke. But over time, Amelia Jenks Bloomer, Elizabeth Cady Stanton, and other *Lily* contributors came to articulate what I call "the sensible woman." The *Lily* began to provide historical and contemporary, as well as fictional, examples of women who were intelligent, self-reliant, and practical. Jenks Bloomer conceived of this new woman as energetic, healthy, and capable of considerable activity. In part, this "sensibility" was promoted and visibly symbolized by wearing sensible, practical dress; the "pantaloons" that quickly came to bear Bloomer's name were modeled for and by new women.

Bloomer and the other *Lily* writers skillfully contrasted this new woman with the older style, a conception they somewhat exaggerated in order to revile and repudiate it. They clearly distanced themselves from frivolous, simpering gossips who were both physically and mentally weak. As Cady Stanton wrote in the *Lily*, "I do hate a sickly, sentimental, half-developed, timid needle-loving woman."[10]

The *Una*'s audience, origins, and especially its lofty, philosophical literary tone differed markedly from the *Lily*'s. In fact, in an 1856 editorial announcing the purchase of the *Una*'s subscription list, the

Lily's editor explicitly distinguished the *Una*'s approach from her own, although noting that their cause was the same: while the *Lily* dealt primarily with "living active wrongs," the *Una* "dealt more with the principles and policy . . . in high-toned, scholastic essays. . . ."[11] On the other hand, like Jenks Bloomer, Paulina Wright Davis, having rejected prevailing models as unsatisfying and constraining, also lacked a precisely worked-out conception of the alternatives. My view is that she extended the scope of the sensible woman. As Tonn notes, the *Una*'s concerns included women's enfranchisement and active involvement in moral reform, as well as physical education and excercise, hygiene and nutrition. (Wright Davis was, however, unsympathetic toward dress reform.) This dramatized a commitment to a new woman who is first a clear thinker but also an energetic actor. This nascent ideal, too, was partly defined in terms of what the new woman is not. She is *not* submissive and silly. She is not dwarfed or silenced by an all-powerful and superior husband. A similarly poised, sensible woman, it may be added, was addressed around the same time by Elizabeth A. Aldrich, editor of the Cincinnati-based *Genius of Liberty*. Aldrich published an ambitious eighteen-point program that included not only suffrage but also equal rights, equal pay, coeducation, dress reform, and physical exercise. Her goal, she said, was a nation of sensible, natural, free women.

The transformation of the *Lily* from a "woman's journal devoted to Temperance and Literature" to one "devoted to Emancipation of Woman from Intemperance, Injustice, Prejudice, and Bigotry" was more evolutionary than radical. Sensible women did not reject the notion of femininity itself. Nor did they oppose all aspects of domestic life; as they articulated it, the central issue was being wholly confined to a narrow and marginalized domestic sphere. Wright Davis explicitly called for moderation and patience in both strategy and style, since "a victory won by persuasion and argument is more certain of good results than a triumph wrung from weakness or extorted from fear."[12]

The Strong-minded Woman as Critic: The *Revolution*

The *Revolution*, as Dow shows, self-consciously set out to argue for a radical model for the new woman. Although the periodical lasted only three years, it succeeded in putting onto the national agenda a definition of the "strong-minded" woman—a term used then by both the *Revolution*'s supporters and opponents. The *Revolution* was not surprised by the "sneers of the weak and the thoughtless at the 'strong-minded' who are trying to rouse them from their lethargy of death."[13] Its title and credos, as well as other rhetorical strategies, vigorously proclaimed a breed of women who were always assertive, sometimes willful, and often dogmatic. Cady Stanton's aggressive, provocative rebuttals to those who criticized her political and financial connections suggest that the woman the *Revolution* represented was secure about her identity and pragmatic about her cause. The actual women who tried to follow the *Revolution*'s prescriptions for the strong-minded style may not, after all, have been quite so confident, and the political philosophy dramatized in the *Revolution* was often contradictory. But from the vantage of strong-minded women, the point was not consistency (or winning the vote per se) but woman's right to express herself forcefully on all the important issues of the day.

The periodical's name (the fact that it was not *Rosebud* or *Lily* was drawn to readers' attention) and its editorial style were self-consciously militant. Cady Stanton frequently advised would-be correspondents to be "sharp, short, and spicy." Likewise, readers repeatedly congratulated their hard-edged paper on being "so different from the namby-pamby, milk-and-water journals that dare not publish the truth."[14] They used the language of religious conversion and of physical transformation to describe the paper's impact: "Since the *Revolution* has removed the bandages from our eyes and the scales have fallen also, we begin to see women as 'trees walking'. . . ."[15]

Although they denied they were fanatics and fire-eaters, a primary rhetorical strategy of strong-minded readers of the *Revolution* was to compare themselves to the great heretics, from Galileo on. They described themselves as an avant-garde of a better civilization to come. As have other reformers (such as members of the Women's Christian Temperance Union), the *Revolution*'s writers also used military vocabulary, replete with references to an army of able-bodied women ready to fall into rank and file. They were eager to wage war. And they exploited the metaphors of natural history to explain both women's problems and indifference or opposition to their sacred cause. Just as trees shed leaves before growing fruit, so society would discard obsolete customs; women were like oaks planted in a flower pot—but natural rights would ultimately restore women's true status in society; the suffrage movement needed opposition just as vegetation needs winds and storms to drive its roots down into the earth, they said.

Another major rhetorical strategy of the strong-minded was to recast as odious what their enemies regarded as virtuous. They contrasted themselves to women who are "viney, and twiney, and whiney throughout. . . ."[16] Not prepared to renounce femininity, they certainly reframed or recast it. They attacked the frivolity and extravagance of "fashion butterflies" and claimed for themselves tasteful appearance, graceful manners, melodious voices. That is, by describing the voice, dress, posture, manners, and cultural preferences of women attending suffrage conventions and meetings, they prescribed an ideal type. Cady Stanton clearly enjoyed refuting the myth of suffragists as bearded Amazons, presenting herself and her seven children as proof that strong-minded women were also wise mothers, attentive daughters, and contented wives; they were charming neighbors and thrifty housekeepers. By the *Revolution*'s reckoning, the choice was one of ballots, brains, and babies, against bonnets, balls, and brocades. So the *Revolution* reversed the prevailing question. The issue was not whether strong-minded women were unsexed, but whether women should remain—and remain content to be—driveling, dependent imbeciles.

Put this way, then, the racist tone to which Dow refers expressed in part Cady Stanton's undisguised and increasingly bitter impatience, frustration, and resentment that honor and status (in the form of enfranchisement) were extended to men with little education or political sophistication but were withheld from strong-minded women. To be identified with convicts, lunatics and children—the remaining classes of nonvoters—was demeaning.

Interestingly, the *Mayflower*, the only woman suffrage paper published during the Civil War, had already noted in 1861 how abolitionists welcomed women as allies, so long as they did only the work men gave them. Its editor, Lizzie Bunnell, predicted that "when they are done with us, they will turn us over to our former occupations and abuse us just as handsomely as ever."[17] The *National Anti-Slavery Standard* did not oppose woman's rights, but it refused to advocate woman's suffrage until African-Americans were enfranchised. And in 1866, Lucy Stone and Henry Blackwell sent out a prospectus for a publication to be called *Universal Suffrage*, which Stone hoped would simultaneously "effect the enfranchisement and complete recognition of the industrial and social and political equality of women and Negroes"; but it failed to get off the ground for lack of support.[18]

In any case, as many historians have often indicated, many suffragists remained uncomfortable with militancy. They were horrified that Cady Stanton's strong-minded organization and paper should pretend to speak for them and claim national legitimacy. Already from January 1869 to May 1870, Lucy Stone and Henry Blackwell (as well as his brother and sister-in-law) had sought an alternative by providing the dominant editorial and stylistic tone of the *Woman's Advocate*, published in New York City by William

Tomlinson. Even Cady Stanton admitted that Tomlinson's dignified philosophy and narrow focus on enfranchisement attracted readers who rejected the *Revolution*'s breadth and eccentricity. The emphasis in both the *Advocate* and in Mary Livermore's *Agitator* on patience and quiet steps toward reform marked the repudiation not only of the *Revolution*'s tactics and strategies but also of its pointedly militant ideals, visions, and values.

The Responsible Worker: The *Woman's Journal* and the *Woman's Tribune*

Not surprisingly, one of Lucy Stone's first actions, after she successfully called for a more widely representative organization dedicated to "the orderly and efficient prosecution of the woman suffrage movement," was to establish an organ to symbolize and give voice to that organization's particular membership. The achievement of the *Woman's Journal* was not simply that it lasted so long but that it articulated an alternative "responsible" style, which was intellectually plausible and affectively satisfying to its adherents, and which the larger society was eventually willing to accord respect. The ability of the Boston-based weekly to attract subscribers, stockholders, and advertisers was a sign not simply of the publishers' business acumen but also of the growing acknowledgment of the legitimacy of a particular kind of new woman. The issue is again self-esteem, mutual esteem, and national esteem.

Huxman correctly points out that pragmatic suffrage leaders realized the need to reject "destructive Radicalism" if enfranchisement were to be won. This entailed jettisoning causes and values that proved alienating. The *Journal* also faced the trickier task of affirmatively defining an identity for middle-class woman that imbued her life with meaningfulness and significance. The paper's name, inspired by the *English Woman's Journal*, was selected specifically because it was neither sensational nor restrictive. According to Henry Blackwell, "It stands for the thing we propose."[19] Analogously, the *Journal* consistently reminded its readers about the symbolic value of their own names and cautioned women at least not to accept silly, trivializing nicknames. Furthermore, the *Journal*'s neat, tight layout, its graphics, its choice of an editorial board top-heavy with well-known national leaders, as well as its editorial and linguistic choices, all proclaimed its essential commitment to a reasonable, calm, sensible version of the new woman, a progressive woman who worked alongside men for the benefit of all humanity.

In some sense, dramatizing a "responsible woman" demanded negotiating a more treacherous tightrope than the one Cady Stanton had walked. After all, Cady Stanton made no claims to consistency and nobility, instead availing herself of the more fiery rhetoric available at the extremes. Conversely, even Harriet Beecher Stowe, while approving of the *Journal*'s conservative tone and respectful attention to domestic life, once objected to its "high-falutin'" descriptions of a "reformeress' marble brows."[20] Nonetheless, the *Journal* generally maintained its tone of decorum, nobility, politeness, and dignity. For example, the *Journal* once advised a new subscriber that being mannish, coarse, or defiant was unnecessary; one could advocate equality and still be a "genuine woman, gentle, tender, refined, and quiet."[21]

The strategic and stylistic accomplishments of the *Woman's Journal* inspired the emergence of other papers. The *Journal* wanted—needed—to unify progressive women nationally and to argue for a style that would not alienate potential adherents. But in so doing, it ignored or downplayed certain possibilities. As Huxman notes, the *Journal*'s editors spoke to and from different positions; this both attracted and sustained additional converts (readers' letters and articles testified to the appropriateness of the language of religious conversion) and energized the organization. Still, with increasing interest in new definitions of womanhood came increasing difficulty in embracing all the potential variations. Furthermore, specific communities—defined both stylistically and geographically—were bound to develop competing papers. Only these more particularized communications could effectively address their specific interests and symbolize their own intellectual abilities, mobilize and sustain their more local constituencies. Especially for those not interested in profit but wholly committed to a cause, printing and distribution technologies and economics of the late nineteenth century continued to permit relatively easy access into the publishing business.

The *Woman's Tribune* shows that an individual—a free-lancer with a message but without institutional support or connections—could position herself and her paper as speaking to and for an audience not specifically addressed by the *Journal*. Clara Bewick Colby perhaps comes across as stubborn and egocentric, but she was no more so than many suffragists and most suffrage editors or publishers, and she was no less committed to the movement. She had staked her own identity and status to a cause, which itself could in part be defined in terms of its ability to provide women outside the inner circle of suffrage leaders with a sense of significance, importance. New women of the late nineteenth and early twentieth century demanded suffrage not because they had realistic hopes of using the ballot box to end their own political oppression or to enact other reforms. Rather, they needed to proclaim the legitimacy of their emerging style of life. So Bewick Colby drew upon common strategies for bolstering the image of suffragists—in their own eyes as well as in others'—by educating them on political issues and by glorifying their participating in a historic nationwide cause.

British-born Bewick Colby saw herself as acting on behalf of western, nonurban women, taking up the slack left by the suspension of the *Western Woman's Journal*, begun in 1881 in Lincoln, Nebraska. Ironically, Abigail Scott Duniway, not long after her own return to Oregon, denounced the "untimely invasion of Mrs. Clara B. Colby and other self-imported Eastern Suffragists."[22] In any case, as Jerry implies, midwestern and western suffragists might well feel isolated from the suffrage leadership, being on the fringes of political action; many of them were quite literally without contact with suffrage sisters. With their reprints of speeches, discussions of convention business, and visual and narrative portraits of individual women, then, such papers as the *Tribune* made newcomers and residents appreciate their self-consciously adopted community. Bewick Colby's personal experiences undoubtedly confirmed her call to women outside the inner circle.

The Local Activist: The *Farmer's Wife* and the *Woman's Exponent*

Rural and agricultural women, as well as poor women, did not experience the same cultural disruption and trauma described earlier in this chapter as besetting middle-class urban women. Given its origins, one might expect that both farm women and industrial workers would initially greet the suffrage movement with some degree of cynicism. For example, the *Woman's Advocate*, a weekly Philadelphia paper begun in January 1855, emphatically stuck to the concerns of the "toiling majority who must work to survive." The *Advocate*'s motto boasted that it was "devoted to the elevation of the Female Industrial Classes, and produced exclusively by the joint stock capital, energies, and industry of females." It openly mocked woman suffrage "upper-ten-dom . . . who complains that our hard work is not ultra enough for their taste. . . ."[23]

As farm women picked up the signals of emerging claims made for and by women, they wanted to participate in their own way. As Burkholder notes, farm women understood themselves as culturally isolated and geographically dispersed. The *Farmer's Wife*, then, first emphasized their "special" commonality. The *Farmer's Wife* cultivated their growing conviction that this specific community deserved social (cultural, political, economic) recognition and status. It also dramatized their membership in and contributions to a larger community.

Burkholder notes that most *Farmer's Wife* contributors defended enfranchisement primarily on the grounds that it was necessary to achieving Populist goals; women needed to be able to vote for Populist candidates, if they were to win and thus be able to work for farmers' interests. But embedded in this language was a view of farm women as capable, intelligent, pragmatic, hard-nosed, and politically astute. Family members, as well as livestock and vegetables, depended on their care. They had a sophisticated knowledge of and responsibility for nutrition, hygiene and medicine, education, and their children's total well-being. While the "mainstream" feminist journals concentrated on middle-class women in high status occupations, such as medicine, teaching, and business administration, farm women could persuasively argue that they also managed all these duties. In sum, the woman celebrated in the *Farmer's Wife* confronted the same moral, political, and social issues described in the *Woman's Journal*, but the form of the argument and was adapted to farm women's interests.

Mormon women were even less well represented by the national suffrage press than farm women. The *Woman's Exponent* was not simply an organ for Utah women, but for Mormon women, who well recognized that "gentile" suffragists were unlikely to respect or sympathize with their defense of polygamy.

Certainly eastern suffragists had asserted their conviction that the practice of multiple wives was insulting to all women and intolerable to responsible women. They understood that Utah's predominantly Mormon population had enfranchised women specifically to help protect Mormon social structure and values; "responsible" suffrage leaders certainly preferred the family-centered industriousness of Mormon culture to the coarse, "uncivilized" culture of the non-Mormon mining population in Utah. But they chose to believe that Mormon women would eventually recognize and resist their subjugation. Peterson's description of the *Exponent*'s defense of polygamy, which was unwavering until the church hierarchy finally reversed its position, shows how wrong easterners were on this point. The *Woman's Journal* essentially walked a tightrope on the Utah issue, avoiding too much discussion of Mormon morality and concentrating on the issue of rights. It published stories detailing the evils of polygamy (with such headlines as "Led into Captivity") but also reprinted articles from the *Exponent*.

Peterson's analysis of the *Woman's Exponent*'s proposed triumvirate of piety, purity, and independence suggests that the Mormon "real" woman was not altogether different from the woman celebrated by most suffragists in the final decades of the nineteenth century. The *Exponent* also defined woman as "a responsible being, capable of judging for and maintaining herself." Apparently the Mormons' grounds for creating and sustaining their paper had less to do with their rejection of the *Journal*'s philosophy, politics, or style, and more to do with a belief that Mormon women had additional concerns and interests ignored by the secular press, the woman's press, and by other Mormon communication channels.

Even its defense of polygamy deemphasized divine origin and biblical precedence, highlighting instead the assertion that plural marriage provided women more time for independent thinking and action. At the least, the rationale that polygamy made woman an equal partner implied that women should not be subordinate and subservient. The *Exponent* was certainly concerned with the status of Mormon culture; it was arguing that the Mormon way of life was legitimate and honorable. But it was also pleading the case of a woman who was capable of intelligent thinking, judging, acting— who could make useful contributions both within and outside the home. The paper's connections to the church, to Mormon activities, and to Mormon leaders, as well as its general sense of religious mission, were unique, but its structure and organization, topics and scope, and financing scheme were not. Finally, its rejection of purple prose and exaggerated sentimentality in favor of straightforward arguments punctuated by militancy and satire suggests its rhetorical commonality with such suffrage publications as the *Journal*.

The Pragmatic Politician: The *Woman's Column*

Alice Stone Blackwell, daughter of the editors of the *Woman's Journal* and American Woman Suffrage Association leaders, guided the *Woman's Column* for its sixteen-year run; so the latter journal's philosophic and stylistic inheritance from the former is predictable. Alice Blackwell had first published (a poem) in the *Journal* when she was fifteen and had been active in the leadership of the *Journal* since her graduation from Boston University in 1881. Alice Blackwell had neither the inclination nor the mandate to forge an identity for new women that was subtly—much less substantially—different from the one evolving in the *Journal*.

With a subscription rate set at a quarter a year, its pithy, matter-of-fact, tightly edited style, and its studied avoidance of controversy and passion, the *Column* was not even intended for converts themselves, except perhaps as an effective, inoffensive tract they could afford to give away or send in bulk. Recognizing the doldrums from which the movement was suffering (neither its own number of members nor the number of states enfranchising women was increasing dramatically or sufficiently), the Stone-Blackwell family experimented with several strategies and organizational tools. For example, from 1895 to 1900 and from 1915 to 1917, the national suffrage organization also published a monthly bulletin. Sent to state and local auxiliaries, it included organizational tips and recommendations on techniques and activities. The *Column* represented a commonsense effort to win favorable publicity in the mainstream press and to achieve some standing with club women and other women who considered themselves modern but not necessarily "new." It was also designed to be distributed in enormous volume during state or local referenda campaigns. Either way, a tract that generally condensed reports of recent activities and reviewed positive developments was not likely to endorse or embrace radicalism.

What is interesting about the pragmatic moderation dominating the *Column* is its willingness to conjoin a number of rhetorical-political strategies, arguing both from expedience and social justice. Repudiating militancy in style and in strategy, it effectively positioned women's enfranchisement alongside a number of reform causes and social interests that the modern woman of the 1890s might be expected to accept.

Equally successful were the papers inaugurated around this time by state suffrage associations as outreach and organizational tools. For example, in 1886, Iowa suffragists began their *Woman's Standard*, issued monthly (except for a two-year suspension) until 1911, "in the Interest of the Home, Purity, Woman and her right to the franchise." The four-page monthly *Illinois Suffragist* began in 1891; the *Wisconsin Citizen* was published from 1887 through 1916; and the *Michigan Suffragist* was published from 1914 to 1917. After the turn of the century, several suffrage papers appeared in New York and on the West Coast.

With some exceptions, most of the post-1900 suffrage periodicals followed the lead of the *Woman's Column* and the *Woman's Journal* and also emphasized organizational, tactical, and procedural matters. They neatly steered away from disputes over marriage, divorce, education, careers, dress reform, and the nature and relationship of women and men. It was as if these new women had temporarily accepted a certain vision of womanhood. Now they could settle down in earnest to fight for status—not achieved until 1920, with the states' ratification of a Constitutional amendment enfranchising women.

Perhaps the new women were not entirely satisfied with the extent to which they had become the women they wanted to be. Women continued to redefine themselves; their models for new womanhood were no more static than was their social context or, for that matter, the image of the "true woman" that they repudiated. The woman's rights editors themselves were not self-conscious about this historical process. Furthermore, as the various authors here have illustrated, the woman's rights periodicals often lacked a self-consciousness about other biases. Most notably, they failed to attend to problems of class and race. But women were able in their newspapers and magazines to construct meaningful, if only provisional, definitions for themselves. Their rhetorical passion and sincerity brought forth an alternative identity that conferred on their daily lives a vital sense of significance and excitement. They dramatized this transformed woman in a way that was satisfying to them, appropriate to the emerging modern culture, and warranting honor and deference.

The passage of the Nineteenth Amendment, which effectively concluded the early phase of the woman's rights movement, marked symbolic affirmation of a "new woman" who was responsible, competent, and intelligent, yet still "womanly." This identity represents a compromise with certain ideals developed at various stages in the movement, a compromise made at least partly in the interests of political expedience. Women today continue the struggle to develop a still more satisfactory image of and identity for themselves.

Notes

Chapter 1: The Role of the Suffrage Press

1. Jane Rendall, *The Origins of Modern Feminism: Women in Britain, France, and the United States 1780–1860* (London: Macmillan, 1985), 7–33.

2. Two problems of usage confront those who write about the American suffrage movement. First, the temptation is to refer to the movement in modern terms as *feminist*. But, as Nancy Cott points out, this is a fairly recent term that was not used by the women themselves. Thus, the following chapters will avoid that usage and employ the terms *woman's movement* and *woman suffrage*, both because that is how the persons involved identified themselves and also because those terms suggest their feeling that "the singular *woman* symbolized, in a word, the unity of the female sex. It proposed that all women have one cause, one movement" (Nancy Cott, *The Grounding of Modern Feminism* [New Haven: Yale University Press, 1987], 3–4). We will also use the term *suffragist*, rather than *suffragette*, to refer to the American workers. Although some younger women embraced the term *suffragette*, with its associations with the more militant and confrontational British movement, most older women preferred the term *suffragist*, which they felt was a less inflammatory and more decorous designation.

Second, how to refer to the women themselves is somewhat problematic. We will follow the practice outlined by Karlyn Kohrs Campbell of referring to the women either by the names they used for themselves, e.g., Carrie Chapman Catt, or by a combination of their birth and married names, e.g., Cady Stanton [Karlyn Kohrs Campbell, *Man Cannot Speak for Her: A Crit-*

ical Study of Early Feminist Rhetoric [New York: Praeger, 1989], 1:3; vol. 2, *Key Texts of the Early Feminists*, contains texts of speeches]. One exception to this principle will be Paulina Kellogg Wright Davis, who will be identified as Wright Davis. Since she is typically referred to as Paulina Wright Davis rather than Paulina Kellogg Davis, we will use both husbands' names for clarity and brevity.

3. Elizabeth Cady Stanton, *Eighty Years and More* (New York: T. Fisher Unwin, 1898; New York: Schocken, 1971), 147–48.

4. Campbell, *Man Cannot*, 1:50.

5. Eleanor Flexner, *Century of Struggle: The Woman's Rights Movement in the United States* (Cambridge: Belknap Press of Harvard University Press, 1975), 77.

6. One invaluable resource for details of the woman suffrage movement in particular is *The History of Woman Suffrage*. Volumes 1 through 3 were edited by Elizabeth Cady Stanton, Susan B. Anthony, and Matilda Joslyn Gage and were published in New York in 1881. Volume 4 was edited by Susan B. Anthony and Ida Husted Harper and published in Rochester in 1902. Volumes 5 and 6 were edited by Ida Husted Harper and published in New York in 1922.

7. Charles J. Stewart, Craig Allen Smith, and Robert E. Denton, Jr., *Persuasion and Social Movements* (Prospect Heights, Ill.: Waveland Press, 1984), 14.

8. Herbert W. Simons, "Requirements, Problems, and Strategies: A Theory of Persuasion for Social Movements," *Quarterly Journal of Speech* 56 (February 1970): 3. See also John Wilson, *Introduction to Social Movements* (New York: Basic Books, 1973), 8.

9. Chapter 5 in Stewart, Smith, and Denton, "A Functional Approach to Persuasion in Social Movements," 73–84, highlights the particular tasks facing social movements.

10. Simons, 7.

11. Ernest G. Bormann, *The Force of Fantasy: Restoring the American Dream* (Carbondale: Southern Illinois University Press, 1985), 11.

12. For example, STOP ERA worked largely through established groups to generate supporters. The West Virginia textbook described by Barbara Warnick is an example of geographically based membership ("The Rhetoric of Conservative Resistance," *Southern Speech Communication Journal* 42 [Spring 1977]: 256–73). The Civil Rights Movement in its earliest stages in Montgomery had the advantages of both geographical closeness and the strong church network (Donald H. Smith, "Martin Luther King, Jr., 'In the Beginning in Montgomery,'" *Southern Speech Communication Journal* 34 [Fall 1968]: 8–17).

13. Joseph R. Gusfield, *Community: A Critical Response* (New York: Harper & Row, 1975), 34.

14. Gusfield, *Community*, 35.

15. Stewart, Smith, and Denton, 75.

16. Leland Griffin, "A Dramatistic Theory of the Rhetoric of Movements," in *Critical Responses to Kenneth Burke*, ed. William H. Rueckert (Minneapolis: University of Minnesota Press, 1969), 456–78.

17. Nancy F. Cott, *The Bonds of Womanhood: "Woman's Sphere" in New England, 1780–1835* (New Haven: Yale University Press, 1977), 3.

18. Rendall, 3, 4.

19. Barbara Welter, *Dimity Convictions: The American Woman in the Nineteenth Century* (Athens: Ohio University Press, 1976), 21.

20. Mrs. E. Little, "What Are the Rights of Women?" *Ladies Wreath* 2 (1848–49): 133; Rev. Mr. Stearns, *Female Influence and the True Christian Mode of Its Exercise: A Discourse Delivered in the First Presbyterian Church in Newburyport, July 30, 1837* (Newburyport, 1837), 114–15. Both quoted in Welter, *Dimity*, 40.

21. Cott, *Bonds*, 99–100.

22. Joseph Buckminister, "A Sermon Preached before the Members of the Boston Female Asylum. September 1810." Boston Public Library Rare Book Room. Quoted in Cott, *Bonds*, 148.

23. Cott, *Bonds*, 5.

24. Flexner, 42.

25. Campbell, *Man Cannot*, 1:9.

26. Flexner, 76. For a complete text of this document, see Campbell, *Man Cannot*, 2:33–41.

27. Flexner, 76.

28. Campbell, *Man Cannot*, 1:46–69.

29. For a complete text, see Campbell, *Man Cannot*, 2:187–234.

30. Ibid., 1:71–85.

31. Charles Conrad, "The Transformation of the 'Old Feminist' Movement," *Quarterly Journal of Speech* 67 (August 1981): 284–97.

32. Flexner, 106–7.

33. Ibid., 147–48.

34. Ibid., 150.

35. Laura Ballard, "What Flag Shall We Fly?" *Revolution*, October 1870, 265. Quoted in William L. O'Neill, *Everyone Was Brave: The Rise and Fall of Feminism in the United States* (Chicago: Quadrangle Books, 1969), 19–20.

36. Flexner, 249.

37. Harriot Stanton Blatch and Alma Lutz, *Challenging Years: The Memoirs of Harriot Stanton Blatch* (New York: G. P. Putnam's Sons, 1940), 92. Quoted in Flexner, 251.

38. Flexner, 253.

39. Campbell, *Man Cannot*, 1:172.

40. Ibid., 1:165. See Flexner, 279–82, for a full discussion of this effort.

41. Flexner, 292.

42. Campbell, *Man Cannot*, 1:9.

43. Ibid., 1:17.

44. Flexner, 42.

45. Quoted in Campbell, *Man Cannot*, 1:24–25.

46. Quoted in Flexner, 47.

47. Campbell, *Man Cannot*, 2:31–32.

48. Karlyn Kohrs Campbell, "Femininity and Feminism: To Be or Not To Be a Woman," *Communication Quarterly* 31 (Spring 1983): 101–8. This

article outlines the rhetorical strategies of consciousness-raising in the early feminist movement.

49. For example, Campbell notes that she was unable to include Lucy Stone in her volumes, despite Stone's pioneering and apparently quite well-known work for woman's rights because of the paucity of remaining texts. Those that do survive, according to Campbell, "do not display the great talents she evidently had" (*Man Cannot*, 1:8).

50. Quoted in Miriam Gurko, *The Ladies of Seneca Falls: The Birth of the Woman's Rights Movement* (New York: Macmillan, 1974), 103, 165.

51. Campbell, *Man Cannot*, 1:49–50.

Chapter 2: The Role of Newspapers

1. Elizabeth Cady Stanton, Susan B. Anthony, and Matilda Joslyn Gage, eds., *History of Woman Suffrage*, vol. 1: 1848–1861, 2d ed. (Rochester, N.Y.: Charles Mann, 1886), 49.

2. George P. Rowell, ed., *Geo. P. Rowell & Co.'s American Newspaper Directory* (New York: Rowell, 1873), 15. Subsequent entries refer to volumes published between 1870 and 1890.

3. Frank Luther Mott, *American Journalism: A History of Newspapers in the United States through 260 Years, 1690 to 1951*, rev. ed. (New York: Macmillan, 1950), 304. Postal rates were lowered from two cents per pound for dailies and weeklies and three cents per pound for monthlies in 1875 to one cent per pound for all second-class material in 1877. See Mott, *American Journalism*, 508.

4. Rowell, 1885, iv. This growth would continue. In 1880, ten percent of American adults were newspaper subscribers; in 1900, twenty-six percent. Edwin Emery and Michael Emery, *The Press and America: An Interpretive History of the Mass Media*, 5th ed. (Englewood Cliffs, N.J.: Prentice-Hall, 1984), 238.

5. Quoted in Willard Grosvenor Bleyer, *Main Currents in the History of American Journalism* (Boston: Houghton, 1927), 242.

6. Gurko, 103–4.

7. Frank Luther Mott, *A History of American Magazines 1865–1885* (Cambridge: Harvard University Press, 1938), 90–91.

8. Lillian O'Connor, *Pioneer Women Orators: Rhetoric in Ante-bellum Reform Movements* (New York: Vantage, n.d.; rpt. 1952), 127.

9. Ibid., 128–29.

10. Michael Schudson, *Discovering the News: A Social History of American Newspapers* (New York: Basic Books, 1978), 100.

11. Bertha-Monica Stearns, "Reform Periodicals and Female Reformers 1830–1860," *American Historical Review* 37 (1932): 678–79.

12. Stanton, Anthony, and Gage, 45.

13. Stearns, "Reform," 679, 681, 688.

14. *Genius of Liberty*, 15 February 1881, 36.

15. Stanton, Anthony, and Gage, 46.

16. Ibid., 221–22.

17. *Proceedings of the Woman's Rights Convention Held at the Broadway Tabernacle in the City of New York on Tuesday and Wednesday, Sept. 6th and 7th, 1853* (New York: Fowlers and Wells, 1853), 4, 19; the Gerritsen Collection of Woman's History, microfilm ed., no. 3168.

18. Susan B. Anthony and Ida Husted Harper, *History of Woman Suffrage*, vol. 4, 1883–1900 (Indianapolis: Hollenbeck, 1902), 14. Rpt. New York: Arno and the New York Times, 1969.

19. After the Civil War, the woman's rights movement had, in great measure, narrowed to the woman suffrage movement, many of the leaders believing that the vote would lead to the other rights they sought. For example, Lynne Masel-Walters has argued that this transformation took place because Progressive politics had led to attainment of many of the other goals of woman's rights, such as advances in educational and employment opportunities and the removal of many legal disabilities. See Masel-Walters, "Their Rights and Nothing Less: The History and Thematic Content of the American Woman Suffrage Press, 1868–1920" (Ph.D. diss., University of Wisconsin–Madison, 1977), 18.

20. Flexner, 150.

21. *Revolution*, 14 May 1868, 296.

22. Lynne Masel-Walters, "Their Rights and Nothing More: A History of *The Revolution*, 1868–1870," *Journalism Quarterly* 53 (Summer 1976): 251.

23. Marion Marzolf, *Up from the Footnote: A History of Women Journalists*, Communication Arts Books (New York: Hastings House, 1977), 225.

24. Ibid., 231.

25. Anne Mather, "A History of Feminist Periodicals, Part 1," *Journalism History* 1 (1974): 84, University Microfilm ed.

26. Marzolf, 229.

27. When the *Revolution* went under, Susan B. Anthony was left with a $10,000 debt, which took her ten years to repay.

28. Rowell, 1873, 257.

29. Rowell, 1874, 251. The new ones were *Homestead*, published in Oakland, California, and *Woman's Right* from Wadesboro, North Carolina.

30. Rowell, 1879, 475. The *Pioneer* and *Woodhull & Claflin's Weekly* were not listed; added were *Truth for the People* (Detroit), Matilda Joslyn Gage's *National Citizen and Ballot Box*, and an Indianapolis weekly, the *Woman's Tribune*.

31. Rowell, 1884, 583.

32. Rowell, 1870–90.

33. The National American Woman Suffrage Association (NAWSA), *Victory, How Women Won It: A Centennial Symposium, 1840–1940* (New York: Wilson, 1940), 72. Park reported that there had been limited local activity: "Only in partial suffrage was there any permanent advance between 1869 and 1890. The first step of that kind had been taken as far back as 1838, when Kentucky gave school suffrage to widows with children of school age. In 1861 Kansas had gone a little further by giving school suffrage to all women. In the 70's and 80's similar grants were made by fifteen states; and

New Hampshire, Massachusetts and Montana gave to taxpaying women the right to vote upon questions submitted to the taxpayers. Then in 1887, Kansas granted municipal suffrage to its women" (73–74).

34. Leslie Wheeler, ed., *Loving Warriors: Selected Letters of Lucy Stone and Henry B. Blackwell, 1853 to 1893* (New York: Dial, 1981), 311. One common bond that was acknowledged by parties on both sides of the controversy was the role Lucy Stone played in bringing women into the movement. At the 1888 International Council of Women, Susan B. Anthony, Julia Ward Howe, and Frances Willard "all told how they had been converted to woman suffrage by Lucy Stone. . . ." This was reported by Alice Stone Blackwell, *Lucy Stone: Pioneer of Woman's Rights* (Boston: Little, Brown, 1930), 266.

35. Blackwell, 240.

36. Olympia Brown, ed., *Democratic Ideals: A Memorial Sketch of Clara B. Colby* (n.p.: Federal Suffrage Association, 1917), 34–35.

37. Ida Husted Harper, ed., *History of Woman Suffrage*, vol. 5: 1900–1920 (New York: National American Woman Suffrage Association, 1922), 337.

38. For a discussion of the antisuffrage forces, see Flexner; Alan P. Grimes, *The Puritan Ethic and Woman Suffrage* (New York: Oxford University Press, 1967); Carrie Chapman Catt and Nettie Rogers Shuler, *Woman Suffrage and Politics: The Inner Story of the Suffrage Movement*, Americana Library, ed. Robert E. Burke (1923; rpt. Seattle: University of Washington Press, 1970); Aileen S. Kraditor, *The Ideas of the Woman Suffrage Movement, 1890–1920* (New York: Columbia University Press, 1965; New York: W. W. Norton, 1981).

39. Catt and Shuler, 107.

40. NAWSA, 133.

41. These numbers are adapted from a chart in Masel-Walters, "Their Rights and Nothing Less," 379–80. The *Woman's Journal* is considered to have ceased in 1917, when its identity was merged into the *Woman Citizen*.

42. Anne F. Scott and Andrew M. Scott, *One Half the People: The Fight for Woman Suffrage*, The America's Alternatives Series, ed. Harold M. Hyman (Philadelphia: Lippincott, 1975), 35.

43. Anne Messerly Cooper, "Suffrage as News: Ten Dailies' Coverage of the Nineteenth Amendment," *American Journalism* 1 (1983): 80.

44. Lauren Jeanne Kessler, "A Siege of the Citadels: Access of Woman Suffrage Ideas to the Oregon Press, 1884–1912" (Ph.D. diss., University of Washington, 1980), 5–6.

45. Ibid., 178.

46. NAWSA membership had grown dramatically, as Kraditor documented: ". . . it may be inferred that the NAWSA grew from 13,150 in 1893; to 17,000 in 1905; to 45,501 in 1907; to over 75,000 in 1910; to 100,000 in 1915; to 2,000,000 in 1917" (7).

47. "The Female Rebellion," *Perspectives on Greatness*, series owned by King Features Entertainment, 1963 production; KTWU rebroadcast, 27 April 1986.

48. This analysis is based primarily on external factors. Suffrage publishers did not cease publication consciously, intentionally, or with ad-

vanced notice; typically, the newspapers folded quietly. For example, the *Wisconsin Citizen* died with so little fanfare that months after its last issue a letter was sent to former recipients informing them that they were no longer receiving the paper because it had folded, not because of a postal or clerical error (files of *Wisconsin Citizen*, State Historical Society Library of Wisconsin).

49. *Woman's Tribune*, March 1885, 2; November 1886, 2.

50. Linda Claire Steiner, "The Women's Suffrage Press, 1850–1900: A Cultural Analysis" (Ph.D. diss., University of Illinois, 1979), 80, University Microfilm ed.

51. Steiner, 32–33.

52. Lauren Kessler, *The Dissident Press: Alternative Journalism in American History*, Sage COMMTEXT Series, vol. 13, ed. F. Gerald Kline (Beverly Hills: Sage, 1984), 86.

53. Lucy L. Correll, "Suffrage in Nebraska," in *Collection of Nebraska Pioneer Reminiscences*, issued by Nebraska Society of the Daughters of the American Revolution (Cedar Rapids, Iowa: Torch, 1916), 277.

54. See E. Claire Jerry, "Clara Bewick Colby and the *Woman's Tribune*: Strategies of a Free Lance Movement Leader" (Ph.D. diss., University of Kansas, 1986).

55. *Woman's Tribune*, 4 January 1902, 2; 23 December 1905, 89.

Chapter 3: The *Lily*

1. Joseph R. Gusfield, *Symbolic Crusade: Status Politics and the American Temperance Society* (Urbana: University of Illinois Press, 1963), 46. See John A. Krout, *The Origins of the Prohibition* (New York: Alfred A. Knopf, 1925), 183.

2. The Washingtonian reform movement was a significant factor in the decision to publish a temperance journal. See "To the Patrons of the *Lily*," *Lily*, January 1849, 3.

3. See Dexter C. Bloomer, *Life and Writings of Amelia Bloomer* (Boston: Arena, 1895; New York: Schocken, 1975), 39.

4. Ibid., 41.

5. Frances E. Willard and Mary A. Livermore, eds., *American Women* (New York: Mast, Cromwell, and Kirkpatrick, 1897; Detroit: Gale Research, 1973), 99–100.

6. Allen Johnson, ed., *Dictionary of American Biography*, vol. 1 (New York: Charles Scribner's Sons, 1946), 385.

7. Information concerning circulation comes from the *Dictionary of American Biography*, 385. See also Bloomer, 145–56.

8. Willard and Livermore, 99.

9. Flexner, 124–25.

10. See, for example, from the *Lily*: "Shun the Wine Cup," January 1849, 4; "The Miseries of Intemperance," April 1849, 28; "Fourth of July," July 1849, 53; "O! Young Man," July 1849, 54; "Alcohol for Pickels," September 1849, 67; "The Place You Should Shun," December 1849, 91.

11. See J. Robert Cox, "The Die Is Cast: Topical and Ontological Dimensions of the Locus of the Irreparable," *Quarterly Journal of Speech* 68 (August 1982): 227.

12. "Intemperance—An Extract," May 1849, 33.

13. "Pencil Sketches—No. 2," June 1849, 44.

14. Other examples of such news reports from the *Lily*: "Death from Intemperance," February 1849, 11; "Another Victim" (reprinted from the *Cayuga Chief* of 8 March 1849), April 1849, 30; "Drunkenness," May 1849, 35; "A Horrible Sight—Rum's Doings and Death's Doing's," June 1850, 45.

15. For example, see "Temperance in the U.S.," February 1849, 15, and March 1849, 22; "Light Breaking," May 1849, 37; "New Law in Wisconsin," May 1849, 38; "Right Has Triumphed" and "Temperance," June 1849, 45; "Progress," August 1849, 62; "A Good Law," March 1850, 20; "Temperance and Politics," April 1850, 29.

16. For an example, see the *Lily*, April 1849, 30, for an announcement of an upcoming lecture in Auburn, New York, by John B. Gough, a relatively well-known temperance orator of the time.

17. Volume 2 of the *Lily* contained articles that related to woman's rights in important respects, but that volume can most effectively be treated in the final section of this chapter, which discusses the impact of the temperance rhetoric on the early woman's rights movement and discusses the ways in which the *Lily* contributed to the early woman's rights movement as a journal devoted primarily to the issue of woman's rights. This final section on the content of the *Lily* describes the kinds of arguments that can be found in issues from volumes 3 through 7.

18. Barbara Welter, "The Cult of True Womanhood: 1820–1860," *American Quarterly* 18 (1966): 151–74.

19. Suzanne Langer, *Philosophy in a New Key*, 3d ed. (Cambridge: Harvard University Press, 1978), 79–102. Although it was unacceptable for women to argue in discursive terms because of the prohibition of female advocates, women could use nondiscursive appeals in the form of poetry and literature because narrative modes of discourse were consistent with the traditional role of "true womanhood."

20. Ibid., 100.

21. Ibid., 263.

22. "Temperance and Politics," September 1849, 69.

23. According to Willard and Livermore, "Mrs. Bloomer was indebted to Mrs. Stanton, Miss Anthony and others for contributions" (99). Johnson says that "Mrs. Stanton became an early contributor writing over the name of 'Sunflower'" (385). The pages of the *Lily* became a regular forum for Cady Stanton's writings on issues related to woman's rights.

24. "The Miseries of Intemperance," April 1849, 28.

25. "Light Breaking," May 1849, 37.

26. "Gentleman Wine Drinkers," May 1849, 37.

27. "Caroline M. Sweet," August 1849, 61.

Chapter 4: The *Una*

1. Flexner, 82.
2. Robert E. Riegel, *American Feminists* (Lawrence: University of Kansas Press, 1963; rpt. 1968), 52.
3. Carol Hymowitz and Michaele Weissman, *A History of Women in America* (New York: Bantam Books, 1984), 99.
4. Flexner, 82.
5. Riegel, 48, 128–29, 191; Hymowitz and Weissmann, 99, 108.
6. These views echo statements by Aristotle in the *Poetics* 9.1451a.35–1452b.7.
7. Lynne Masel-Walters, "To Hustle with the Rowdies: The Organization and Functions of the American Suffrage Press," *Journal of American Culture* 3 (Spring 1980): 171.
8. Ibid., 180.
9. Campbell, "Femininity," 101–9.
10. Flexner, 75.
11. *Ladies Companion* 11 (1838): 238, as quoted in Welter, "Cult," 154.
12. Masel-Walters, "To Hustle," 175.

Chapter 5: The *Revolution*

1. Elisabeth Griffith, *In Her Own Right: The Life of Elizabeth Cady Stanton* (New York: Oxford University Press, 1984), 131.
2. Ibid., 129.
3. Much of the interest in woman suffrage had come from its connection with abolition, an important issue for the press. In 1867, however, most abolitionists were concerned solely with obtaining the vote for freed male slaves, and many viewed connections with woman suffrage as a hindrance. Consequently, efforts to promote suffrage for former slaves in the press overshadowed coverage of woman suffrage issues. See Flexner, 148–49.
4. Masel-Walters, "Their Rights and Nothing More," 244.
5. Alma Lutz, *Susan B. Anthony: Rebel, Crusader, Humanitarian* (Boston: Beacon Press, 1959), 139.
6. Marzolf, 228.
7. Ibid.
8. Masel-Walters, "Their Rights and Nothing More," 250.
9. Flexner, 156.
10. Marzolf, 228; see also *Revolution*, 23 April 1860, 248.
11. Marzolf, 227; Masel-Walters, "Their Rights and Nothing More," 242.
12. Ida Husted Harper, *Life and Work of Susan B. Anthony* (Indianapolis: Hollenbeck Press, 1898), 309–10.
13. See Flexner, 154; Marzolf, 225; Masel-Walters, "Their Rights and Nothing More," 242.
14. Flexner, 154.
15. Kraditor, 260.

16. Lutz, 169; Masel-Walters, "Their Rights and Nothing More," 242.

17. See Conrad, "Transformation," 289.

18. Katharine Anthony, *Susan B. Anthony: Her Personal History and Her Era* (Garden City, N.Y.: Doubleday, 1954), 226.

19. Griffith, 147.

20. Ibid., 138–39; Lutz, 169; Masel-Walters, "Their Rights and Nothing More," 242.

21. Flexner, 155.

22. Masel-Walters, "To Hustle," 168.

23. For an explanation of consciousness-raising techniques in feminist rhetoric, see Campbell, "Femininity," 105–6.

24. Kraditor, 44–45, n. 1.

25. Conrad, "Transformation," 289.

26. Ellen Carol DuBois, *Feminism and Suffrage: The Emergence of an Independent Woman's Movement in America, 1848–1869* (Ithaca: Cornell University Press, 1978), 147–53.

Chapter 6: The *Woman's Journal*

1. Catt as quoted in Agnes Ryan, *The Torch Bearer: A Look Forward and Back at the* Woman's Journal, *the Organ of the Woman's Movement* (Boston: Woman's Journal and Suffrage News, 1916), 15.

2. Existing scholarship on the *Woman's Journal* includes Lynne Masel-Walters, "A Burning Cloud by Day: The History and Content of the *Woman* [sic] *Journal*," *Journalism History* 3, no. 4 (Winter 1976–77): 103–10; Ryan; and Conrad, "Transformation."

3. For biographical data and financial information of the *Woman's Journal*, see Ryan, 11–20; and Blackwell, 242, 300–301.

4. 8 January 1870, 1, and every subsequent issue.

5. *Harper's Weekly* review, as quoted in "Opinions from the Press," *Woman's Journal*, 25 February 1870, 64.

6. Ryan, 21.

7. M.E.W.S., "One Woman's Experiences," 20 February 1875, 60.

8. Marzolf, 231; Gurko, 235.

9. J.C.N., "Women Not Satisfied," 5 January 1878, 2; "Letters," 9 April 1870, 107; Inez Haynes Irwin, *Angels and Amazons: A Hundred Years of American Women* (Garden City, N.Y.: Doubleday, Doran, 1933), 260.

10. *Chicago Post*, as quoted in "Opinions of the Press," 26 February 1870, 64.

11. B.B.H., "Ladies Column," 22 May 1880, 160.

12. "Enough Said," 6 February 1875, 45.

13. Ryan, 42.

14. Blackwell, 238–39.

15. Ryan, 11–20; Blackwell, 242, 300–301.

16. Flexner, 68–69; Gurko, 135.

17. Higginson, as quoted in Riegel, 85.

18. Wheeler, 380; Irwin, 259; Steven M. Buechler, *The Transformation of*

the *Woman Suffrage Movement: The Case of Illinois, 1850–1920* (New Brunswick, N.J.: Rutgers University Press, 1981), 65.

19. For more information on the four assistant editors, see Wheeler, Gurko, Irwin, Buechler, and Riegel.

20. Letter from Lucy Stone to Abby Kelley Foster, 24 January 1867, explaining Wendell Phillips's, William Lloyd Garrison's, and the Republican party's justifications for abandoning woman suffrage. Quoted in Wheeler, 215–16.

21. Conrad, "Transformation," 285; Stewart, Smith, and Denton, 44–45.

22. Wendell Phillips, "The Divorce Debates of 1860," speech to the New York Woman's Rights Convention urging pragmatic, uncontroversial goals for the movement. Reprinted in Stanton, Anthony, and Gage, 716–40. The major speeches in the "divorce debate" are reprinted in Campbell, *Man Cannot*, 2:187–234.

23. As respective leaders of the two wings of the movement, the relationship between Anthony and Stone was decidedly competitive. But when the racist Train and the eccentric Woodhull joined forces with the NWSA and when the *Revolution* impugned the character of Beecher, then president of the AWSA, the two became bitter rivals, occasionally exchanging accusations in print. For a one-sided view of the personality conflict, see Blackwell, 214–31.

24. Lucy Stone, "Miss Anthony's Case," 28 June 1873, 204.

25. Annegret S. Ogden, *The Great American Housewife: From Helpmate to Wage Earner 1776–1986* (Westport, Conn.: Greenwood, 1986), 184–85.

26. T. W. Higginson, "Fair Play," 1 March 1873, 1; Lucy Stone, "Mrs. Tilton," 29 August 1874, 278.

27. Riegel, 92.

28. "Our Third Birthday," 4 January 1873, 4.

29. Henry B. Blackwell, "Political Organization," 8 January 1870, 8.

30. Jerry, 45.

31. For other newspapers that were competing for women's attention, see Beverly Beeton, *Women Vote in the West: The Woman Suffrage Movement 1869–1896* (New York: Garland, 1986), 161.

32. See Buechler, 101; Jerry, 65–66.

33. Susan E. Dickinson, "Women Journalists in America," in *What America Owes to Women*, ed. Lydia Hoyt Farmer (Buffalo: Charles Wells Moulton, 1893), 208.

34. Stewart, Smith, and Denton, 73–83.

35. Ibid., 75.

36. Karlyn Kohrs Campbell, "The Rhetoric of Women's Liberation: An Oxymoron," *Quarterly Journal of Speech* 59 (February 1973): 74–86. While Campbell's analysis is limited to the rhetorical constraints of the contemporary women's movement, her findings explain the rhetorical difficulties of the early movement as well.

37. Scott Duniway, as quoted in Nancy Woloch, *Women and the American Experience* (New York: Alfred A. Knopf, 1984), 333.

38. Florence Howe Hall, *Julia Ward Howe and the Woman Suffrage Movement* (New York: Arno and the New York Times, 1969), 17.

39. Charles Conrad, "Agon and Rhetorical Form: The Essence of 'Old Feminist' Rhetoric," *Central States Speech Journal* 32 (Spring 1981): 53.

40. J.C.N., "Women Not Satisfied," 5 January 1878, 2.

41. T. W. Higginson, "Educating Self-Respect," 10 January 1874, 1; "Woman's Lack of Self-Appreciation," 16 April 1870, 116.

42. Campbell, "Femininity," 101–8.

43. Herbert W. Simons, James W. Chesebro, and C. Jack Orr, "A Movement Perspective on the 1972 Presidential Election," *Quarterly Journal of Speech* 59 (April 1973): 168–78. These authors argue that inherent tensions develop when movements connect themselves to established organizations in order to effect change. Specifically, when movements endorse a political party within the established two-party system, they: (1) admit to the satisfactory state of the established order; (2) close nontraditional rhetorical options for protest; (3) force themselves into a maintenance stage, which dampens enthusiasm for the cause; and (4) are no longer newsworthy by the media.

44. Henry B. Blackwell, "How To Succeed," 28 January 1871, 29; "Letter from Mrs. Campbell," 3 August 1872, 248.

45. Long after the 1872 presidential elections, the *Woman's Journal* continued to print in a prominent corner of the paper the fourteenth plank of the Republican platform; Lucy Stone, "The Elections," 2 November 1872, 348; T. W. Higginson, "Women in Politics," 3 August 1872, 248.

46. Rebecca Hazard, "What Party Shall Suffragists Support," 11 September 1880, 292.

47. Elizabeth Boynton Harbert, "Woman's Duty in the Campaign," 4 September 1880, 281.

48. Lucy Stone, "Sins against Women," 2 August 1884, 248; Wheeler, 286; Mary A. Livermore, "From a Woman's Point of View," 9 August 1884, 208; T. W. Higginson, "Tell the Truth," 9 August 1884, 208.

49. T. W. Higginson, "Honest Differences," 9 October 1880, 321.

50. T. W. Higginson, "A New Year's Greetings," 8 February 1873, 44.

51. T. W. Higginson, "How to Speak," 12 July 1873, 217.

52. T. W. Higginson, "After Fifteen Years," 27 December 1884, 417.

53. Ibid.

54. Henry B. Blackwell, "The Legislative Hearing," 8 February 1873, 44.

55. Lucy Stone, "Republicans and Woman Suffrage," 25 September 1880, 308.

56. Lucy Stone, "The Ladies' Centennial Commission," 1 May 1875, 140.

57. Alice B. LeGeyt, "Correspondence," 8 July 1871, 211.

58. M.E.W.S., "One Woman's Experience," 20 February 1875, 60.

59. "What Women Are Doing," 5 March 1870, 67, and 8 January 1870, 3.

60. Conrad, "Transformation," 288.

61. "Woman's Lack of Self-Appreciation," 16 April 1870, 116.

62. T. W. Higginson, "Educating Self-Respect," 10 January 1874, 1.

63. Ibid.

64. "What Is the Aim of the Woman's Movement?" 9 April 1870, 108.

65. Lucy Stone, "Legal Issues," 8 January 1870, 8.

66. Lucy Stone, "Never Forget It," 17 June 1876, 196.

67. T. W. Higginson, "The New Year," 3 January 1880, 1.

68. Eric Hoffer, *The True Believer* (New York: Harper & Row, 1951), 67.

69. Julia Ward Howe, "Salutory," 8 January 1870, 4; see also J.W.H., "The New Year," 2 January 1875, 4; J.W.H., "Our Annual Meeting," 1 February 1873, 36; J.W.H., "Mothers Day," 1 March 1873, 68.

70. Lucy Stone, "To the Women of Massachusetts," 1 March 1873, 68.

71. Julia Ward Howe, "The New Year," 2 January 1875, 4.

72. 8 January 1870, 4. Significantly, the suffrage defeat was reported without title or author.

73. Wheeler, 282.

74. J.L.H., "What the Wild Waves Say," 9 August 1870, 110.

Chapter 7: The *Woman's Tribune*

1. Brown, 32.

2. *Woman's Tribune*, January 1886, 3.

3. *Woman's Tribune*, January 1885, 2.

4. Brown, xi; Abigail Scott Duniway, *Pathbreaking: An Autobiographical History of the Equal Suffrage Movement in Pacific Coast States*, 2d ed. (1914; rpt. New York: Kraus Reprint, 1971), 229.

5. The *Woman's Tribune* is a sound choice for such an examination for several reasons. The *Tribune*'s lack of official backing and affiliation is significant in explicating Bewick Colby's leadership role. For example, she should have been freer to explore a variety of issues related to woman's rights from a broader spectrum of women's viewpoints than were other editors, and the *Tribune* strove to be more varied in its topics and departments. In other words, the *Tribune* was in a different and perhaps slightly better position to represent the very women who were not involved in mainstream movement activity. Moreover, because Bewick Colby was a "free lance," a study of the *Tribune* offers one of the few opportunity to analyze the influences of a newspaper independent from any influence attached to an editor who was elected to movement leadership. Geography is also a factor in the choice of the *Tribune*. Eastern women did not have the same needs for a suffrage organ as did women on the western frontier. The *Tribune* was in a position to be supplying women who were outside the more traditional communication channels within the movement. Finally, the *Tribune* had one of the most overtly political orientations of any woman's publication, due in part to the close relationships Bewick Colby attempted to maintain with the United States Congress. Indeed, Bewick Colby may well have been the only suffragist publisher to strive so hard for acceptance as a general circulation newspaper.

6. Kathie Sarachild, theorist and historian on the early stages of twentieth-century feminism, is one of the few movement theorists to observe the critical importance of activists' being in charge of their own movement's records. She has argued that those in charge of the history ultimately become the most powerful leaders in the movement. See Sarachild, "The

Power of History," in *Feminist Revolution*, ed. Redstockings, 13–43, abg. ed. (New York: Random House, 1978).

7. Susan B. Anthony and Matilda Joslyn Gage, eds., *History of Woman Suffrage*, vol. 3: 1876–1885 (Rochester, N.Y.: Charles Mann, 1886), 671.

8. 2 February 1885, HC Folder 34, Elizabeth Boynton Harbert Collection, Henry E. Huntington Memorial Library.

9. Daniel Anthony Fus, "Persuasion on the Plains: The Woman Suffrage Movement in Nebraska" (Ph.D. diss., Indiana University, 1972), 74. For one year, Bewick Colby was assisted financially by "a joint stock publication company" (*Woman's Tribune*, 1 January 1884, 1). She explained the relationship: "The stockholders of the N.W.S. Publishing Company held a meeting at Lincoln, May 2d. A board of directors, consisting of Mrs. S. M. Moore, Mrs. Jane F. Holmes, Mrs. Mollie K. Maule, Mrs. A. M. Pruitt and Mrs. I. D. Evans, was elected. The proceeds arising from the assessments of this year were voted to the support of THE WOMAN'S TRIBUNE. . . . While not assuming the direct responsibility of THE TRIBUNE, this company aims to assist in its publication this year and to accumulate a fund which may be used in the publication of suffrage literature or the advancement of the work as may be deemed best" (1 June 1884, 2). No further mention was ever made of this company in the pages of the *Tribune*.

10. 22 November 1885, HC Folder 34, Elizabeth Boynton Harbert Collection, Henry E. Huntington Memorial Library.

11. Thomas D. Clark, "Rhetoric, Reality, and Rationalization: A Study of the Masking Function of Rhetoric in the London Theosophical Movement," *Communication Quarterly* 26 (Fall 1978): 30.

12. Thomas Chalmer Coulter, "A History of Woman Suffrage in Nebraska, 1856–1920" (Ph.D. diss., Ohio State University, 1967), 111.

13. This concern with painting pictures of events for women who could not attend had begun early in Bewick Colby's public life. For example, she presented a talk in Beatrice after the Chicago World's Fair, in which she described in great detail the art that was displayed in the central exposition hall. See Clara Bewick Colby Manuscripts, MSS 379, State Historical Society of Wisconsin.

14. Brown, 37.

15. Ibid., 57.

16. 14 December 1898, Clara Bewick Colby Collection, CC 3 (86), Henry E. Huntington Memorial Library.

17. Brown, 39.

18. The *Geo. P. Rowell & Co.'s American Newspaper Directory* listed the *Woman's Tribune* as a woman suffrage newspaper. For an example of the *Tribune*'s advertising, see September 1886, 4.

19. See the following letters from Anthony to Bewick Colby: 1 December 1895, CC 3 (42), and 26 February 1896, CC 3 (56), Clara Bewick Colby Collection, Henry E. Huntington Memorial Library.

20. Bewick Colby also included a short interesting story about the first woman's temperance convention in the United States, one held by Iroquois women in 1802 (21 November 1891, 305).

21. Bewick Colby occasionally wrote about the history of less famous

women. For example, she told about the first woman to refuse to be taxed without representation, Miss Sarah Wall in 1850 (4 December 1897, 93).

22. Anthony was involved in the best known of the court cases involving women's attempts to vote. For a discussion of her trial, see Flexner, 168–72.

23. Twenty-five Cady Stanton speeches were printed in the *Tribune*.

24. Bewick Colby insisted upon complete recognition of her special position, for example: "All persons are warned against reproducing the Reminiscences of Mrs. Stanton, which are being published in THE TRIBUNE, as they are copy-righted. The next chapter will have the notice in legal form."

25. Fus, 75–76.

26. See letter from Anthony to Bewick Colby, 12 February 1897, Clara Bewick Colby Collection, CC 3 (63), Henry E. Huntington Memorial Library.

27. Brown, 35.

Chapter 8: The *Woman's Column*

1. National American Woman Suffrage Association Papers, Library of Congress, Washington, D.C.

2. Anthony and Harper, 431.

3. Masel-Walters, "To Hustle," 180.

4. Clinton Rossiter, *Conservatism in America* (New York: Alfred A. Knopf, 1956), 12.

5. DuBois, 197.

6. Flexner, 156, 222; Barbara Sinclair Deckard, *The Women's Movement: Political, Socioeconomic, and Psychological Issues*, 2d ed. (New York: Harper and Row, 1979), 278–79; DuBois, 197–200.

7. Mari Jo Buhle and Paul Buhle, eds., *The Concise History of Woman Suffrage: Selections from the Classic Work of Stanton, Anthony, Gage, and Harper* (Urbana: University of Illinois Press, 1978), 19–21. Buhle and Buhle provide a detailed analysis of how the AWSA's leaders worked within a context of broad moral reform for several oppressed groups, maintaining ties with the Republican party even when woman's rights were abandoned for African-American rights.

8. Rossiter, 11–12.

9. Flexner, 156; DuBois, 104.

10. Buhle and Buhle, 19.

11. Ibid., 23; DuBois, 104.

12. Deckard, 282.

13. Anthony and Harper, 431, 465, 708.

14. Ibid., 708.

15. Blackwell played an important role in a variety of woman suffrage organizations between 1880 and 1920. She served as the chairperson of the State Board of Directors of the Massachusetts Woman Suffrage Association, recording secretary of the NAWSA, and editor of journals for the AWSA and NAWSA. Blackwell actively supported a number of state woman suffrage associations, speaking regularly before New England state conventions and

donating funds to support state suffrage initiatives. She frequently served as spokesperson and delegate on behalf of the NAWSA to a variety of U.S. Senate committees and other agencies.

16. Blackwell's votes in the NAWSA conferences repudiating Stanton's *Woman's Bible* and against resolutions specifically advocating African-American women's rights were evidence of her dedication to safeguard woman's suffrage from association with unpopular or radical positions. For further discussion of Blackwell's stand on the race question and on the *Woman's Bible*, see Kraditor, 200; and Anthony and Harper, 265.

17. Elinor Rice Hays, *Those Extraordinary Blackwells: The Story of a Journey to a Better World* (New York: Harcourt, Brace and World, 1967), 256; and Flexner, 226.

18. Masel-Walters, "To Hustle," 180.

19. Ibid., 172.

20. National American Woman Suffrage Association Papers.

21. Flexner, 182–85.

22. Ibid., 185.

23. Kraditor, 5.

24. For an explanation of how Frances Willard dealt with this perception in the Women's Christian Temperance Union, see Flexner, 185–89.

25. Rossiter, 12.

26. Kraditor, 56–57.

27. Campbell, *Man Cannot*, 1:4–6.

28. Ibid.

29. Although no feature was consistently included within the *Column*, one column appeared frequently. Titled "Women in the Churches," the articles covered the ordinations and activities of women ministers.

30. Anthony and Harper, 431.

31. Deckard, 281.

32. Marzolf, 221.

33. Ibid., 233.

34. For a detailed analysis of woman suffrage arguments from expediency, see Kraditor, 52–74.

35. Ibid., 66.

36. Campbell, *Man Cannot*, 1:14–15.

37. Kraditor, 66.

38. Flexner, 223.

39. Marzolf, 227–30.

40. Ibid., 224, 227.

41. Ibid., 234.

42. Buhle and Buhle, 33.

43. Edwin Black, "The Second Persona," *Quarterly Journal of Speech* 56 (1970): 113.

44. Ibid.

45. Kraditor, 67.

46. Flexner, 222–23.

47. Gusfield, *Community*, 64.

48. Stewart, Smith, and Denton, 44–45.

49. Flexner, 167.

50. For further discussion of the relationship between empowerment and collective action, see Marsha L. Vanderford, "Vilification and Social Movements: A Case Study of Pro-Life and Pro-Choice Rhetoric," *Quarterly Journal of Speech* 75 (1989): 176–77; Luther P. Gerlach and Virginia H. Hine, *People, Power, and Change: Movements of Social Transformation* (Indianapolis: Bobbs-Merrill, 1970), 163–65; and Smelser, 94–100.

51. Marzolf, 234.

52. Ibid.

53. Flexner, 224.

Chapter 9: The *Farmer's Wife*

1. Masel-Walters, "To Hustle," 167.

2. Ibid., 177–78.

3. Among those efforts are Leland M. Griffin, "The Rhetoric of Historical Movements," *Quarterly Journal of Speech* 38 (April 1952): 184–88; Griffin, "Dramatistic Theory," 456–78; Simons, 1–11; Dan F. Hahn and Ruth M. Gonchar, "Studying Rhetorical Movements: A Rhetorical Methodology," *Speech Teacher* 20 (January 1971): 44–52; Robert S. Cathcart, "New Approaches to the Study of Movements: Defining Movements Rhetorically," *Western Speech* 36 (Spring 1972): 82–88, and "Movements: Confrontation as Rhetorical Form," *Southern Speech Communication Journal* 43 (Spring 1978): 233–47; Charles A. Wilkinson, "A Rhetorical Definition of Movements," *Central States Speech Journal* 27 (Summer 1976): 88–94; and Stewart, Smith, and Denton.

4. Simons, 3–4.

5. Stewart, Smith, and Denton, 73–84.

6. Campbell, "Femininity," 107.

7. Ibid., 105.

8. Ibid., 106.

9. Masel-Walters, "To Hustle," 175.

10. Marilyn Dell Brady, "Populism and Feminism in a Newspaper by and for the Women of the Kansas Farmer's Alliance, 1891–1894," *Kansas History* 7 (Winter 1984–85): 280–90.

11. Ibid., 281.

12. "Personal Paragraphs Pertinent to Populist Women among Kansas Reformers," *American Nonconformist*, 23 February 1893. This journal was published in Indianapolis. The clipping is on file at the Kansas State Historical Society Library in Topeka.

13. Brady, 282.

14. Ibid.

15. Flexner, 149.

16. See Wilda M. Smith, "A Half Century of Struggle: Gaining Woman Suffrage in Kansas," *Kansas History* 4 (Summer 1981): 84–85.

17. Brady, 282.

18. Ibid.

19. Ibid., 288.

20. Frances I. Garside, "A Frontier Farmer's Wife," 28 January 1893, 3.

21. Ibid.

22. Fannie McCormick, "A Kansas Farm," September 1891, 1.

23. For a discussion of the influence of natural rights philosophy on the rhetoric of the early feminist movement, see Campbell, "Femininity," 102.

24. Bina A. Otis, address at Rossville, Kansas, 4 July 1893, in August 1893, 1.

25. Otis, address at the Kansas State Fair, in October 1893, 1.

26. Mrs. Crumb, response to the welcome delivered by Bina A. Otis, in June 1893, 1.

27. M. Katherine Gernen, "An Address Delivered at the Commencement Exercises of the Russell, Kansas, Graduating Class of 1894," August 1894, 4.

28. September 1981, 1.

29. McCormick, "Fourth of July Address at Manhattan, Kansas," in August 1891, 1.

30. Nettie S. Nutt, "Woman's Opportunity," November 1891, 1.

31. Mary A. Livermore, "Let Women Study Politics," September 1891, 1.

32. Nutt, "Educate the Mothers," February 1892, 1.

33. Emily E. Lathrop, "The National Children's Home Kindergarten and Industrial Alliance," December 1891, 5.

34. Ibid.

35. Ibid.

36. Frances F. Allen, "Women in Politics," October 1891, 1.

37. Ibid.

38. Brady, 290.

39. Ibid., 283.

40. Elizabeth N. Barr, "The Populist Uprising," in *A Standard History of Kansas and Kansans*, ed. William E. Connelley (Chicago: Lewis Publishing, 1918), 1148–49.

41. "An Eye-Opener," June 1894, 5.

Chapter 10: The *Woman's Exponent*

1. Louisa Lula Green to Zina S. Whitney, 20 January 1893, Louisa Lula Green Richards Papers, Historical Department, Church of Jesus Christ of Latter-day Saints, hereinafter cited as LDS Church Archives; Lula Green Richards, "How the Exponent Was Started," *Relief Society Magazine* 14 (December 1928): 607; Sherilyn Cox Bennion, "The *Woman's Exponent*: Forty-two Years of Speaking for Women," *Utah Historical Quarterly* 44 (Summer 1976): 226–27; Carol Cornwall Madsen, " 'Remember the Women of Zion': A Study of the Editorial Content of the *Woman's Exponent*, a Mormon Woman's Journal, 1872–1914" (M.A. thesis, University of Utah, 1977), 7–8.

2. *Woman's Exponent*, 15 October 1873, 64; 1 December 1875, 72; 1 August 1877, 29. The activities of the "Committee of Consultation" are somewhat ambiguous. However, it did continue to function for several

years. Committee members solicited subscriptions and discussed *Exponent* policy. Emmeline B. (Woodward) Wells, diary, 27 September 1888, Brigham Young University Library, hereinafter cited as BYU Library.

3. Cooperative Retrenchment Association Meeting Minutes, 1872–74, [date missing] and 23 November 1872, 10 May 1873; Mary Horne, Salt Lake State Relief Society Minutes, 21 and 22 March 1879, Conference Records 1868–1903, LDS Church Archives.

4. Bennion, 237.

5. Madsen, "Remember," 45.

6. Bennion, 228.

7. Ibid., 227.

8. Louisa Lula Green to Eliza R. Snow, 20 February 1872, Louisa Lula Green Richards Papers, LDS Church Archives.

9. Madsen, "Remember," 19–21.

10. Madsen's "Mormon Woman in Victorian America" (Ph.D. diss., University of Utah, 1985) provides a detailed and sympathetic biography of Emmeline B. Wells.

11. Wells, diary, 2 March 1883, BYU Library.

12. "Heartfelt Farewell," *Exponent*, February 1914, 100.

13. "The Power of the Press," *Millennial Star*, 7 May 1877, 297; Special Collections, University of Utah Library, hereinafter cited as U of U Collection.

14. The following editorials provide examples of attempts at reader "education": *Exponent*, 15 May 1888, 188; 15 May 1880, 188; 15 April 1889, 172; 15 November 1889, 92; June 1901, 4.

15. Madsen, "Remember," 41.

16. "Miss Eliza R. Snow, President of the entire Female Relief Societies, cordially approves of the journal." Quoted from "Woman's Exponent," *Exponent*, 1 June 1872, 4; Cooperative Retrenchment Association, 13 April 1872, LDS Church Archives.

17. Sarah M. Kimball, Salt Lake Stake Relief Society, 22 June 1878, LDS Church Archives.

18. Relief Society Minutesbook, 28 April 1842, LDS Church Archives.

19. The following sources provide discussions of women performing ordinances: Dr. Ellis R. Shipp, 16 June 1882, and Mary Horne, 9 March 1883, Salt Lake Stake Relief Society; Cooperative Retrenchment Association Meetings, LDS Church Archives; Wells, diary, 27 July 1894, BYU Library.

20. Cooperative Retrenchment Association; Salt Lake Stake Relief Society, LDS Church Archives.

21. Leonard J. Arrington, *Great Basin Kingdom: Economic History of the Latter-day Saints, 1830–1900* (Lincoln: University of Nebraska Press, 1958); Tarla Rai Peterson, "Justifying Ideological Conflict: Mormon Abandonment of Polygamy," paper delivered at the Annual Meeting of the Speech Communication Association, Boston, November 1987.

22. Peterson.

23. Remarks of Mattie H. Tingey, read by Cornelia H. Clayton, *"Mormon" Women's Protest: An Appeal for Freedom, Justice and Equal Rights* (pamphlet

containing full account of proceedings of Salt Lake Ladies Meeting, held 8 March 1886), U of U Collection.

24. Madsen, "Mormon Woman," 210.

25. Wells, diary, 23 January 1891, BYU Library; Wells, report in *Transactions of the National Council of Women of the United States* (Philadelphia: J. B. Lippincott, 1891), 258–60; Madsen, "Mormon Woman," 195–238.

26. Wells, diary, 30 September 1874, BYU Library.

27. Wells, diary, 28 September 1888 and 8 October 1890, BYU Library.

Chapter 11: Evolving Strategies and Identities

1. Volume 1 of her study is devoted to a close analysis of this process.

2. Stewart, Smith, and Denton, 75.

3. Ibid., 78.

4. Black, 113.

5. Campbell, 6.

6. *Woman's Journal*, 4 February 1882, 35.

7. Black, 113.

8. Ann Douglas, *The Feminization of American Culture* (New York: Alfred A. Knopf, 1977), 44–79.

9. *Lily*, November 1852, 82.

10. *Lily*, May 1852, 39.

11. *Lily*, 15 April 1856, 60.

12. *Una*, December 1853, 182.

13. *Revolution*, 15 January 1868, 25–26.

14. *Revolution*, 29 October 1868, 260.

15. Ibid.

16. *Revolution*, 15 January 1868, 17.

17. *Mayflower*, August 1861, quoted in Louise Noun, *Strong-minded Women: The Emergence of the Woman Suffrage Movement in Iowa* (Ames: Iowa State University Press, 1969), 25.

18. Noun, 79.

19. *Woman's Journal*, 22 January 1870, 27.

20. *Woman's Journal*, 3 September 1870, 273.

21. *Woman's Journal*, 29 July 1871, 236.

22. Duniway, 195.

23. *Woman's Advocate*, 27 January 1855, 2.

Bibliography

Manuscript Collections

Brigham Young University Library Special Collections.
    Emmeline B. Woodward Wells Diary.
Cincinnati Historical Society.
Henry E. Huntington Memorial Library, San Marino, California.
    Clara Bewick Colby Collection.
    Elizabeth Boynton Harbert Collection.
Latter-day Saints Church Archives, Historical Department. Salt Lake City
    Utah.
    Cooperative Retrenchment Association Meeting Minutes, 1872–1874.
    Louisa Lula Green Richards Papers.
    Relief Society Conference Records, 1868–1903.
    Relief Society Minutesbook, 28 April 1842.
National American Woman Suffrage Association Papers. Library of Con-
    gress, Washington, D.C.
State Historical Society of Wisconsin, Madison, Wisconsin.
    Clara Bewick Colby Manuscripts.
University of Kansas, Lawrence, Kansas.
    Gerritsen Collection (Microfilm Edition, Spencer Research Library Col-
    lection).
University of Utah Special Collections.

Sources: Books and Essays

Anthony, Katharine. *Susan B. Anthony: Her Personal History and Her Era.* Garden City, N.Y.: Doubleday, 1954.

Anthony, Susan B., and Matilda Joslyn Gage, eds. *History of Woman Suffrage.* Vol 3: 1876–1885. Rochester, N.Y.: Charles Mann, 1886.

Anthony, Susan B., and Ida Husted Harper. *History of Woman Suffrage.* Vol. 4: 1883–1900. Indianapolis: Hollenbeck, 1902; New York: Arno and the New York Times, 1969.

Arrington, Leonard J. *Great Basin Kingdom: Economic History of the Latter-day Saints, 1830–1900.* Lincoln: University of Nebraska Press, 1958.

Barr, Elizabeth N. "The Populist Uprising." In *A Standard History of Kansas and Kansans,* ed. William E. Connelley, 1115–1595. Chicago: Lewis Publishing, 1918.

Beeton, Beverly. *Women Vote in the West: The Woman Suffrage Movement 1869–1896.* New York: Garland, 1986.

Bennion, Sherilyn Cox. "The *Woman's Exponent*: Forty-two Years of Speaking for Woman." *Utah Historical Quarterly* 44 (Summer 1976): 222–39.

Black, Edwin. "The Second Persona." *Quarterly Journal of Speech* 56 (1970): 109–19.

Blackwell, Alice Stone. *Lucy Stone: Pioneer of Woman's Rights.* Boston: Little, Brown, 1930.

Blair, Karen J. *True Womanhood Redefined, 1868–1914.* New York: Holmes and Meier, 1980.

Blatch, Harriot Stanton, and Alma Lutz. *Challenging Years: The Memoirs of Harriot Stanton Blatch.* New York: G. P. Putnam's Sons, 1940.

Bleyer, Willard Grosvenor. *Main Currents in the History of American Journalism.* Boston: Houghton, 1927.

Bloomer, Dexter C. *Life and Writings of Amelia Bloomer.* Boston: Arena, 1895; New York: Schocken, 1975.

Bormann, Ernest G. *The Force of Fantasy: Restoring the American Dream.* Carbondale: Southern Illinois University Press, 1985.

Brady, Marilyn Dell. "Populism and Feminism in a Newspaper by and for Women of the Kansas Farmer's Alliance, 1891–1894." *Kansas History* 7 (Winter 1984–85): 280–90.

Brown, Olympia, ed. *Democratic Ideals: A Memorial Sketch of Clara B. Colby.* N.p.: Federal Suffrage Association, 1917.

Buechler, Steven M. *The Transformation of the Woman Suffrage Movement: The Case of Illinois, 1850–1920.* New Brunswick, N.J.: Rutgers University Press, 1981.

Buhle, Mari Jo, and Paul Buhle, eds. *The Concise History of Woman Suffrage: Selections from the Classic Work of Stanton, Anthony, Gage, and Harper.* Urbana: University of Illinois Press, 1978.

Campbell, Karlyn Kohrs. "Femininity and Feminism: To Be or Not To Be A Woman." *Communication Quarterly* 31 (Spring 1983): 101–8.

———. *Man Cannot Speak for Her: A Critical Study of Early Feminist Rhetoric.* 2 vols. New York: Praeger, 1989.

———. "The Rhetoric of Women's Liberation: An Oxymoron." *Quarterly Journal of Speech* 59 (February 1973): 74–86.

Cathcart, Robert S. "Movements: Confrontation as Rhetorical Form." *Southern Speech Communication Journal* 43 (Spring 1978): 233–47.

———. "New Approaches to the Study of Movements: Defining Movements Rhetorically." *Western Speech* 36 (Spring 1972): 82–88.

Catt, Carrie Chapman, and Nettie Rogers Shuler. *Woman Suffrage and Politics: The Inner Story of the Suffrage Movement.* Americana Library, ed. Robert E. Burke. 1923; rpt. Seattle: University of Washington Press, 1970.

Clark, Thomas D. "Rhetoric, Reality, and Rationalization: A Study of the Masking Function of Rhetoric in the London Theosophical Movement." *Communication Quarterly* 26 (Fall 1978): 24–30.

Conrad, Charles. "Agon and Rhetorical Form: The Essence of 'Old Feminist' Rhetoric." *Central States Speech Journal* 32 (Spring 1981): 45–53.

———. "The Transformation of the 'Old Feminist' Movement." *Quarterly Journal of Speech* 67 (August 1981): 284–97.

Conway, Jill K. *The Female Experience in 18th and 19th Century America: A Guide to the History of American Women.* Princeton, N.J.: Princeton University Press, 1985.

Cooper, Anne Messerly. "Suffrage as News: Ten Dailies' Coverage of the Nineteenth Amendment." *American Journalism* 1 (1983): 75–91.

Correll, Lucy L. "Suffrage in Nebraska." In *Collection of Nebraska Pioneer Reminiscences,* issued by Nebraska Society of the Daughters of the American Revolution, 277–78. Cedar Rapids, Iowa: Torch, 1916.

Cott, Nancy. *The Bonds of Womanhood: "Woman's Sphere" in New England, 1780–1835.* New Haven: Yale University Press, 1977.

———. *The Grounding of Modern Feminism.* New Haven: Yale University Press, 1987.

Coulter, Thomas Chalmer. "A History of Woman Suffrage in Nebraska, 1856–1920." Ph.D. diss., Ohio State University, 1967.

Cox, J. Robert. "The Die Is Cast: Topical and Ontological Dimensions of the Locus of the Irreparable." *Quarterly Journal of Speech* 68 (August 1982): 227–39.

Deckard, Barbara Sinclair. *The Women's Movement: Political, Socioeconomic, and Psychological Issues.* 2d ed. New York: Harper and Row, 1979.

Dickinson, Susan E. "Women Journalists in America." In *What America Owes to Women,* ed. Lydia Hoyt Farmer, 205–11. Buffalo: Charles Wells Moulton, 1893.

Douglas, Ann. *The Feminization of American Culture.* New York: Alfred A. Knopf, 1977.

DuBois, Ellen Carol. *Feminism and Suffrage: The Emergence of an Independent Women's Movement in America, 1848–1869.* Ithaca: Cornell University Press, 1978.

Duniway, Abigail Scott. *Pathbreaking: An Autobiographical History of the Equal Suffrage Movement in Pacific Coast States.* 2d ed. 1914; rpt. New York: Kraus Reprint, 1971.

Emery, Edwin, and Michael Emery. *The Press and America: An Interpretive*

History of the Mass Media. 5th ed. Englewood Cliffs, N.J.: Prentice-Hall, 1984.

"The Female Rebellion." *Perspectives on Greatness,* series owned by King Features Entertainment, 1963 production. KTWU rebroadcast, 27 April 1986.

Flexner, Eleanor. *Century of Struggle: The Woman's Rights Movement in the United States.* Rev. ed. Cambridge: Belknap Press of Harvard University Press, 1975.

Fuller, Paul E. *Laura Clay and the Woman's Rights Movement.* Lexington: University of Kentucky Press, 1975.

Fus, Daniel Anthony. "Persuasion on the Plains: The Woman Suffrage Movement in Nebraska." Ph.D. diss., Indiana University, 1972.

Gerlach, Luther P., and Virginia H. Hine. *People, Power, and Change: Movements of Social Transformation.* Indianapolis: Bobbs-Merrill, 1970.

Griffin, Leland. "A Dramatistic Theory of the Rhetoric of Movements." In *Critical Responses to Kenneth Burke,* ed. William H. Rueckert, 456–78. Minneapolis: University of Minnesota Press, 1969.

———. "The Rhetoric of Historical Movements." *Quarterly Journal of Speech* 38 (April 1952): 184–88.

Griffith, Elisabeth. *In Her Own Right: The Life of Elizabeth Cady Stanton.* New York: Oxford University Press, 1984.

Grimes, Alan P. *The Puritan Ethic and Woman Suffrage.* New York: Oxford University Press, 1967.

Gurko, Miriam. *The Ladies of Seneca Falls: The Birth of the Woman's Rights Movement.* New York: Macmillan, 1974.

Gusfield, Joseph R. *Community: A Critical Response.* New York: Harper and Row, 1975.

———. *Symbolic Crusade: Status Politics and the American Temperance Society.* Urbana: University of Illinois Press, 1963.

Hahn, Dan F., and Ruth M. Gonchar. "Studying Rhetorical Movements: A Rhetorical Methodology." *Speech Teacher* 20 (January 1971): 44–52.

Hall, Florence Howe. *Julia Ward Howe and the Woman Suffrage Movement.* New York: Arno and the New York Times, 1969.

Harper, Ida Husted. *Life and Work of Susan B. Anthony.* Indianapolis: Hollenbeck Press, 1898.

———, ed. *History of Woman Suffrage.* Vol. 5: 1900–1920. New York: National American Woman Suffrage Association, 1922.

Hays, Elinor Rice. *Those Extraordinary Blackwells: The Story of a Journey to a Better World.* New York: Harcourt, Brace and World, 1967.

Hoffer, Eric. *The True Believer.* New York: Harper and Row, 1951.

Hymowitz, Carol, and Michaele Weissman. *A History of Women in America.* New York: Bantam Books, 1984.

Irwin, Inez Haynes. *Angels and Amazons: A Hundred Years of American Women.* Garden City, N.Y.: Doubleday, Doran, 1933.

Jerry, E. Claire. "Clara Bewick Colby and the *Woman's Tribune*: Strategies of a Free Lance Movement Leader," Ph.D. diss., University of Kansas, 1986.

Johnson, Allen, ed. *Dictionary of American Biography.* Vol. 1. New York: Charles Scribners's Sons, 1946.

Kessler, Lauren Jeanne. *The Dissident Press: Alternative Journalism in American History.* Sage COMMTEXT Series, vol. 13, ed. F. Gerald Kline. Beverly Hills: Sage, 1984.

———. "A Siege of the Citadels: Access of Woman Suffrage Ideas to the Oregon Press, 1884–1912." Ph.D. diss., University of Washington, 1980.

Kraditor, Aileen. *The Ideas of the Woman Suffrage Movement, 1890–1920.* New York: Columbia University Press, 1965; New York: W. W. Norton, 1981.

Krout, John A. *The Origins of the Prohibition.* New York: Alfred A. Knopf, 1925.

Langer, Suzanne. *Philosophy in a New Key.* 3d ed. Cambridge: Harvard University Press, 1978.

Lutz, Alma. *Susan B. Anthony: Rebel, Crusader, Humanitarian.* Boston, Beacon Press, 1959.

Madsen, Carol Cornwall. "A Mormon Woman in Victorian America." Ph.D. diss., University of Utah, 1985.

———. " 'Remember the Women of Zion': A Study of the Editorial Content of the *Woman's Exponent,* a Mormon Woman's Journal, 1872–1914." M.A. thesis, University of Utah, 1977.

Marzolf, Marion. *Up from the Footnote: A History of Women Journalists.* Communications Arts Books. New York: Hastings House, 1977.

Masel-Walters, Lynne. "A Burning Cloud by Day: The History and Content of the *Woman* [sic] *Journal.*" *Journalism History* 3, no. 4 (Winter 1976–77): 103–10.

———. "Their Rights and Nothing Less: The History and Thematic Content of the American Woman Suffrage Press, 1868–1920." Ph.D. diss., University of Wisconsin–Madison, 1977.

———. "Their Rights and Nothing More: A History of *The Revolution,* 1868–1870." *Journalism Quarterly* 53 (Summer 1976): 242–51.

———. "To Hustle with the Rowdies: The Organization and Functions of the American Suffrage Press." *Journal of American Culture* 3 (Spring 1980): 167–83.

Mather, Anne. "A History of Feminist Periodicals, Part 1." *Journalism History* 1 (1974): 82–85. University Microfilm ed.

Mott, Frank Luther. *American Journalism: A History of Newspapers in the United States through 260 Years, 1690–1951.* Rev. ed. New York: Macmillan, 1950.

———. *A History of American Magazines 1865 to 1885.* Cambridge: Harvard University Press, 1938; rpt. 1957.

National American Woman Suffrage Association. *Victory, How Women Won It: A Centennial Symposium, 1840–1940.* New York: Wilson, 1940.

Noun, Louise R. *Strong-minded Women: The Emergence of the Woman Suffrage Movement in Iowa.* Ames: Iowa State University Press, 1969.

O'Connor, Lillian. *Pioneer Women Orators: Rhetoric in Ante-bellum Reform Movements.* New York: Vantage, n.d.; rpt. 1952.

Ogden, Annegret S. *The Great American Housewife: From Helpmate to Wage Earner 1776–1986.* Westport, Conn.: Greenwood, 1986.

O'Neill, William L. *Everyone Was Brave: The Rise and Fall of Feminism in America.* Chicago: Quadrangle Books, 1969.

"Personal Paragraphs Pertinent to Populist Women among Kansas Reformers." *American Nonconformist* (Indianapolis), 23 February 1893. Clipping on file at the Kansas State Historical Library in Topeka.

Proceedings of the Woman's Rights Convention Held at the Broadway Tabernacle in the city of New York on Tuesday and Wednesday, Sept. 6th and 7th, 1853. New York: Fowlers and Wells, 1853. The Gerritsen Collection of Woman's History, microfilm ed., no. 3168.

Rendall, Jane. *The Origins of Modern Feminism: Women in Britain, France, and the United States 1780–1860.* London: Macmillan, 1985.

Riegel, Robert E. *American Feminists.* Lawrence: University of Kansas Press, 1963; rpt. 1968.

Rosenberg, Rosalind. *Beyond Separate Spheres: Intellectual Roots of Modern Feminism.* New Haven, Conn.: Greenwood, 1986.

Rossiter, Clinton. *Conservatism in America.* New York: Alfred A. Knopf, 1956.

Rowell, George P., ed. *Geo P. Rowell & Co.'s American Newspaper Directory.* New York: Rowell, 1870–90.

Ryan, Agnes. *The Torch Bearer: A Look Forward and Back at the* Woman's Journal, *the Organ of the Woman's Movement.* Boston: Woman's Journal and Suffrage News, 1916.

Sarachild, Kathie. "The Power of History." In *Feminist Revolution,* ed. Redstockings, 13–43. Abg. ed. New York: Random House, 1978.

Schudson, Michael. *Discovering the News: A Social History of American Newspapers.* New York: Basic Books, 1978.

Scott, Anne F., and Andrew M. Scott. *One Half the People: The Fight for Woman Suffrage.* The America's Alternatives Series, ed. Harold M. Hyman. Philadelphia: Lippincott, 1975.

Simons, Herbert W. "Requirements, Problems, and Strategies: A Theory of Persuasion for Social Movements." *Quarterly Journal of Speech* 56 (February 1970): 1–11.

Simons, Herbert W., James W. Chesebro, and C. Jack Orr. "A Movement Perspective on the 1972 Presidential Election." *Quarterly Journal of Speech* 59 (April 1973): 168–78.

Smith, Donald H. "Martin Luther King, Jr., 'In the Beginning in Montgomery.'" *Southern Speech Communication Journal* 34 (Fall 1968): 8–17.

Smith, Wilda M. "A Half Century of Struggle: Gaining Woman Suffrage in Kansas." *Kansas History* 4 (Summer 1981): 74–95.

Stanton, Elizabeth Cady. *Eighty Years and More.* New York: T. Fisher Unwin, 1898; New York: Schocken, 1971.

Stanton, Elizabeth Cady, Susan B. Anthony, and Matilda Joslyn Gage, eds. *History of Woman Suffrage.* Vol. 1: 1848–1861. 2d ed. Rochester, N.Y.: Charles Mann, 1886.

Stearns, Bertha-Monica. "Early Western Magazines for Ladies." *Mississippi Valley Historical Review* 18 (1931): 319–30.

———. "Philadelphia Magazines for Ladies." *Pennsylvania Magazine of History and Biography* 69 (1945): 207–19.

———. "Reform Periodicals and Female Reformers 1830–1960." *American Historical Review* 37 (1932): 678–99.

Steiner, Linda Claire. "The Women's Suffrage Press, 1850–1900: A Cultural Analysis." Ph.D. diss., University of Illinois, 1979.

Stewart, Charles J., Craig Allen Smith, and Robert E. Denton, Jr. *Persuasion and Social Movements.* Prospect Heights, Ill.: Waveland Press, 1984.

Vanderford, Marsha L. "Vilification and Social Movements: A Case Study of Pro-Life and Pro-Choice Rhetoric." *Quarterly Journal of Speech* 75 (1989): 166–82.

Warnick, Barbara. "The Rhetoric of Conservative Resistance." *Southern Speech Communication Journal* 42 (Spring 1977): 256–73.

Wells, Emmeline B. Woodward. Report in *Transactions of the National Council of Women of the United States,* 258–60. Philadelphia: J. B. Lippincott, 1891.

Welter, Barbara. "The Cult of True Womanhood: 1820–1860." *American Quarterly* 18 (1966): 154–71.

———. *Dimity Convictions: The American Woman in the Nineteenth Century.* Athens: Ohio University Press, 1976.

Wheeler, Leslie, ed. *Loving Warriors: Selected Letters of Lucy Stone and Henry B. Blackwell, 1853 to 1893.* New York: Dial, 1981.

Wilkinson, Charles A. "A Rhetorical Definition of Movements." *Central States Speech Journal* 27 (Summer 1976): 88–94.

Willard, Frances E., and Mary A. Livermore, eds. *American Women.* New York: Mast, Cromwell, and Kirkpatrick, 1897; Detroit: Gale Research, 1973.

Wilson, John. *Introduction to Social Movements.* New York: Basic Books, 1973.

Woloch, Nancy. *Women and the American Experience.* New York: Alfred A. Knopf, 1984.

Wood, Ann D. "The 'Scribbling Women' and Fanny Fern: Why Women Wrote." *American Quarterly* 23, no. 1 (1971): 2–24.

Contributors

Thomas R. Burkholder is Assistant Professor of Speech Communication at Southwest Texas State University. His research interests are primarily in nineteenth-century American public address. He has published articles in *Communication Studies* and the *Southern States Communication Journal*.

Bonnie J. Dow is Assistant Professor of Communication at the University of Cincinnati. Her research interests include the role of rhetoric in social movements, women as political speakers, and feminist criticism of entertainment television.

Edward A. Hinck is currently the Director of Forensics at Central Michigan University. He is working on *Enacting the Presidency: Political Argument, Presidential Debates, and Presidential Character*, a book to be included in the Praeger Series in Political Communication. He has taught previously at California State University, Fullerton, where he was the Assistant Director of Forensics.

Susan Schultz Huxman is Assistant Professor of Communication in the Elliott School of Communication, The Wichita State University. Her research publications and interests include the rhetoric of apologia, religious movements, and early American public address.

E. Claire Jerry is Assistant Professor of Speech Communication at

Butler University. Her research interests include nineteenth-century women's rhetoric, contemporary political rhetoric, and rhetorical epistemology.

Tarla Rai Peterson is Assistant Professor of Speech Communication at Texas A&M University. She has published articles about the rhetorical dimensions of social change in the *Howard Journal of Communications*, the *Southern Speech Communication Journal*, and *Western Journal of Speech Communication*. She has written chapters on women and culture in *Communication and the Culture of Technology* and *Feminist Critiques in Communication Studies* (forthcoming).

Martha M. Solomon is Professor in the Department of Speech Communication at the University of Maryland, College Park. She has published articles on the rhetoric of social movements, women's rhetoric, and rhetoric and social change in the major journals in the field of speech communication. In addition, she has written rhetorical biographies of Emma Goldman (1987) and Anna Howard Shaw (with Wil Linkugel, 1990). She is past editor of the *Southern Speech Communication Journal* and is currently editor of the *Quarterly Journal of Speech*.

Linda Steiner is Assistant Professor of Journalism at Rutgers University. She has published several essays on nineteenth- and twentieth-century women's alternative media. Her more recent work concentrates on journalism ethics, and, in particular, the contributions of feminist theorizing to the development of an applied ethics.

Mari Boor Tonn is Assistant Professor of Speech Communication at the University of New Hampshire. Her research involving social movement rhetoric includes critical analyses of the rhetoric of Mary Harris "Mother" Jones, an early labor union agitator, and the rhetoric of pro-choice advocates surrounding the *Webster v. Reproductive Health Services* decision of the Supreme Court.

Marsha L. Vanderford is Associate Professor of Communication at the University of South Florida. Her academic interests focus on the role of rhetoric in empowering audiences. Her published work examines the rhetoric of women's novels, the contemporary abortion controversy, and television news coverage.

Index

Blackwell, Elizabeth, 52

Blackwell, Henry B., 108, 129, 131, 147, 156, 190; founding of American Woman Suffrage Association, 9, 10, 23, 88; support for "Negro's hour," 22; editor of *Woman's Journal*, 92, 93, 104, 191; contribution to *Woman's Journal*, 96, 102, 104, 108; views in 1872 election, 100; work on *Woman's Column*, 129, 147; role on *Woman's Advocate*, 190; founding of *Universal Suffrage*, 191

Blatch, Harriot Stanton: founding of League of Self-Supporting Women, 10

Bloomer, Amelia Jenks, 29–48, 187, 188; founding of Ladies Temperance Society, 30; founding of and work on *Lily*, 31–32, 37, 39, 40, 48, 187. See also *Lily*

Bloomer, Dexter, 31

Brown, Olympia, 110, 118, 119, 156

Bullard, Laura J., 73

Bunnell, Lizzie, 190

Cary, Alice, 75

Catt, Carrie Chapman, 25; president of NAWSA, 10; "winning plan" of, 11; endorsement of *Woman's Journal*, 87

Civil War: impact on woman's rights movement, 21, 94, 105, 202 (n. 19); women's activities during, 21; role of Woman's National Loyal League and Sanitary Commission during, 8, 92

Colby, Clara Bewick, 15, 28, 29; editor of *Woman's Tribune*, 110–28, 192–93; goals for readers, 113–19; accomplishments of, 128

Congressional Union (National Woman's Party), 11

Consciousness-raising, 13, 15, 16, 98, 99, 154; in *Una*, 52, 65–70; in *Revolution*, 83–85; in *Woman's Journal*, 97–99; in *Farmer's Wife*, 157–64; in *Woman's Exponent*, 173–74, 178; in Utah women's protest meetings, 175

Cook, Eliza, 61

Cornell, Lucy L., 29

"Cult of domesticity," 5, 7, 42; deconstructed in *Woman's Exponent*, 165–81. See also True Womanhood

Cutler, H. M. Tracy, 62

Dall, Caroline Healy: work on *Una*, 48, 54, 55, 60, 64

Davis, Paulina Kellogg Wright, 29; editor of *Una*, 48–70, 188; background of, 49–50; commitment to natural rights philosophy, 49–50, 56–58; sympathy for poor women, 65–66; work on *Revolution*, 72, 74

Davis, Thomas, 49

"Declaration of Sentiments," 7

Diggs, Annie L., 156

Divorce and marriage: as issues in woman's rights movement, 8, 9, 50, 57, 75, 77, 134; "Divorce debate" at 1860 Woman's Rights Convention, 8, 22, 50, 57, 78, 208 (n. 22)

Duniway, Abigail Scott, 29, 98, 128, 193; editor of *New Northwest*, 23, 24, 29

"Emma": letters from in *Una*, 55–56, 66–69

Expediency arguments, 32, 43–46, 57–58, 63, 78, 83, 137–43, 160, 161, 213 (n. 34). *See also* National rights arguments

Farmer's Alliance and Industrial Union. *See* Populism

Farmer's Wife, 15, 153–64, 193–94; background of, 153–56; populism and, 156, 160, 161, 162–63, 164; contents of, 156–57; model of activist woman in, 193–95

Fry, Elizabeth, 36, 41

Gage, Frances D.: contributions to *Una*, 51, 52, 55

Gage, Matilda E. Joslyn, 74

Garrison, William L., 52, 74, 202 (n. 30); views of in 1860 divorce debate, 8; support for "Negro's hour," 22, 78; editor of *Woman's Journal*, 23, 92–93; contribution to *Una*, 55, 58; work on *Liberator*, 93

Genius of Liberty, 20, 22, 188

Gougar, Helen, 117, 121

Grange, the, 155

Greeley, Horace, 19; views of in debate over 14th amendment, 9

Grimke, Sarah: *Letters on Equality of the Sexes*, 12

Grimke sisters, 7, 12, 142

Harbert, Elizabeth Boynton, 111, 116; Bewick Colby's description of, 116

About the Series

STUDIES IN RHETORIC AND COMMUNICATION
General Editors:
E. Culpepper Clark, Raymie E. McKerrow, and David Zarefsky

The University of Alabama Press has established this series to publish major new works in the general area of rhetoric and communication, including books treating the symbolic manifestations of political discourse, argument as social knowledge, the impact of machine technology on patterns of communication behavior, and other topics related to the nature or impact of symbolic communication. We actively solicit studies involving historical, critical, or theoretical analyses of human discourse.